# THE
# AMERICAN
# WRITER

# THE
# AMERICAN
# WRITER

*Shaping a Nation's Mind*

## JACK CADY

ST. MARTIN'S PRESS ✿ NEW YORK

FOR CAROL ORLOCK, AN AMERICAN WRITER

Edited by Gordon Van Gelder
Production Editor: David Stanford Burr

Design by Nancy Resnick

Library of Congress Cataloging-in-Publication Data

Cady, Jack.
    The American writer : shaping a nation's mind / Jack Cady.—
1st ed.
        p.   cm.
    Includes bibliographical references.
    ISBN 0-312-20274-1
    1. American literature—History and criticism.  2. National
characteristics, American, in literature.  3. Literature and
history—United States—History.  4. United States—Intellectual
life.  I. Title.
PS169.N35C33    1999
810.9'358—dc21                                          99-15928
                                                           CIP

First Edition: October 1999

10  9  8  7  6  5  4  3  2  1

# ACKNOWLEDGMENTS

TWO OF MY fellow writers, Carol Orlock and Larry Karp, read early manuscript and took me to task as needed. It is difficult to be both ruthless and kind at the same time, but they managed. I am deeply grateful. Equally grateful, if it could speak, is the book.

Librarians of the Port Townsend (Washington) Public Library, and the Pacific Lutheran University Library, stepped forward, most kindly, with magic methods for finding obscure books. They once more demonstrated that mine would be a dreadfully unhappy world without librarians. I also extend thanks to bookstores in Port Townsend: The Imprint, William James Books, Melville & Company; and in Port Angeles, Port Book and News; in Seattle, Violet Books.

From our small towns and libraries on the West Coast to the roar of New York is (according to William Saroyan) 3,333⅓ miles. Any book traveling that great distance needs champions when it arrives, and this book has two: Clyde Taylor is my friend and agent of many years. Gordon Van Gelder has been my friend and editor for the last three books. I am a very lucky writer.

And, finally, any misstatements found in these pages are mine, alone. If caught with them, I'll own up.

Sing unto Him a new song;
play skillfully with a loud noise.

—Psalm 33

She could still recite them [the poems in McGuffey's Readers] in full when she was lying helpless and nearly blind, in her bed, an old lady. Reciting, her voice took on resonance and firmness, it rang with fervor, ferocity even. She was teaching me one more, almost her last, lesson; emotions do not grow old. I knew that I would feel as she did, and I do.

—Eudora Welty, *One Writer's Beginnings*

# PART I

# MORNING THOUGHTS

PERFECTLY NORMAL STORYTELLERS, as they advance in age, begin writing nonfiction. I've watched it happen to at least a dozen of my elders, who, after a lifetime of yarning, departed from tale spinning to deliver messages reading: "What I really meant to say was . . ."

I would read their words, shake my head in knowing manner, smile most kindly, and say: "These writers fought the good fight. If one of them now wishes to reminisce about the old Brooklyn Dodgers, or another wishes to write a history of women in South Dakota, surely we have no reason to quarrel." Then, and with only a tiny ray of unconcealed pride, I would murmur: "Of course, I shall never do such a thing." I was a good deal younger in those days.

Because, I discover that my elders were doing what writers and artists always seem to do: trying a new way (for them it's new) to infuse the world with another jolt of good sense. They may have a broad point of view, or a narrow one, but we can pretty well trust it as unique and earned.

My point of view sees a world where the young are hard-pressed, but still hold the idealism and beauty of youth. I see young writers and artists alight with inner vision, yet beset by confusions. They are not wrong to be confused. It's tough enough to be young and talented in this noisy world at the end of the twentieth century. Add to the noise the chaos of a growing and changing society, and it's wonderful that most stay reasonably sane.

Yet, writers and artists have traditionally gone eyeball-to-eyeball with situations so confused as to seem senseless. Creating order in the midst of chaos is one part of the job. I see these young ones' situation as holding great opportunity, but also know their lives will not be easy.

Perhaps, I tell myself, I can make their task a little easier, while paying back a bit of what I've received. Writing has been awfully good to me, as have art, theater, and music, together with writers and other artists.

This book, then, is written as a road map for young writers, artists, and other creative minds. It deals in the context of storytelling for two very good reasons. I know more about storytelling than anything else. I could add little about art since Ben Shahn wrote *The Shape of Content* and Sam Hunter wrote *Modern American Painting and Sculpture*. In theater, Arthur Miller's introduction to his *Collected Plays,* in combination with *Act One,* Moss Hart's autobiography, gives most of the insights we need in theory and practice of theater.

The young writer or artist already knows, or will soon discover, there's not much difference in the way honest artists and writers go about matters. Painters use paint, sculptors use stone, writers use words, playwrights use the three dimensions of a stage; but the basic problems and attitudes required by all arts are much the same. It's those problems and attitudes, the demands they make, and where they originate, that are chief subjects of this book.

Literature and art in America operate under influences as old as the times of Puritans and Pilgrims. Our literature also rises from legends and myths of other countries because few nations have had the numbers and varieties of immigration enjoyed by America. It is commonly said, and rightly, that we are a nation of immigrants.

Equally, we are a nation that, from its beginnings, has searched for a utopia we will never find. We won't find utopia because, at base, America is still an idealistic nation. Idealists never fully achieve their ideals because their ideals stand too high for a democracy to handle. (This assertion sounds obscure and abstract, but will seem less so as we go along.) The glory of America is that we have a nation that keeps hungering for, and striving after, ideals, even though many ideals are often offended.

I offer this book to young minds on the assumption that it is much easier to work on behalf of the American people if one understands what formed our society. The young writer's and artist's problem, and mine, is that society traditionally loves easy answers, while art and literature give complete answers; and blamed few of those answers are easy.

This book tells things I wish someone had told me. We won't deal with techniques (for many books about techniques of writing and art are available), but with basic assumptions about storytelling, and thus art in general. We'll then follow main highways of thought, explore some byways not generally thought of as polite places to be seen, and ask only that those byways serve as context for young genius.

We'll watch the American writer putting together a written culture on which we of the twentieth century have largely depended; and we'll see the need for a new mythology. A lot of wonderful words, plus a lot of pure foolishness, prepared the stage on which we tread.

One caution seems necessary. What you read here is a single opinion, although an educated one. Goodspeed, and trust your own judgment.

# THE STORY

LET'S START BY thinking of what stories do for people, because stories function in different ways at different times. We'll look at the story as:

Entertainment and news
Giving identity
Imparting integrity
Creating myths on which a civilization depends[1]

## ENTERTAINMENT AND NEWS

Back in the Dark Ages of Europe (dark for most people, although learning and discovery were still alive), storytellers abounded. They could not write. If they could, they would not have copied their stories down. Their stories were their stock in trade.

In those old, dark days, night came without apology or interference. Darkness surrounded, cut only by illumination from camp or lodge fires, or the moon. Storytellers went from camp to camp, or, later, on the coasts, from ship to ship. They were always welcomed. They received food, lodging, and, sometimes, sex. Nothing about the commercial aspect of the business has changed.

In return, the storyteller brought news and entertainment. There

---

[1]Later, at an appropriate point, we'll also see the story as a form of history.

were no books, radio, television, operas, or symphonies; although there were jugglers, clowns, and sometimes traveling actors who performed morality plays. Generally, though, there were only the storytellers. As storytellers ourselves, we can imagine some directions in which they drifted; because, as you have doubtless already discovered, it is wrong to allow facts to get in the way of the story:

"I've come from a far country many leagues beyond the sea. . . ." (He actually came from a kingdom in the next valley, twenty miles away, over a range of high hills from which ran a stream he had to jump across.) ". . . a land of rare spices and great castles where a just king has heretofore ruled over a loyal and happy kingdom. . . ." (Most kings in those days had a principality of about ten thousand acres, and were sufficiently civilized to make Macbeth look like a holy saint.) "But, alas, of late they have been having dragon problems. A dragon named Loathsome has been devouring maidens." (In those societies a maiden was a girl under age twelve.) "The king has reserved the hand of his daughter, the princess, who is of beauty beyond belief. . . ." (In this sort of storytelling, it is illegal to have a princess who is a bowser.) ". . . and her hand will be given in marriage to the warrior who slays the dragon. . . ." (Nobody ever asks the princess for her opinion because she might give it.) "Many and many a stalwart knight has sallied forth to engage Loathsome in battle. The knights carried swords tempered with magic by a guy named Merlin. No knights have returned. Dragon magic defeats human magic. . . ." (The tension mounts. The kingdom is clearly in a dreadful fix if it faces superior magic.) "But still there is hope. The king has recruited a new boy named Lancelot, who is nine-and-oh against dragons. . . ." (And at this point our storyteller wraps up the story, because the next time he comes through town, he'll be more than welcome. His audience will be all sweaty to see how things turned out.)

In later days, this sort of storytelling would be called a serial, and, in my youth, would star Tom Mix, or Sergeant Preston of the Royal Canadian Mounted Police.

On this level the story largely entertains, although the storytellers did mix local news in with their tales. They might tell of births and deaths among the aristocracy, or gossip surrounding a local parish.

What the storyteller did then, and does now, is enlist the audience. The audience commits itself to the story, and to the people in the story. As the story goes on and becomes elaborate, people in the audience do their own creating. On a subconscious level, they say, "I am afraid of dragons. I love my daughter, who is a maiden. I wish I were someone brave and strong who could defeat dragons. This Lancelot is a hero, and I want to be as much like him as possible." Some listeners/readers will use a lot of creativity, and some will use little; but, either way, the story functions on the level of entertainment, not amusement. There is an important difference.

The story is different from simple amusement because amusement requires nothing from the audience. For example: one may feel obligated to laugh at a joke, but one is not obligated to become a part of the joke. Or, ask yourself how much you remember of what was reported on yesterday's television news. The vast part that you don't remember amounts only to amusement.

Stories generally entertain, and generally should. However, there are other important functions of the story.

## IDENTITY

The story is probably as old as language, and is certainly as old as the cave paintings in northern Spain and southern France; which is to say, twenty thousand years. Painting and language are tied so closely that it's probably impossible to have one without the other. In this business of giving identity, stories and paintings even function in much the same ways.

The story gives people a sense of themselves, a past and a future. This is true of the story in all languages and nations. Because of the story, people are not trapped in themselves, nor are they trapped in the present.

Here are two examples. The first complex:

In the beginning God created the heaven and the earth.

So begins the Hebrew Bible, and even the gravest doubter must admit it is one whale of an opening sentence. It is only when we look at the full record that we realize the genius of those old Hebrew storytellers.

They had a nation of people who could be pretty feisty and capable of scrapping among themselves. They were a tribal culture. In tribal cultures, infighting often proves deadly.[2]

The Hebrew people may have been largely illiterate in those days, but they were not simple. Their storytellers did not come up with short and easy answers for a nation that could divide and break apart. Instead, they dealt with history. The books of Genesis, Exodus, Leviticus, and Numbers tell how the world was made, how it was peopled, and how the Hebrews were anointed by God. The books tell of mistakes, of captivity, of exodus, of battle. In other words, they create an entire world from which the Hebrews derive. Those four books are a workup to the great book of Deuteronomy.

In Deuteronomy, the Hebrews finally get a complete sense of who they are, because Deuteronomy is a book of definitions. (It looks, at first, like only a book of rules.) If seen as the logical result of the first four books, then the business of definition for the Hebrews becomes obvious. A complex people learned of themselves through a complex set of tales.

Different peoples need different mixtures of stories. Our second creation-story deals with tribal people who lived at a later time than the ancient Hebrews, although they derived from origins at least twelve thousand years old. They were forest Indians, and their context was more than a little mystical.

Here is the Cherokee story of creation:[3]

## How the World Was Made

The earth is a great island floating in a sea of water, and suspended at each of the four cardinal points by a cord hanging

---

[2]Tribal culture is generally insular, secluded, and argumentative. For example, in Klawock, Alaska, a Tlingit gentleman once told me: "If we heard that an army was coming to kill our children, we'd let it happen because we'd be too busy arguing." Elements of tribal culture exist wherever one finds insularity, be it the contemporary Middle East or early America.

[3]As taken from *The Nineteenth Annual Report of the Bureau of American Ethnology to the Secretary of The Smithsonian Institution, 1897–98,* by J. W. Powell, director.

down from the sky vault, which is of solid rock. When the world grows old and worn out, the people will die and the cords will break and let the earth sink down into the ocean, and all will be water again. The Indians are afraid of this.

When all was water, the animals were above in Galunlati, beyond the arch; but it was very much crowded, and they were wanting more room. They wondered what was below the water, and at last Dayunisi, "Beaver's Grandchild," the little Water-beetle, offered to go and see if it could learn. It darted in every direction over the surface of the water, but could find no firm place to rest. Then it dived to the bottom and came up with some soft mud, which began to grow and spread on every side until it became the island which we call the earth. It was afterward fastened to the sky with four cords, but no one remembers who did this.

At first the earth was flat and very soft and wet. The animals were anxious to get down, and sent out different birds to see if it was yet dry, but they found no place to alight and came back again to Galunlati. At last it seemed to be time, and they sent out the Buzzard and told him to go and make ready for them. This was the Great Buzzard, the father of all the buzzards we see now. He flew all over the earth, low down near the ground, and it was still soft. When he reached the Cherokee country, he was very tired, and his wings began to flap and strike the earth. When the animals saw this, they were afraid that the whole world would be mountains, so they called him back, but the Cherokee country remains full of mountains to this day.

When the earth was dry and the animals came down, it was still dark, so they got the sun and set it in a track to go every day across the island from east to west, just overhead. It was too hot this way, and Tsiskagili, the Red Crawfish, had his shell scorched a bright red, so that his meat was spoiled: and the Cherokee do not eat it. The conjurers put the sun another hand-breadth higher in the air, but it was still too hot. They raised it another time, and another, until it was seven hand-breadths high and just under the sky arch. Then it was right, and they left it so. This is why the conjurers call the highest place Gulkwagine Digalunlatiyun, "the seventh height," because it is seven hand-breadths above the earth. Every day the sun goes along under this arch, and returns at night on the upper side to the starting place.

There is another world under this, and it is like ours in every-thing—animals, plants, and people—save that the seasons are different. The streams that come down from the mountains are the trails by which we reach this underworld, and the springs at their heads are the doorways by which we enter it, but to do this one must fast and go to water and have one of the under-ground people for a guide. We know the seasons in the under-world are different from ours, because the water in the springs is always warmer in winter and cooler in summer than the outer air.

When the animals and plants were first made—we do not know by whom—they were told to watch and keep awake for seven nights, just as young men now fast and keep awake when they pray to their medicine. They tried to do this, and nearly all were awake through the first night, but the next night several dropped off to sleep, and the third night others were asleep, and then others, until, on the seventh night, of all the animals only the owl, the panther, and one or two more were still awake. To these were given the power to see and to go about in the dark, and to make prey of the birds and animals which must sleep at night. Of the trees only the cedar, the pine, the spruce, the holly, and the laurel were awake to the end, and to them it was given to be always green and to be greatest for medicine, but to the others it was said: "Because you have not endured to the end you shall lose your hair every winter."

Men came after the animals and plants. At first there were only a brother and a sister until he struck her with a fish and told her to multiply, and so it was. In seven days a child was born to her, and thereafter every seven days another, and they increased very fast until there was danger that the world could not keep them. Then it was made that a woman should have only one child in a year, and it has been so ever since.

As with the Hebrew story, the Cherokee story is accompanied by other stories in the mythology: the first fire, how the moon and sun came into being, how evil entered the world, et cetera. The difference between the stories is the difference between groups.

The patriarchal Hebrew society needed clear and definite answers. It had to be in control because it existed in a harsh land that did not forgive mistakes. The Cherokee society, living in a much easier land, did not need to be as precise. In the Cherokee stories there is more room for mystery, and for individual interpretations of the world. Still, those stories do for the Cherokee exactly what the books of the Bible did for the Hebrews.

## INTEGRITY

Our storytellers have done the same thing as did Hebrew and Cherokee storytellers. Since we are American storytellers, let us take a quick look at our first American storytellers and a snapshot from American history.

The first writers we see as fully American were born within a generation or so after the Revolution: roughly 1780 through 1820. In this group are Thoreau, Emerson, Margaret Fuller, Herman Melville, Edgar Allan Poe, and one of our best, Nathaniel Hawthorne. John Greenleaf Whittier was born in those days, as were Longfellow, William Cullen Bryant, James Russell Lowell, and Harriet Beecher Stowe. Walt Whitman was born then, as were Washington Irving and James Fenimore Cooper.

These were the first fully American writers for the reason that their few predecessors were English colonists. From 1607 (the founding of the Jamestown colony) until the American Revolution in 1775, our writers thought of themselves as loyally English.

Even among the generation born after the American Revolution, that English way of thinking carried some influence. Washington Irving was a fine writer and an able historian, but he mostly followed English literary models. James Fenimore Cooper believed and behaved like an English squire. Still, and in spite of a tendency to overstate everything to the point of contradiction, he produced some very American books.

Those first American writers were raised on their parents' tales of the American Revolution. They read poetry by hotshots like John Trumbull, the poet of the Revolution. They discussed the brilliant and revolutionary thought of Thomas Paine. They came from a background where writing had become intense, always important, and generally defiant.

Recall that in those days the way of life was not so different from five hundred years before. In outlying areas, night still descended like black drapes. In cities, houses held oil-burning lamps, but a lot of illumination came from the fireplace around which families gathered; parents, children, grandparents, uncles, and aunts.

People had spare time in evenings and on Sunday afternoons. Main entertainments were talk, reading, tracing family history, and a certain amount of bulling around that has gone on since the invention of language—and in every nation.

Those young writers, sitting and listening, were among the first people on these shores to know themselves as completely American. As they grew and began telling stories, their stories sought to show an American identity, not British. They had a great deal of new material to work with, material no English writer owned: the frontier, issues of Indian/white/black, and an overreaching (and fairly humorless) religious heritage. In addition, they had the romance of the American land.

Now we arrive at the process by which our early storytellers helped civilization gain integrity and become honorable. It can be done by comparing the problems of Thomas Jefferson in 1807 with the problems of Daniel Webster in 1850. Jefferson enjoyed little American identity. Webster would enjoy a lot.

During his second term, in 1807, Jefferson faced tough opposition. Federalists, and plenty of others, were convinced that Jefferson would destroy this newly formed nation. They howled in absolute frenzy. Powerful groups acted in savage opposition. In one of our first dirty political campaigns, opponents spread a tale that Jefferson sired children by his slaves; a story that has since been greatly generalized among those motivated by politics or prejudice.[4]

Jefferson did stand for questionable national policies, and he never got completely clear on the issue of slavery. As president he made some mistakes. England reigned as the major world power on the seas. France fielded the major armies on land. Jefferson attempted to juggle both facts, and caused people to say the country would soon be at war with

---

[4]Jefferson may very well have sired children with Sally Hemings, who was a slave. Recent DNA findings show a high probability that this is true, and a near certainty that some man in that gene pool was involved. Studies of Jefferson have troubled over the question since the early nineteenth century. The greatest likelihood says that Thomas and Sally engaged in a love affair of many years.

both nations. When Jefferson embargoed trade in an attempt to avoid war, he pretty well wrecked the economy in northern seaports. At the same time, Jefferson cut the U.S. Navy back to a minor force. Later, during the War of 1812, the nation could have used a bigger navy. Tumult popped around Jefferson's ears. Some of his friends began to desert him.

We need now ask what Jefferson had going:

He had his personal integrity as a Southern gentleman. He had the integrity of his thought. He had a few friends, and that was the whole cake. He had no great sense of an American identity, although he had memory of a revolutionary presence. In fact, he was one big portion of what American identity then existed. When he fought back and ran a sometimes brilliant administration, he seems to have done it largely on nerve.

Now we'll reel history ahead to 1850, and here comes Daniel Webster, one of the most respected, and even well-loved, men of his generation. He would die owning the hatred of great numbers of people.

In 1850, Congress already knew that the Union could crack in a civil war. Texas had been annexed after the Mexican War. A congressional battle ensued over the extension of slavery to Texas, to California, and to the New Mexico and Utah territories. Senator Henry Clay of Kentucky introduced a compromise bill, partly the creature of Stephen A. Douglas, senator from Illinois.

Unfortunately, one provision of Clay's compromise was known as the Fugitive Slave Act, which returned escaped slaves to the South. In spite of the powerful Stephen A. Douglas, the Northern states were going to have nothing to do with that compromise unless it was backed by a great statesman. Webster, who had spent a good part of his life opposing Clay, saw that the only way to save the Union was to support Clay.

Tired and ill, Webster, then a man of sixty-eight years, delivered his greatest speech in behalf of the compromise. The compromise passed. Webster gave his life in behalf of the Union.

His speech drove Northern intellectuals, abolitionists, and writers to a point of frenzy.[5] They gave incendiary speeches. They damned Web-

---

[5]The only decent piece of writing from the affair—or at least the only one I've found—is "Ichabod," a poem by John Greenleaf Whittier that compares Webster to Noah after the biblical flood. (Noah kind of deteriorated after that flood. He became a drunk, and had some good times and gray times.)

ster in the press, the least nasty word used being "traitor." They achieved a sort of mindless howl where facts, motives, and reasons meant nothing. There is no possible way to know, but had the Northern intellectuals and writers remained rational—and had Southern slave hunters not trotted north, inflaming the situation—men of good-will might well have ended slavery and avoided the Civil War.[6]

The hated compromise would hold for ten years. Meanwhile, Webster's nerve and conscience passed from the scene. There had been no way for him to delude himself. He knew his speech would not simply make him dead politically, but would kill him. He died in less than two years, during which he served as secretary of state.[7]

Now we may ask what Daniel Webster had going.

He had an American presence. He was completely American, a child of revolution, but not an English revolutionary. Webster had the con-gregated voices of two generations of American writers, and those voices were explaining what it meant to be an American. A lot of those voices would come to hate Daniel Webster, but that is not the point. Those voices gave Webster his identity as an American statesman. In part, they allowed him to make his decision.

He had other American voices. He had the emerging Hudson River School of painting. Those fine artists were explaining the romance of America, a nation that often runs on romance, albeit sometimes darkly. Webster had two generations of American theologians behind his un-derstanding. (Theology remained important in the country until after the Civil War.) Webster had an emerging American music, and though much of it derived from slavery in the form of the minstrel show, nearly all of it was better than the tunes of the Revolution.

We cannot know how much strength came to Daniel Webster be-cause of his American identity; but when we compare his problems to those of Thomas Jefferson, we get this business of integrity in perspec-tive.

Jefferson made a tough, uphill fight. During the American Revolu-tion, he had pledged his life, his fortune, and his sacred honor. There

---

[6]Except in the South, anyone who thought about matters could see slavery was dying. English mills already tried to get away from dependence on Southern cotton. Slavery was becoming economically impractical, as the sharecropping system would soon demonstrate.

[7]This is the historic picture of Webster. If you would like to meet the real flesh-and-blood hero, read "The Devil and Daniel Webster," by Stephen Vincent Benét.

is no reason to doubt he would have given his life and fortune for America. There is plenty of reason to doubt he would ever have taken much of a chance with his sacred honor. After all, honor was nearly his whole source of identity.

Webster gave his life. He took a chance with his honor—or, rather, with being misunderstood. He died in dishonor. We honor him today through the comfortable gauze of history. We can also know he had such courage because of a complete American identity, and with it the strength of a moral man.

## WORKING MYTHS

Every nation, and every people, own mythology. When the myths are working, people and society get along pretty well. When the myths no longer work, people and society find themselves in a world of hurt. A good bit of the trouble you see in our present society comes because we're trying to run a twentieth-century urban world on a nineteenth-century rural mythology.

You, the young and talented, are among this nation's best hopes for survival as an enviable civilization. You can do what national leaders will not, and probably cannot; you can create a new mythology.

Here are a few of the old myths:

The frontier, with Conestoga wagons, Indian wars, cowboys, loggers, railroad building; pioneer and the settler, the notion of "growing up with the country," and the great love of the American land. Heroes: Lewis and Clark, trail bosses, Paul Bunyan, John Henry.

Writers from James Fenimore Cooper to Zane Grey helped build this myth, and pulp writers also contributed. Popular painters like Frederic Remington and Charles M. Russell helped as well. The myths rose from stories told on the trail, and many rose from popular music.

There are also farm myths expressing love for the land. As Steinbeck's character George puts it in *Of Mice and Men,*

> "... Someday—we're gonna get the jack together and we're gonna have a little house and a couple of acres ... we'll have a big vegetable patch and a rabbit hutch and chickens. And when it rains in the winter, we'll just say the hell with goin' to work, and we'll build up the fire in the stove and set around it an' listen to rain comin' down on the roof...."

Southern myths centered around English traditions, and arose from the plantation system. The myths for white people are best seen as expressions of English country life. As we'll later see, myths for black people held all sorts of magic. The mythology of slavery was rural, and its music would be both rural and religious. A lot of Southern music helped form myths. Stephen Foster's minstrel songs are one example, the spiritual is another.

The nation had other mythologies, from songs of the Erie Canal to Western adventures by Bret Harte to riverboat stories by Mark Twain.

The point is that our nation's mythology centers around places where most Americans no longer live, because these days most Americans live in cities. Specifically, fifty years ago, half of our people lived on farms or in towns of under ten thousand. Today only 5 percent of our population lives in those places.

Perhaps the strongest myth is that of the American individualist; rough, woolly, going-his-own-way, and finally being elected judge or president, or appointed general of an army because he didn't pay attention to anyone but himself. In this category we traditionally see people of the caliber of Thomas Edison, Teddy Roosevelt, and Henry Ford.

## MYTHMAKERS, YOUNG WRITERS AND ARTISTS

You can understand the problem. The nation has a mythology symbolized by cowboys and individualism, while needing a mythology that allows people of many cultures to live happily cheek by jowl.

You can measure your own importance by the size of the task. You can also measure your importance as you read further and see what other creators before you faced, and what they accomplished. This business of working in literature and art is one of the toughest, but most rewarding, jobs in the world. I hasten to explain:

The mythic voice rising from literature and art allows us to be humane. We are not humane because of political power, or education, or even religion. We are humane because we recognize the humanity of others. The writer and the artist appeal to that humanity. For that reason, literature and art are the bones of civilization.

Here is a demonstration that you can understand with your heart, but not necessarily with your logic; although on a deep level it is completely logical:

Assume, as legislatures and senators and citizens' committees and PTAs sometimes do assume, that literature and art are useless. They have no practical purpose. They put no beans on the plate. No one wants his child to be a writer or an artist, because many writers and artists cannot even make a living unless they take a secondary job. Let us put the writer and the painter—also the musician, the actor, the composer, and the sculptor—back into the workforce. Let's rid the world of these unprofitable endeavors.

First, let us burn all the plays of Shakespeare and Marlowe. Let us take Nefertiti from the Berlin Museum and sink her back in the Nile. Let us finish the job the Turkish and Greek armies started, and blow up the remains of the Parthenon. Let us raid the museums of Europe, burning the *Mona Lisa,* the Rembrandts, the Renoirs.

We do that. We lift our heads and look around. Civilization still proceeds. The cars still run, the highways function, and the trains are nearly on time.

Good. Now let us destroy every recording by Louis Armstrong, Keely Smith, Janis Joplin. Let's get rid of *Rhapsody in Blue.* Burn the works of Beethoven, and turn all the guitars in the world into planters for geraniums. We will burn the paintings of Rubens and the novels of Dostoyevsky. We will dispose of Jane Austen, Ernest Hemingway, Martin Anderson Nexö. We will get rid of Shohi Ooka, Nikos Kazantzakis.

We do this. We lift our head. Nothing has changed. The trains still run almost on time.

Let us torch the work of Auden, cummings, Frost, Arnold, Amy Lowell, Donne, Emily Dickinson. Let us take the Elgin marbles and use them for the foundation of a motel. Let us renovate the Sistine Chapel, turning it into a useful place for the sale of merchandise. Let us ban dancing in Hawaii, ban dancing in China and Japan and Austria. Let us murder the work of Abram Tertz.

We do this. We lift our heads. Something has changed.

Somewhere, at some time in the destruction, something awful happened. We stopped our forward move toward being humane, and are slipping quickly backward to the state of animals.

The trains still run nearly on time, but we do not. What sustained our hearts and hopes is gone.

The story, the painting, the play, and the song are single bones in the intricate skeleton of a civilization composed of yea-sayers and nay-sayers. The nay-sayers enjoy bombs, superficial power, tons of wealth and influence.

The yea-sayers like humanity. They tell their joys and griefs with stories, plays, music, painting, theology, and pure science. They are not afraid of design, and they are not afraid of content. You are one of them.

# The American Writer in World Literature

I TEACH AT a small university in America's Northwest. My beloved university is happily peopled by multitudes of Norwegians, together with representatives of about every other nationality and ethnic group; but the preponderance is Norwegian. Norwegians are not shy about telling jokes on themselves, and one story they favor tells of the traditional standoff between Norwegians and Swedes:

Once there was an international conference on *The Elephant*. Representatives of all the nations got together and wrangled. After two weeks of infighting, no one could come to any conclusions. The nations voted to suspend the conference. They agreed that at the end of a year, each nation would submit a book about the elephant. These books would form the basis for a new conference.

The year passed. The books came in. This is how it went:

The British book was bound in royal blue with eighteen-karat-gold-embossed title: *The Elephant as an Emblem in Heraldry*.

The German book was three volumes; large, heavy tomes in thick covers of black and royal purple titled: *Tactical and Strategic Uses of the Elephant in Land Warfare*.

The French book was a slim volume bound in limp leather, and with a little ribbon for use as a bookmark. It was titled: *The Love Life of the Elephant*.

The American book was in practical, green library binding and was titled: *How to Breed Bigger and Better Elephants and More of Them.*

The Swedish book was titled: *Seventeen Recipes for Preparing Elephant Steak.*

And the Norwegian book carried a cover of red and orange, titled: *Norway Is Just as Big as Sweden If You Flatten Out the Mountains.*

Norwegians find this hilarious. The point for us is that each nation has a personality, and is known for certain characteristics and interests. These national personalities come about because of a nation's geographic location, its relations with its neighbors, its religions, its art and literature and history. Some nations resemble each other, as do some literatures. What matters for us is the American position:

The American writer has a few companions in the world's literatures. Our closest cousins are Russians and Japanese. American literature is far closer in spirit to the literatures of those nations than to English or European literatures. There are probably dozens of reasons why this is true, but one dominates.

American, Russian, and Japanese literatures are, in a broad and general sense, religious. Most literatures are—but what is different about these is: they are unforgiving. Other literatures gladly take on the clash between good and evil (as do American, Japanese, and Russian literatures), but few take on the specter of sin. I use the term *sin* not in a preacherly sense, but in the intimate sense of the writer in close communion with his or her characters, discovering how those characters feel about their actions.

Pick up a book by an American, Russian, or Japanese, and this question will likely appear: "In a world containing good and evil, what is the proper behavior for a man or woman in a given situation?"

This is not an overwhelming question in French literature. When it appears in English literature, it is usually asked in the context of nationality, not religion. The Spanish are not riddled with the question. Although there are plenty of exceptions, most European literatures see characters as pressed by outside forces. This is why Europe has produced some fine existential writing in the manner of the gloomy French, while America (with the exception of a few Hemingway stories and such) has not. Even our Beat Generation, back in the 1950s when praise of existentialism was at its height, produced little existential silliness, although it did produce an extremely unbeat Allen Ginsberg.

Since anything that attains to the condition of art is, in at least an abstract sense, religious, I have to guess that the idea of sin rises in literatures not heavily influenced by Catholicism. In Catholic countries, the Church serves as an eraser. A person sins, feels guilty, goes to confession, pays off the sin with Hail Marys and Our Fathers. The unworthy behavior does not lie like a warty toad in the subconscious. In America, we have not had the heavy influence of the Catholic safeguard. We brood, feel guilty, and paw at our consciences.

This also happens in America because of our Puritan history. In Japan, the cause doubtless comes from the old ethics of Bushido, the samurai code of chivalry that valued honor above life. In Russia, the problem seems more complex. The Russian Orthodox Church has not traditionally had the same relationship between church and government as state churches in other countries. In addition, life in Russia has been a dark and awfully private experience for the majority. Most likely, that privacy contributes to questions of conscience.

In addition to religion, there's another important difference: America, Russia, and Japan have no Roman history in the European tradition. Where nations beyond Europe have developed—or discovered—a sense of order, it has been order that did not come from the stable Roman influence that links the European background.[1]

Exceptional writers who do not fit the pattern come to mind. From England we hear Graham Greene. From Poland to England, Joseph Conrad. From Greece, Nikos Kazantzakis, one of the spiritual fathers of any honest writer. Great writers break the pattern, but that does not mean the pattern doesn't exist.

In American writing the two most obvious examples of writers preoccupied with sin are Hawthorne and Faulkner, but there is probably no serious American writer who has not at one time or other wrestled the angel of sin.

It is an important wrestling match, and it makes the clash of good and evil seem remote. The whole business of personal responsibility to a code called "right" makes American literature a main structure in moral (not moralistic) attitudes of our civilization. Since our literature

---

[1] I thank religious historian Patricia Killen for this insight.

is a main moral structure, it's also apparent that the serious writer is engaged in building—and sustaining—the American character.

A few words about *good* and *evil,* before turning to the origins of the American writer. You've heard those two words all your life, and heard them, no doubt, to the point where they've become nearly meaningless. It's worth noting that in the history of thought, those two words have produced tons of philosophy, theology, social analysis, and psychology. Nearly every thinker who deals with those words comes to different conclusions. For what it's worth, and as an American writer, I'll give you mine.

Good and evil may run through history, but they are forces that do not cause revolutions. They rescue starving children, or burn witches, and both too often pontificate. In a global sense, good and evil are rather silly, although their effects are often mighty serious.

They are forces knowing little of each other. Each has a direction. Sometimes their directions cause them to collide. When that happens, we usually observe catastrophe, not classical tragedy. For example: During the 1970s, 2 million people died of starvation in Biafra, partly because international oil companies played politics to control offshore oil, and partly because internal political forces tried to take power in the name of good. The resulting starvation was not literary, and it was not theater.

Evil is banal. It has no imagination, is essentially weak, and gets by because it is a bully with a loud mouth. Evil is a force in history. Madmen like the Nazis can sometimes prompt that force. In general, though, all that the most so-called evil men can hope to become are poor dopes whose insecurities get inflicted on a world, because, for sociological reasons, they stumble into power.

Of good, a lot that is optimistic may be said. Goodness is not banal, but is common. It exists around us every day. Perhaps as writers we are more aware of goodness because it's something in which we take an interest. Fiction is not necessarily about spectacular things, but often about usual things.

As writers we discover one or more characters in a situation. We follow those characters with complete respect, watching their decisions while being delighted or appalled. When they foul up, and when ugliness enters their worlds, we allow them to make their mistakes. The anger that we'll later discover among American writers largely exists because their idea of "good" or "right" became offended.

Thus, as writers we love the picture of a small boy walking home at nightfall through a darkening alley, and the boy is whistling. We love shadows that do not darken, but illuminate, the face of an old woman who spoons cereal into her great-grandchild. The little things, and the chance for those things to become central to the story, are an absolute mainstay of writers.

Because America concerns itself with the great themes of good and evil, the American writer has a great advantage in the world's literatures. With advantage comes responsibility. Most of our writers handle that responsibility pretty well, and one strong reason lies in our history, to which it is time to turn.

# THE ORIGINS

A HISTORY TEACHER may have once told you that we study history in order to avoid the mistakes of history. It's a tidy idea that ought to work, but often doesn't. You can study history until your eyeballs wrinkle, then look up, only to discover that someone else already made a mistake for you; and the guy who made the mistake will most likely tell you how fortunate you are to fight a war he began, or suffer an economic depression caused by his excess.

The better answer is that we study history in order to understand ourselves, and thus understand the minds and emotions of our characters.

Here is an illustration showing how you have perceptions, thus understandings, that are not, strictly speaking, uniquely yours. They derive from history.

Ask yourself, "How did my parents learn to be parents?" You'll answer variously, depending on your relationship with your parents. About the only answer you won't give will be "I came with a book of instructions." The best answer will probably be "They learned from having been raised by their own parents." And, having said that, you will realize that your grandparents learned to be parents from their parents, your great-grandparents. And your great-grandparents learned from your great-great-grandparents. And so on.

For those lucky enough to have great-grandparents still living, I invite you to listen carefully to them. Watch for attitudes. Listen for slang.

Get a feel of who they might have been when younger. Then look at your grandparents. Then look at your parents. Then look at yourself. You'll find that more than genes are passed down generations.

I am quite fond of saying that we are the products of forgotten words spoken by forgotten ancestors. You will find more basic perceptions in common with your great-grandfather than you'll find differences. The differences will lie in opinions, because you confront the contemporary world and your great-grandfather remembers other times. There's a difference, though, between basic perceptions and opinions. Perceptions dictate how you see the world, and opinions are changing reflections of your changing world.

This same principle applies to nations. America has changed on its surface in the past 350 years, but the marrow in its bones has changed but little. That's why much of what you see in our present world seems without reason. Or, where reasons are given, a lot of what goes on seems silly. Let's look at five examples that seem silly:

1. Sex is not something the human race discovered but recently; yet the various media, and especially television, treat it that way. Sex is also touted as the sole key to success in commerce, adventure, weight loss, scientific research, grocery shopping, and, possibly, the training of the family dog. About the only thing it is not good for, according to the media, is as an expression of love between two people. We'll soon see that such sexual preoccupation is very American, and has an American spin.

2. High schools and colleges hype the single purpose of education as a method for making money; as if the cultivation of the mind was a waste if not accompanied by bank balances.

3. Local, regional, and national governments supposedly "... of the people, by the people, and for the people. ..." treat the people as problems obstructing the exercise of power. This is generally done by indiscriminate use of rules accompanying bureaucracy.

4. Multitudes (certainly not all) of religions claim to be humane, but manage to preach division, amusement, and, perhaps only 1 percent, messages of understanding.

5. Pressure groups, ranging from corporate interests to ethnic and social interests, claim their rights are offended unless they are given even more than they can reasonably get.

None of this is as senseless as it seems, and nothing is especially new, except for means of expression. These days we have more ways to broadcast messages, but television, for example, did not invent sensationalism about sex, nor did radio or newspapers; sensationalism being nothing but supercharged gossip. Through public and economic pressures, high schools and colleges have been forced into the role of professional schools all during this century. Machinations by government stem from days before the American Revolution. Religions are institutions, and they suffer from flaws attending institutions; generally flaws stemming from the exercise of power. And pressure groups ask for more than they can get, knowing that if they ask for the stars, they'll get at least the moon.

If you look at the confusion of our contemporary American world, the justification for writers and artists to deal with history becomes evident.

## PURITANICAL BEHAVIOR

You've probably heard that the United States is a Protestant nation. You've probably heard that it is, or was, a Puritan nation. Those were good things to hear, but I doubt if anyone explained how Protestant or Puritan mythology forms actions. Let's start by looking at one piece of foolishness that, in another time, made sense in America.

Every few decades, prissiness enters the American world. You will lately have experienced tight-lipped self-righteousness from people who do not know you, but who tell you how *not* to live. They tell you how *not* to dress, how *not* to think, and how *not* to express a well-thought opinion (just on the off chance that you didn't listen and actually did some original thinking). They tell you that certain words must never be used, although many of those words (such as, for example, "Occidental," "Oriental," "Caucasian," "Negro," "Indian") are as bland as custard. In some parts of the country, and especially on college campuses, it has become practically impossible to express a thought without offending someone who is "politically correct." Those who are offended probably believe they are on the cutting edge of change. They are, in fact, only antiques. America has seen their dreary type for three-and-a-half centuries.

Most people are not this way because most people have good sense. However, America is presently seeing more than its share of prissiness. It's easier to ignore the pettiness of prissy people, both in your life and on the page, if you know that in terms of olden times they are (and I'm honestly not trying to be humorous here) like Puritans without a god.

They are terribly frightened, and are acting in the same way as those New Englanders who once hanged witches. They act that way because a once-Puritan nation retains a large memory of its past. The differences between them, and those old witch-hunters, arrive because our contemporaries are not really Puritan but only puritanical. In addition, our contemporaries have mostly themselves to fear, while the New Englanders (as we'll later see) had very good reason to be afraid.

Especially in America, such behavior inevitably occurs when people feel insecure. They traditionally surround themselves with tons of rules. As long as they can enforce the rules on someone, they feel at least nominally in control. I suppose such people are frightened by their inadequacies. There's an old saying: "Either you eat life, or life eats you." Life, I fear, is eating them.

A second possibility is that they are simply inarticulate, and wish to inflict misery because that sort of action makes them feel powerful. Our history is full of such people, and our writers have combatted them for at least two centuries.

Here is a wonderful example of a writer taking on the problem, from *The Fiddler in Barly* (1926), a novel by Robert Nathan. A fiddler has come to town. He is talking with a youngster, Metabel, who is the subject of a lot of tsk-ing among the good citizens of Barly. Those citizens suspect Metabel of dancing in the woods.

"Oh," said Metabel with a gasp, "I'm not a dancer." And she looked about fearfully to see if the preacher, or anyone, had heard him [the fiddler]. "I'm nothing but a little girl."

The fiddler left the garden, and came and sat down beside her. "Why are you afraid of what gives you joy?" he asked. "Is it a sin to be happy, and to dance? Then we must all of us sin a little bit, my child. I do not believe you are any more wicked than a rose-bush."

And he added gravely, "It is wicked to be envious, or to make people unhappy. But it is not wicked to dance like a little tree in the wind, or a beetle with a green coat. There are so many who cannot dance or sing in the world, and so they go about scolding those who can. That is what is wicked, as a matter of fact."

Nathan's theme is both as old as puritanism, and as new as today. We may now forge ahead on this Puritan business and see why it became so strong in our history.

I'll have to go at it roundabout, because it will not serve you if I make a bunch of summary statements and ask you to trust that they are true. Anyone can offer information, but art and literature offer understanding. Writers and artists need to experience the process by which things come into being, because that's the process they use in their own work.

## Colonial America

Let's first note that colonial America was not especially interested in politics from 1607 until 1750, or thereabouts. America was motivated by religion and commerce. Local politicians might wrangle; but for the most part, our country did not become overtly political until just before the American Revolution.

Thus, the struggle for the American mind, and for the minds of America's writers, began not as a political battle, but as a battle between gods; a battle every bit as titanic as anything bequeathed by ancient mythology. The resulting losses and victories would combine and form mainstreams of American thought, literature, and art.

## Sources of American Thought

Mainstreams of thought, literature, and art rose from three great ideas:

Original Sin
Original Possibility
Original Good

The first, Original Sin, was religious, and especially Puritan. The second, Original Possibility, was both religious and philosophic in roughly equal amounts. The third, Original Good, was largely philosophic, but a little bit religious.

## Original Sin

The American experience begins with Original Sin. I'm certain most readers, even those with no religious background, have heard of Original Sin. I'm also pretty sure most readers will not regard it as a great idea, because, practically speaking, Original Sin evolved through centuries to become the biggest fraud ever perpetrated on Western history; a shabby doctrine used for political and social control. By the time it got to America, the idea would become so strong it would influence the American mind—apparently, forever.

In its beginnings, and long before it reached America, the idea was not a fraud. To look at Original Sin as an originating—instead of controlling—idea, we have to go back many centuries; but it's worth the digression.

In the days of the early church, the idea of Original Sin was used to explore the difference between humans and all other life. One important spin-off from thoughts about Original Sin held that all creatures have souls, but only humans need redemption. Thus, a case could be made that your cat, at least, is bound for Glory.

Original Sin was once a great idea because it was an attempt to explain and to understand human behavior. The very roots of modern psychology go all the way back to at least the fifth and sixth centuries.

As centuries rolled past, and as religion gained political and economic power, priests and preachers peddled this simpleminded version of Original Sin:

The serpent in the Garden of Eden tempted Eve with forbidden fruit, and Eve tempted Adam. They both fouled up royal. Because of this, God introduced death into the world, along with Heaven and Hell. In other words, if that easily conned girl—who had only just been fashioned from a somewhat obtuse guy's rib—had not been euchred by a serpent (who stood to make no profit on the deal, and who up until that time walked about on legs; but who would ever after have to wriggle on his belly), you might live forever without any problems at all.

If there is ever a need to demonstrate the power of mythology, for good or ill, the Adam-and-Eve story will do nicely. It lies at the base of sorrows that are summed up in a widely circulated ancient rhyme: "In Adam's fall, / We sinned all." In other words, everyone was supposedly born flawed, sinful, and thus subject to political and economic control by a priesthood.

This version of Original Sin held on for centuries. As the church used it to wield power, and as social and economic conditions changed, some people rebelled. As far back as the tenth century, revolutionary movements rose against the church. Some of those movements took the form of satanic worship. The whole concept of the Devil, accompanied by witches, warlocks, demons, and unclean spirits, spread in opposition to established religious and economic systems.[1]

At the same time, fear began to rise because, while Heaven was sort of unreal, you may be sure the clergy made Hell just as real as real could be. That kind of reality caused fairly continual religious preoccupation among many—perhaps, most people. Much later, when it got to America, the reality of Hell lived as a constant terror among Puritans.

## THE REALITY OF HELL

I first understood how real was this ancient business of Heaven and Hell when I visited the cathedral in Haarlem, Holland. In fact, I think that cathedral started me on a study of the origins of American thought. At the time, I knew just enough history to understand that Holland had played a pretty strong role in the life of Pilgrims in Massachusetts.

The Haarlem cathedral is enormous, towering into those gray and windy skies. Down the street still stands the poorhouse where the painter Franz Hals died, and where his later work is still displayed (my reason for being in Haarlem in the first place). The cathedral sits above

---

[1]The Devil appears in many shapes through history. Six thousand years ago, along the Nile, the Devil took the form of a crocodile. In Hebrew angelology, the Devil is an accusing spirit, not a tempter. The European version of the Devil rose as Christianity encountered elder gods of other religions, and adapted those gods to its own purposes. Dionysus and Pan, for example, were goatlike, having horns and animal sexual proclivities.

a tightly knit square of old, old bricks. It is one heart of ancient darkness.

As I approached, it was so huge. No fire, not the fires of perdition itself, could warm that cathedral. I entered and walked toward one of the distant altars, gradually becoming aware that I walked over mighty curious-looking and enormous slabs of slate. My mind tried to be objective, but my feet did not like what they were about. The slates lay carved with pictures of skeletons, and other pictures. The slates carried dates.

I realized with horror that I walked across a floor containing the dead. My horror came not from the fact of death, which is a normal condition. It came from the horror these vanished corpses must have once felt. With the horror came indignation. I knew I walked in the company of those ancient fat cats who accumulated enough wealth to allow themselves to be buried inside the church. Those fat cats did everything they could to protect against demons, witches, and all things evil that stalk the night. In the sacred depths of the church, behind the powers of prayer, those few felt protected.

## Two Takes on Original Sin That Were Imported to America

After the Protestant Reformation of 1517, two versions of Original Sin begin to take shape. They would shortly make their appearance on the shores of the recently discovered New World. They came from the religious leaders Martin Luther and John Calvin.

### Martin Luther

Martin Luther (1483–1546) figured that people were born without sin, but rapidly developed a taste for it. Specifically, he held the doctrine of *incurvatus se*, the "inner eye" or "inward looking." This means that a baby has no sin until it grows to the point where it starts looking inside itself, instead of looking outward toward God. This was an important idea. Centuries before psychology came up with the idea of the ego, Luther had expressed that concept in religious terms.[2]

---

[2]This idea would not really take effect in America until the early eighteenth century. It was shaped by German Pietist religions: Mennonites, Moravians, and latterly, Amish. In general, Pietists express their faith by quiet devotion and a plain way of life. These religions are not large today, but were powerful in their time.

# John Calvin

John Calvin lived from 1509 through 1564, and thus inherited the responsibilities of a religious man during the Reformation. He also inherited the complete intolerance that marks those days. Calvin, churchman of Geneva, has been described by some theologians as a bookkeeper. A standard theological joke about Calvin is that he was the man who created God in his own image. Both statements are just true enough to be droll, without covering the full range of facts.

By 1530, Calvin established a working theology, and he rapidly established social control in Geneva. Even back then, however, Europeans had a different view from future generations of Americans when it came to churchmanship. Calvin got kicked out of Geneva in 1538. Geneva began backsliding toward what it feared was Hell. Society began to fall apart. Calvin was invited back, and he returned in 1541. He was not the first theocrat in history, but he *was* a theocrat. He wanted government to be concreted in Biblical law, and *he* wanted to interpret the law.[3]

Calvin's theology still leaves theologians shaking their heads with awe, if not with envy. He reasoned thus:

Because of Original Sin, humans are born depraved: he used the term "Original Depravity." People were so low that God was not obligated to save a single one from utter damnation. However, God, being good, would save a few.

Further, if God is all-knowing and omnipotent, then it is clear God has everything traced. He knows centuries before you are born what your name will be. He knows who your parents will be. He knows exactly how you will live your life and what will happen to you. Finally, He knows before you are ever born whether you will go to Heaven or Hell. In a narrow sense, your good works or your bad works mean nothing. God has already predestined you to bliss or damnation.[4]

---

[3]History often offers good advice, and one such piece of advice is: *Never* give political power to preachers or intellectuals, because hell will pop if you do; as witness what will happen next in this book, or, historically, the butchery that happened during the French Revolution, or after the Soviet Revolution in 1917.

Politicians are better at government because politicians live by compromise. Preachers and intellectuals are used to arriving at what they consider *truth*, and are thus uncompromising; an attitude that has proven dangerous.

[4]This was not a new idea. In the fourth and early fifth centuries, it was a concern

These ideas of sin and predestination would become controlling forces in the Puritan congregations of early America. Those congregations, as well as the Pilgrims, would get their beliefs from Calvinism as it developed in Puritan England.

## HOW PURITAN ENGLAND FORMED
## AMERICAN THOUGHT

The late 1500s and early 1600s were wonderful times to be alive, if a person could manage to stay alive. What with periodic epidemics, no sanitation, the misadventures of the Spanish, witch trials, religious intolerance, and the capriciousness of royalty, for many people staying alive became a full-time job.

These were days of Marlowe and Shakespeare. They were also days of preoccupation with religion. The preoccupation grew so great that, to this day, no honest American writer has escaped its effect. While American writers may not be preoccupied with religion, they come from a society founded in preoccupation.

In the seventeenth century a person really could be hanged, burned, beheaded, or drawn and quartered because of religion.[5] Death did not generally come from attempted purges. It came from intolerance rising from theology and dogma. This means that each time the society killed someone, the death was singular, not wholesale. It was generally surrounded by trials and denunciations and encouragement to recant.

If this seems strange today, it will seem less strange if we understand that the concept of tolerance was nearly brand-new in European and English thought. The idea of tolerance was first introduced in 1565, in a book titled *Stratagemata Satanae* or *Satan's Stratagems,* by Jacopo Acon-

---

of St. Augustine and St. John of Damascus. Each had a slightly different take on the matter, but neither denied freedom of will. The predestination that worked for John Calvin seems, at this late date, far less abstract than its predecessors.

[5]I've been advised by teachers I respect to explain why the seventeenth century is spoken of in terms of the 1600s, or why the twentieth century is described in terms of the 1900s. Apparently, this sort of thing is no longer taught in schools.

Dating of centuries is in relation to the birth of Christ. The first century after the birth of Christ ran from the year 1 to the year 100. The second century began in 101. Thus there's a seeming delay of one hundred years when we speak of centuries. The seventeenth century began in 1601, the eighteenth century in 1701, the nineteenth in 1801, and the twentieth in 1901. The twenty-first century will begin in 2001.

cio. He argued that Satan tried to tear Christianity apart by introducing different dogmatic creeds among different religions. His plea for tolerance got him kicked out of the Dutch Reformed Church.

In addition to intolerance, the seventeenth-century world that produced Pilgrims and Puritans was saturated, absolutely saturated, with God and theology. It was a world but little removed from the Middle Ages (roughly speaking, the period from the fifth to the fifteenth centuries).[6] The seventeenth century was still as preoccupied with religion, and its possible consequence of Hell, as was the tenth or thirteenth.

As in all times in history, religious preoccupation in the seventeenth century was not universal. A lot of people drank and laughed, danced and sang, cussed and helled around. The difference is that in the seventeenth, the forces of religion became controlling, and so did preoccupation; because the Reformation had thrown individual responsibility for salvation onto the believer.[7]

Preachers enjoyed followings the way rock stars do today. It was not unusual for people to travel several days on foot to hear a celebrated preacher, who might enjoy audiences of hundreds or even a thousand. A preacher would give a sermon, then take it to the printer. The sermon would sell in the streets in the same way boys would sell newspapers in a later century.[8] In addition, the preachers railed against each other. There were mighty battles of words, scripture, and denunciations. When we look at the overall English and European pattern, we see Western civilization in search of ideas that eventually released Euro-

---

[6]The best picture of Middle Ages thinking that became central to the American experience may be found in *A Distant Mirror*. Historian Barbara Tuchman points out that the sky lay close to earth in those days, and there was little sound except the lowing of cattle and the clank of the church bell. By the seventeenth century, conditions would improve, but not much. In cities some lamplight shone after the sun went down, but darkness remained fear ridden and could not be defeated.

[7]An illustration of preoccupation: The Quaker, George Fox, records that he went to an inn at the end of a workday. A couple of workmen, probably in the trades or apprenticed to them, drank and talked. Those men had probably put in a sunrise-to-sunset day.

Were they talking about where to find a usable shoe, or where to find a tractable woman? No. They were most earnestly discussing the sacred blood of Christ. Religion and God were so commonly a part of life they served as ordinary subjects in barroom conversation.

[8]Even as late as the 1840s, in Boston, preachers still did the same thing, although the newsboy aspect of the business disappeared.

peans from the Middle Ages. Those ideas produced a variety of religions.

Five major forces arose after the Reformation. Those forces were Catholic, Lutheran, Calvinist, the Church of England, and, by the middle of the seventeenth century, Quakers. For our present purpose, we may ignore the Catholics and Lutherans. The American experience would begin with Calvinist Puritans, and that means we have to think about the Church of England. Quakers, who were also main players in early America, will appear later.

## THE CHURCH OF ENGLAND

The Church of England[9] was originally the Catholic church, as modified by King Henry VIII (1491–1547). He modified it for a number of reasons, but principally because he wanted a divorce in order to father a legitimate son. The Pope would not allow such foolishness. In 1533, Henry said, "To hell with the Pope," and married Anne Boleyn.

Too much was at stake in the way of power and the ornaments of power. The Church of England still resembled the Catholic church, with lots of rituals and robes and costumes. As power struggles grew, a group of religionists began to modify the Church of England. They said that they were "purifying" the church. As time rolled along, and purification caused a predictable amount of death and destruction, the Church of England was grabbed by the purifiers, who were now called Puritans.

Some Puritans became even more pure and insisted that there be no churches, only meetinghouses.[10] Everything would be plain. In fact, everything would be simplified to point of discomfort. People sat on backless benches. Light came from small windows, and, of course, there was no heat in winter.

Doctrines and theology were further modified so that the church came in line with the teachings of John Calvin. A new, and awfully rigid, brand of Puritanism arose. The purest of the pure came to America, either because they wanted to practice their brand of Calvinism exclusively, or because they were kicked out of England. For example,

---

[9]Later known as the Anglican/Episcopal church.

[10]The Quakers, whom we'll soon meet, also insisted on meetinghouses. In their beginnings, though, they met at private homes to avoid arrest by the sheriff.

the English preachers wanted the Pilgrims dead. The Pilgrims fled from England to Amsterdam in Holland.

Many groups contained elements of other groups. Politics and power plays within religions formed odd alliances. Thus, "Puritanism," as a term, could describe a state of mind. A lot of the wildest so-called heretics acted every bit as puritan as did their conservative opponents. Sometimes sincere conservatives even got mixed up with scandal, as happened to the Pilgrims after they went to Amsterdam. They got involved with a congregation that had a mild sex scandal, and that (although it wasn't funny then, it's sort of funny now) was headed by a guy named Studley.

Elements of social and economic reform also entered these religions. In the middle of the seventeenth century, religionists called Diggers and Levelers would propose radical economics in the name of religion. The people who came to America were thus products of the modified theology, politics, and economics that restructured the Church of England.

# The American Experience
## Begins

In America, the first two groups to establish their ideas, and make them stick, were Pilgrims and Puritans. The Pilgrims had left England for Amsterdam, then left Amsterdam for Leyden, Holland, then came to Plymouth in America. Puritans came from England to Boston Bay. From our historical distance, we can see three main differences between them:

First, the Pilgrims never developed the hard-line theocracy (control of government by preachers) that occurred in Puritan Boston Bay, partly, perhaps, because they were not economically a very successful colony. They had a hard time keeping preachers because they did not pay as much.

Second, the Pilgrims were what we know as Congregationalists. The congregational stance was an absolute religious proposition with the Pilgrims, although others thought of the position as political. In America, these Congregationalists were called by another name: Separatists. Separatism meant that the Pilgrims wanted religion separate from government, and separate from a hierarchy beyond their own congregations. They did not want bishops and other such churchy paraphernalia. They also wanted no political obligation to England or any other nation (and rightly, in the case of England, which would have hanged every blessed one of them).

Third, the Pilgrims had more generosity and balance. The only witch trial in Plymouth history ended when the complaint was laughed out of court. The Pilgrims wore colorful clothes and had some colorful leaders. In addition, they even showed a sense of humor. I expect this came about because their history was so difficult they had to either laugh or jump off cliffs.

The Calvinist Puritans in Boston, however, were not Separatists. They were perfectly content to keep the sea roads open to England. To them, the idea of separation between church and state was unthinkable. When their own Roger Williams expressed the idea of separation, they kicked him out of the colony.

## PREOCCUPATION AND ITS RESULTS

Our early people learned religious preoccupation in England and Holland. When this preoccupation hit America, it stood unopposed. There were no playwrights—Shakespeares, Marlowes, Dekkers, or Jonsons—to tweak ecclesiastical noses. There were taverns, and we may be glad of that, but there were no satirists. There was no one to scoff, to disbelieve, to scratch sand in the eyes of the status quo. When a scoffer appeared, he was thrown out of the colony.

When conditions like these rise in history, some form of dictatorship rises with them. The disbelievers, the scoffers, the malcontents are the ones who keep the world safe from authoritarianism. That is the main reason why oppressive governments attempt to keep a tight rein on their artists and writers. It is also why the American lunatic fringe howls for the banning of books, and why those who demand "correctness" despise laughter.

## MASSACHUSETTS BAY

In America, the most effective religious oppression began in 1630, when two thousand Calvinist Puritans arrived in Massachusetts Bay. (The colony had already been established in 1628.) These folk became extreme examples of what can happen when a religion gets out of hand.

The Massachusetts Bay people came to these shores chock-full of Calvinist belief. They also confronted a situation for which neither England nor Europe could prepare them.

## FREEHOLD OF LAND

They hit a brand-new continent where land was not allocated. Aboriginal people lived on the land, but the idea of an individual owning land was absolutely alien to the thinking of any American Indian. In contrast, the Puritans arrived from England, where every spoonful of land was owned.

Matters immediately became confusing. Wealth did not happen right away, but it *began* to happen right away. The colonists had unlimited resources and the will to work. They discovered that people who work their own land will just naturally work about three times harder than if they are on someone else's land. In those witchery days of yesteryear, the Puritans got into a theological bind.

This was the bind: They believed they were predestined, but they also began to get rich. Predestination depended on being under the thumb of a harsh God who didn't let common people get away with anything, leave alone allowing them to become rich. Through the seventeenth century, the sneaky notion began to arrive that God had either lost control, or no longer cared.

We read their records, which are plentiful, and see them trying to solve the contradiction between predestination and wealth. Failing to solve it, they turned to their preachers.

Any sensible person, it would seem, would say something like "Well, if I'm predestined, there ain't a whale of a lot anybody can do about it, so I might as well go out and have a good time." Calvinism, as interpreted by American preachers, held a different notion. The preachers kindly explained that while nothing was definite in the way of salvation, a communicant could discover indicators.

First, the preachers argued, a person predestined for Heaven would exhibit behavior reflecting the fact. The person would be awfully, awfully good, and would do exactly as the preacher commanded. Second, if a person was predestined for Heaven, God would surely give some indications in the person's life in this world. In early Massachusetts, this nice bit of casuistry came to mean that wealth could be taken as an indication of God's favor. For that reason, our early people worked terribly hard. As they worked hard, they gradually became richer than man was ever supposed to be.

Preoccupation would sometimes become total. It got so silly and intense that a man might be overjoyed if his cow calved twins, because that was a double indication of God's favor. If the cow dropped only one calf, and that calf stillborn, the man would know despair. Such an event signaled perdition.

It would be a mistake, though, to scoff at those old Puritans. They knew they were in a war, but the war they believed they were in was not the one developing. They believed the enemy was Satan, who occasionally was assisted by depredations of Satan's children, the Indian tribes. The coming war was a war of ideas, but Puritans, stuck as they were with the idea of Original Sin, could not understand that.

They were also stuck with the idea of absolute control by preachers who believed themselves "godly." The Puritans could not understand the ramifications of that, either; although, as we'll shortly see, it is gloriously written that some of them would figure it out.

## HOW THEY LIVED AND WHAT THEY LIVED FOR

I like to think of ancient springtimes, and how people who were young, or old, would wake as dawn colored eastern skies above the Atlantic. People would rub their eyes, feel the cold air of a New England spring, and roll from bed to stir the fire. I like to think of the forest beneath that dawn, the ancient hardwoods beginning to bud into new leaves, and dark conifers like paint across the mountainside.

They rose praying, I suspect, or at least a lot of them did. After prayers, most were probably occupied with thoughts of chores and the work of the day. They did not daily note—although they may have been aware subconsciously—that they had survived one more night unattacked by demons. When they went to milk the cow, they expected her to give milk. They did not daily fear that the milk would be stopped or soured by witchcraft. After all, they paid their preacher a pretty fair price to worry about things like that.[1]

Meanwhile, there was work to do. If prayer was a part of their lives,

---

[1] Interesting sidelight: Hardly anyone drank milk or water. Both were thought unhealthy, and, considering the lack of sanitation in those days, probably were. Milk was used to make cheese. Our early people drank beer, cider, syllabub (made by curdling milk with cider), brandy, flip (made of beer, rum, molasses, and stirred with a hot poker), and, if they could afford it, wine.

and if some religious fear was part of their lives, then how were they different from people of other ages and times? For, in fact, they were different.

## THE MEDIEVAL MIND

The American Calvinist religion represents the final, and, perhaps, highest development of the mind of the Middle Ages in the Western world. That mind did not die with the Renaissance, nor with the Reformation. In fact, to this day it may not be developing, but is not quite dead. It is tenacious as a razorback hog, a real survivor.

Several features show the medievalism of the American Puritan. The theology was at least as rigid as had been religion at the deepest point of darkness in Europe. Like those old Europeans, the Boston people believed as they were told, or disbelieved and kept their mouths shut. While few of the old Europeans could read or write, the Americans were a fairly literate population. They reinforced the theological assumptions and constraints through constant discussion. This had the effect of medievalism because it reinforced preoccupation with Hell and religion.

Another feature was isolation. The isolation of those early towns was even greater than the isolation of peoples during medieval times. In America's seaports, a certain amount of commerce brought ideas from other places, but in the interior the villages stood completely alone. Combine the religious focus of thought with the social control brought through isolation, and the medieval village begins to appear on these shores. At its base, American thought stems from days before the Reformation. We carry a strain of darkness every bit as dark as were those ancient nights when witches and warlocks and the Devil himself rode the winds.

Isolation would remain an important factor for at least two generations. People's lives revolved around the church building, standing in plain sight as had churches of the Middle Ages. Like the people of the Middle Ages, their lives were constrained in the circle of work and home and church. Ability to travel was limited to foot, or horseback. For much of the year, the roads (trails or wagon tracks) were impassable. Each town was a fairly self-supporting, self-contained entity.

While we can easily imagine what went on in those days, imagination is not necessary. Puritans were scrupulous record keepers. It was a duty of their religion. The mind of the Middle Ages is there for anyone who wants to do a bit of reading.

In that reading, we would see the courage displayed by people living in a few towns on the eastern edge of an enormous forest, a forest extending all the way to the long grass prairies later known as Illinois and Iowa. The forest stood everywhere, and as people contacted the Indians, the forest became increasingly dangerous; for the Puritans were most often ham-handed when dealing with Indians. (Recall that the seventeenth century was largely a century of intolerance.)

As the Puritans lived on the edge of that forest, quite a few things developed. For one, they did their God-given best to cut down the forest, and with no small justification. During their early years, the forest was one great cause of fear.

They were also in a battle with land. New England holds some of the world's most beautiful land, but in many places the most difficult: little more than rock held together with sprinkles of soil.

## THEOCRACY

These conditions, combined with the fact that no one could manage much effective scoffing, produced a theocracy. While there were several honest men in pulpits, the theocracy that developed would soon prove itself composed of some of the most bigoted and outrageous power-mongers who ever had the temerity to call themselves preachers. The first American "good old boys" did not come from the South, they came from Massachusetts. The good old boys would anoint themselves as caretakers of that last expression of the medieval mind, and would attend it as a sacred flame; a flame that even today continues to flicker in the deep and often dark recesses of the American mind.

Their society was one of laws that, today, seem either absurd or dangerous. A man and wife were not allowed to kiss in public. Such an act would net two or three hours in the stocks. No one was allowed to sit in a tavern for more than an hour. The punishment was a public whipping. The amount of beer one could drink was strictly limited, although the limit was high. People could be arrested for gossip, for appearing to be lazy, for wearing clothing sewed with colored thread.[2]

---

[2]Two social classes predominated. Freemen had the right to vote; and, together with their wives, wear clothing with gold or silver thread. They were called "Mister," and

If an unmarried man and woman went for a walk without getting permission from her father, arrest was certain if they got caught. People were whipped for cursing. In fact, there was not a single element of Puritan life that was not regulated by laws or rules.

You would think that a society this rigid would be discarded almost immediately, but it was not. For one thing, such a society offers a sense of security, because if you follow the rules, you're home free. People who crave security have no trouble with rules, and isolation gave those folk good reason to crave security. Added to isolation was the awful fear of a Hell they knew was real. If the entire society seems somewhat sadistic, and not a little masochistic, it owned good reasons.

Another reason why their darkness would be tenacious is because Puritans believed in education. No other force would allow a few thousand people spread along a coast of expanding seaports to exercise such enormous influence. The Puritans established schools. They extended their thought through centuries, and their thought underwent little change. In the eighteenth century, when their Harvard College strayed too far from "Truth," they established Yale College in order to correct the damage.[3]

In the late seventeenth century, in Massachusetts Bay, matters would finally develop to a point where the Puritan situation could not last. Too much new information arrived from England, Holland, France, Germany; and too many people with other ideas headed for America. Prosperity stood panting in the wings. Science developed rapidly, and offered new ways of viewing the world.

While Puritanism lasted, it flamed, and Massachusetts was a place where we would not wish to live. As people became afraid, and as the theocracy took control, the Puritan village became completely rigid. Prices were fixed on wages and goods. People could be thrown in jail simply because they were accused, even though there existed no evi-

---

there were few of them (about 4 percent of the population). Common men were called "Goodman." Women did not vote, nor, of course, did slaves or apprentices.

[3](Yale, incidentally, still holds this as one of its main missions. Ask any Yale man.)

We can see the effectiveness of Puritan education by contrasting it with Philadelphia in the late eighteenth century. Quakers of Philadelphia would fail to establish a wide educational system, although among their meetings education was a great concern. This, together with an influx of Calvinists into Pennsylvania, blunted Quaker hopes for social control in the soon-to-be new nation. Quakers also began losing economic control starting in 1758 and ending in 1772, as they released their slaves.

dence to justify the accusation. Anyone who expressed the opinion that a particular preacher was unsound could find himself in deeper trouble than the trouble faced today by people charged with armed robbery. In our day, we don't generally hang armed robbers, but in the Puritan era, you could get hanged if you crossed the wrong preacher.

While the fear of Satan, and the control by theocracy, lasted, the society showed bared teeth. The control lasted in less-than-crippled form from 1620 until the Salem witch trials in 1692. In crippled form, it has lasted ever since, and a Calvinist discipline, a strain of darkness, runs through the work of almost all American writers. If it were the only strain, we would be in deep, deep trouble.

As it turns out, Puritanism, and the crack-up of Puritanism, and the struggle of ideas that caused the crack-up, worked in a happy combination to produce the American writer; who, in turn, produced one of the world's great literatures.

# CRACK-UP

PURITANISM CRACKED FOR several reasons. Partly, it cracked because the theocracy became so extreme that the entire society turned outlandish.

Another reason, as we've seen, was wealth. Within very few years, American ships were trading in ports of the West Indies, Spain, and England. The New England folk used the highways of the sea, where travel was less limited than land travel.

The biggest reason for crack-up had been lurking for over fifty years—the idea of Original Possibility.

## ORIGINAL POSSIBILITY: THE PRELUDE

The first great battle for the American mind, and the mind of American writers, took place in Boston in 1637 when the enemy came down like a lamb on a lion's fold. The lion roared and chomped. It chewed meat, spat out bones, and ended up sending itself to Hell on a bobsled. The lion went in that direction because Hell was its proper place.

In 1637, as the battle opened, there had been a few witchcraft problems in the past. A few people were hanged. Except for that, there had been little official violence. To the preachers' credit (although there is reason to believe they protected their collective posterior), that first battle was mostly theological disputation and spite.

The bare facts are easily told. A preacher named John Cotton, who stands in that American stream of well-educated intellectuals who are less than brilliant (like his namesake, Cotton Mather, and not like our great intellectuals), preached that there was a difference between a religion of works and a religion of grace. In a religion of grace, John Cotton suggested, the worshiper could actually experience some transformation of his original depraved condition. That transformation would come through the actual entry of God into his being.

A highly respected married woman, Anne Hutchinson, the daughter of a minister in England, bought the idea. She formed a meeting of women. It was originally designed to discuss the points of the previous Sunday's sermon for the benefit of women who had been unable to attend. The meeting soon threatened to get out of hand. Hutchinson also started to get out of hand, expressing opinions that sounded much like preaching. The record of comments, even by her enemies, suggests she was brilliant.

John Cotton was minister of the church to which Anne Hutchinson belonged. As Hutchinson's meeting grew to unexpected proportions, it changed. The women were soon comparing the virtues of preachers in and around Boston. They concluded that except for John Cotton, and for Hutchinson's brother-in-law, John Wheelwright of Mount Wollaston, every other Boston preacher walked the authoritarian line of a religion ruled by theocratic law. No matter how loving and understanding a worshiper might be, that worshiper was still a mechanical pawn of God.

The Boston clergy reacted in the way power always reacts when it is weak. It behaved in the same way spiritually weak governments arm to the teeth, or spiritually weak cities promote police riots during political conventions. Although the trial and subsequent excommunication of Anne Hutchinson were couched in theology, the preachers' message was clear to history if not to themselves.

That message said: If Original Depravity can be changed by the grace of God, that will alter the power structure. The preacher will turn from dictator to spiritual adviser, only.

There it was, the first great issue over which the battle for the American mind would be waged. On one side stood nearly every preacher and politician in Boston. On the other side stood Anne Hutchinson, William Coddington, John Coggeshall, William Aspinwall, Nicholas Easton, and Mary Dyer. John Wheelwright had already been thrown out of the colony because of his heretical sermons.

This first battle came early in the eventual war. The old, old men of Boston would not seriously begin destroying lives, hanging people, or tying old women to the back of carts, stripping them to the waist, and whipping them from one town to the next through New England snows until 1658. By that time the old men would prove themselves capable of hanging women, as they would certainly do again in 1692 during the Salem trials. I say "old men," but the establishment stood solid, and the goodwives often proved as bad or worse than their husbands. By 1692, though, there would be a difference. The old men would be hanging their own people.

If it were only a power issue, it might be no more important than shoot-outs between members of the Mafia, or corruption attending some bureaucracies. Yet, a more important wind blew across the scene, and the preachers' messages became hysteric because that wind blew warm. It threatened to thaw an iceberg against which the Western mind had crashed for many-a-hundred year. That warm idea was/is: Original Sin (Depravity) is as outmoded as the Middle Ages.

On the theocracy's side stood an authoritarian god who regulated flawed human beings from the time they were born until the time He sent them to Heaven or Hell.

On Hutchinson's side was an Immanuel god, planting an idea that would later become a developing political philosophy; an idea presenting the human race as an affirming, perfectible race that could take responsibility for its own decisions. A race, under God, that could form a nation hungering after liberty and justice. A race not in a state of Original Sin, but in a state of Original Possibility.

The idea was immense. Original Sin was the first great idea to affect American history. Original Possibility was the second.

I do not want to dwell long on the violence of those days, but any writer knows it is wrong to leave a story dangling from its middle.

Anne Hutchinson was hauled into court and cruelly cross-examined. She got every opportunity to change her opinions—and refused. What infuriated the preachers even more than her refusal was her implication that their doctrines put them on the easy road to Hell. It did not help that one of their own flew the flag of cowardice. John Cotton was that man.[1]

---

[1] In Puritan history, there are two John Cottons, father and son; and neither of them the kind of men you would wish to claim as far-distant cousins. The second John

In some ways, Cotton was notable. He stood strong in the inner circles of Puritan power. He actually tried to deal with the Indians, instead of simply regarding them as the Devil's children. He made converts and attempted to put their language into written form. He proved himself a good organizer and a man of ideas. It was his ideas that sent Hutchinson on her search. Now, when the storm broke, he made a couple of feeble attempts to defend her. Then he turned around, went back on the whole thing, and rushed to join the majority.

The importance of the Hutchinson controversy in the developing mind of America proved twofold. It was the first public breakaway from the medieval mind. It was also the first time that authority attacked a citizen, and the citizen told authority to take its insecure little bag of tricks and go elsewhere. One of the glories of America, and America's writing and art, is that citizens have been telling government where to "place it" ever since.

After her trial and excommunication, Anne Hutchinson was imprisoned at a preacher's house. She was subjected to round-the-clock theologizing by a series of preachers. When the preachers absolutely could not get her to recant, they kicked her out of the colony. She was killed by Indians in 1643 near what would become New Rochelle, New York. When the news made its way back to Boston, the preachers made sanctimonious pronouncements claiming Hutchinson's death showed the vengeance of God on wrong ideas.

If those old-time preachers seem crazy, then it is because they were. They were a dying power structure. All things that sustained their intellects, their bodies, and their hopes were under attack.

From Hutchinson's trial in 1637 until the Salem trials of 1692, there would be no peace for Puritanism. The preachers would get even more crazy as the crack-up approached. The witch trials were a catalyst for crack-up.

---

Cotton would spend time in Plymouth, where he tended to blame most of humanity's trouble on women, which, in his case, turns out to be sort of amusing. His actions caused a major scandal in Massachusetts, a scandal even the Puritan preachers could not cover up. His problem centered around the seduction of one or more women in his congregation. He got kicked out of the church in 1697 and went to Charleston, South Carolina, where he died the next year. While I confess to a great belief in the efficacy of fornication under certain circumstances, I have neither missed nor mourned this particular man.

## THE SALEM TRIALS

The Salem witch trials have taken a large place in American history because they are well documented, and because they were spectacular. Briefly: Young girls were discovered dancing in the forest, which was still believed to be the abode of evil. An old slave named Tituba claimed herself taken in witchery. The girls claimed they were possessed by witches and began naming people who tormented them. People were arrested, tried in court, and twenty-one were hanged. One man, Giles Corey, was pressed to death, stones piled on his body. Two dogs were hanged.

People were convicted for a number of reasons, but the main quoted reason was "spectral evidence." When an accused woman or man entered the court, the girls would scream that they were being hurt, pinched, attacked. Huge welts would rise on the girls' arms. This proved to the judges that the accused could injure the girls from afar.

Modern psychology can explain all this, but modern psychology was two hundred years away. That these physical manifestations were a product of mass hysteria, I have no doubt. My problem with their full dismissal under the heading of "mass hysteria" rises because historians know a good deal more about that seventeenth-century world than do psychologists. The historians, and the Puritan record itself, give me pause.

Let us consider a proposition that may not be as outrageous as it seems.

Start with an illustration: At the end of the twentieth century, we all know that Oldsmobiles exist. We may like the fact, dislike the fact, or be completely indifferent; but, by the Lord Harry, we blamed well know that Oldsmobiles exist.

At the end of the seventeenth century, the Devil was every bit as real in Massachusetts as Oldsmobiles are in our world. Given that fact, and the further fact that creative energy is not restricted to individuals, it is fair to speculate that Salem created the Devil. If manifestations were hellish, it is no surprise.[2]

---

[2]The notion that creativity is limited to individuals has restricted the perspectives of psychologists, sociologists, and some historians. Yet, any jazz musician will attest to the creative ability of groups, as will dancers and actors. In Salem, where creativity was

The importance of the Salem witch trials is not that they were spectacular, or that modern-day Salem makes tourist dollars from a history it does not understand; the importance is that they are the end-mark of total power by the New England theocracy. Preachers would still wield power, but limited power. As the crack-up came with the witch trials, the preachers grew even crazier. Cotton Mather, the best-educated man in America, would turn into a raving maniac.

## Cotton Mather

During the witch trials, Boston preacher Cotton Mather was twenty-nine years old. He was overeducated, by which I mean he had spent those twenty-nine years learning from books while learning absolutely nothing about the work of the world, or about people. He was lopsided. Later, as he aged, he mellowed and became fairly courageous. Experience chastened him. Until he got some experience, though, he was an absolutely despicable person. His great learning caused him to display a variety of ignorant idealism—which is a variety of intellectual pride (probably learned from his daddy, Increase)—and ignorant idealism is one of the most dangerous forces in the world.

When Mather addressed a subject comfortably within the assumptions of his Puritan vision, he was capable of some genius and mastery. The moment he had to entertain assumptions beyond that vision—even those not in opposition—he foamed at the mouth. His preoccupations with sex and death got all mixed up with politics, and what looks like a zest for turmoil.

He would use any means to destroy an enemy, on the grounds that the enemy was Satan. While he had little direct involvement in the witch trials, he exerted a lot of influence. He argued the question of "spectral evidence" and, sensibly, thought it inadequate. If he not been hysterical during the whole affair, his ambivalence might have looked like good sense. As it was, Mather behaved like a psychopath, which indeed he was.

I caution myself to remember, though, that to Mather the Devil was real. Witches were real. There was good reason for hysteria.[3]

---

blocked by harsh conditions, the group created something ugly that reached beyond the simple explanation of mass hysteria.

[3]Other people turned nasty during the trials, including judges of the court, and

After the trials, when everyone else wanted the matter ended, Mather could not, or would not, leave witchcraft alone. In two separate cases, he counseled young women who were believed taken by the Devil. While this went on, two of his own children died. He became not much crazier than a lot of the people around him, and with somewhat better reasons.

## FROM SIN TO POSSIBILITY

After the Salem trials, when the congregations walked in shame, Puritanism changed. There would once more be an opportunity for it to become a strong moral influence on the American mind. Still, the Puritan crack-up was important because there would have been no American Revolution if American ideas were founded only on Original Sin. A Puritan would tell you that the status quo is what God wants, because if God didn't want it that way, it wouldn't be that way.

After the crack-up, the force of Original Possibility became even stronger. It walked widely across the world as one of the strongest ideas in history. In America, ironically, it would become strong because it was tempered by the fires of Puritanism, and buttressed with Puritanism's iron.

There would be another crack-up in Boston, 150 years later. Leading the loyal opposition would be the Transcendentalists, whom we shall meet in a later chapter.

However, that was an entirely different kind of crack-up. It signaled the emergence of the third great idea in American history: Original Good. We will turn to it after a brief look at the further development of that second idea, Original Possibility.

---

people who were paying off old grudges. In some cases, there were economic motives, because property of convicted witches was forfeited. We get a picture of a group of authorities who suspected they were wrong, and thus on the road to Hell. To justify their acts they pursued the course they were stuck with, and pursued it vigorously.

# ORIGINAL POSSIBILITY

AN INVASION BY religionists, now known as the Lambs' War, broke against American shores in 1656, with the appearance in Boston of the Quakers Mary Fisher and Ann Austin. Their books were burned in the public square by the Boston hangman. The women were stripped, examined for marks of witchcraft, and thrown into an unheated cell. A fine of 5 pounds was threatened against anyone who so much as spoke a word to them.[1] One man came forward and offered to pay 5 pounds. He was thrown in jail. Nine weeks later the women were shipped to Barbados. The governor, John Endecott, had been away during those nine weeks. When he returned, he swore the women were lucky because, had he been there, he would have hanged them sure. The two women were not the enemy, but Boston could not admit that.

The enemy was basically the same idea that compelled Anne Hutchinson: There can be direct experience of God in the life of the believer. To the Quakers, there was "that of God" in each person. A believer needed only to listen to the voice of God within. This is why, even today, Quakers sit in silent meeting for worship. They wait until they are moved to speak by a "leading" from God.

This doctrine, originating in England, had fairly taken northern En-

---

[1] Five pounds (100 shillings) amounted to quite a bit. Skilled laborers could support their families on 2 shillings a day.

gland by storm. It rose from slow beginnings in 1648, when George Fox started his ministry.

## GEORGE FOX

To the English and American seventeenth century, George Fox was similar to what Martin Luther King, Jr., would be to the American twentieth century. Both were men of genius who arrived on the scene just as a major transition in thought lay waiting. King was the great man of the twentieth century, and Fox, the great man of the seventeenth. They were also two of the great men in all of Western history.

Fox was of the historical type "messiah." Like most messiahs, he proved dangerous not only to the established order, but sometimes to his own followers. As Quakerism spread, and was opposed by established preachers, the followers of Fox were beaten, imprisoned, tortured, and executed. Fox was himself beaten and imprisoned so many times that his survival through forty-three years of work seems not simply remarkable, but miraculous.

Since there was "that of God" in each man and woman, it followed that no one was better than anyone else. Fox addressed magistrates as "Friend," and refused to take off his leather hat in the presence of temporal power. He always spoke the truth as he knew it. In his journal, he records that, as a boy, he decided to follow the injunction "Let your aye be aye, and your nay, nay." There are no feelings of guilt to be found in the writings of George Fox, and no ambivalence.

Since there was "that of God" in each person, it was clear that preachers were unnecessary and were leeches. Fox did not believe in black robes and black suits. He believed in preachers who dressed plainly and earned their livings at honest work in the world.

As a follower and exponent of Christ, Fox was totally convinced of his own message. He was unswerving, intense, and the record suggests he performed at least a few miracles. To the Puritans of both England and America, a man like Fox had to seem prima facie insane.[2]

---

[2]Like Christ, Fox was a synthesist. Neither dealt in strictly new ideas. Christ's main message, for example, can be found in Deut. 6:5 and Lev. 19:18. The Sermon on the Mount is a nearly verbatim exposition of the teachings of Rabbi Hillel, one of the great teachers of the Pharisees, a generation earlier. Christ's pacifist leanings were standard doctrine among a contemporary Jewish group called the Essenes. Fox's message

Any great idea will generally bring together some mighty interesting bedfellows. In the seventeenth century, and in behalf of a God that existed elsewhere than in Catholic or Puritan services, large numbers of religious, and semireligious, and economic groups surfaced. There were Anabaptists, Diggers, Levelers, Ranters, Antinomians, Fifth Monarchy Men, Howlers, and a long string of Christian mystics with a heritage stretching all the way back to the desert fathers of the early church in the third century.[3]

The idea of God within each person had never seriously threatened history because history had never before produced George Fox.

Fox confused the Puritans and plenty of other religionists. Puritans were accustomed to disputation, and suddenly here was a man with a doctrine over which there was nothing to dispute. No logical argument could be thrown against it. Once the main premise was accepted, the whole business of predestination turned silly; and with it the whole basis for political and social control by theocracy. Worse, perhaps, it made no difference if believers spent their entire lives without hearing a preacher. Given the premise, each person *was* a minister, with complete and indisputable authority.

Of course, if the main premise was rejected, the proponents of the idea looked crazy. Some of them were. The problem the Puritans had is the problem we have with zealots to this very day. Until the smoke of battle fades into the pages of history, it is often quite difficult to tell who is plain nuts, and who is a saint.

Puritans could not believe that anyone could have no sense of sin or guilt. When Quaker guiltlessness entered Boston, the theocracy proved itself capable of hanging women.

---

of "God within" was not new. It had been used and abused by religionists, Anabaptists and others, since the days before the Reformation.

[3]Diggers and Levelers tied religion to economics. The Fifth Monarchy Men saw the imminent return of Christ as the rise of a fifth monarchy; the previous four having been the empires of Assyria, Persia, Greece, and Rome. The Fifth Monarchy Men were prepared to use violence in order to establish Christ's return.

Anabaptists, Ranters, Howlers, and Antinomians were a mixed crew. In general, they held that the truth and purity of the heart stood above law, religion, and morals. If the heart was pure (and we may be sure they believed their hearts were pure), then it followed that their actions were pure: including fornication, violence, and matters unmentionable. Some, however, were pure of heart and many of those eventually ended up in the Quaker camp. This is a simplistic explanation. A complete discussion would take a great many pages.

This is what happened in Boston when Quakers were hearing the voice of God. They told the absolute, scrupulous truth. They actually did love their enemies, as unbelievable as that may seem. They would not raise their hands to defend themselves. They would have nothing to do with killing, with revenge, and they cared not one whit for profit.

Later, some of this would change. Religions, even more than other institutions, show predictable development. The first generation of religious members are unconquerable because they ride the strength of revelation. By the fourth generation, the religion becomes a full institution and has too much to lose. It is no longer unconquerable, and sometimes is a pushover.

That first generation of the guiltless hit the theocracy in Boston, and Boston lay helpless. The ensuing battle became so personal and intense it is easy to see the battle and miss the more important clash of ideas. Yet, the personal lives of the attacked and the attackers are the best illustration of the force of ideas.

What is to be done with a man who comes to your town, is lashed soundly with a whip that opens most of the flesh on his body, and is then kicked beyond your borders? You look up—and here he comes again. You whip him within an inch of death, cut off one of his ears, and kick him beyond your borders. You look up—and here he comes again. You whip, brand him by burning the letter H (heretic) into his flesh with red-hot iron, and kick him out. You look up, and, oh God, here he comes again!

All they could figure to do, in jocund old Boston town, was hang him. Two who were hanged were William Leddra and Mary Dyer. Of Mary Dyer, swinging at the end of rope, a man named Humphrey Atherton joked, "She hangs there as a flag."

## SEXUAL PREOCCUPATION

As conflicting ideas struggled above broken bodies of men and women, another feature of the American mind became all too apparent. That feature was sexual preoccupation, a subject American writers have to deal with much more than do writers of other nations.

Puritan fear and repression caused preoccupation so great not even the seamiest of porn magazines can exceed it. When (and if) Cotton Mather, and his father Increase, sat rubbing a woman's naked breasts, which in some way helped with prayer and protecting her from the

Devil, Puritan preoccupation with sex is evident.[4] Of course, those two men were special cases of weirdness, but other evidence exists. When depositions were taken during the witch trials, several of them suggest sexual preoccupation every bit as perverse. More accurately, perhaps, Puritans were preoccupied, not specifically with sex, but with adultery; sex in marriage suited them just fine.[5] At any rate, American preoccupation with sex did not enter our writing during the Victorian period; it has been there since the seventeenth century.

During the Quaker invasion of Boston, men, but especially women, were stripped and often kept that way for two reasons. The first reason was the then-honest search for signs of witchcraft. With women, the ordinary sign was an extra breast. A few women do develop nonmalignant cysts on their backs or sides that resemble rudimentary breasts. From the time of the Spanish Inquisition, this had been a standard reason for search. An extra breast was believed to be the place for suckling the Devil's young. Through history, some women died because of cysts found during these examinations.

The second reason came with exhibition in public of people stripped at least to the waist. This was not merely a concession to the whip of the hangman. The exhibition gave a vile religious and civil sanction for the display of sex. This was certainly nothing new; and, in all fairness to the Puritans, little happened during the Quaker invasion that could come close to perversities practiced in Europe.

Generally, people were simply whipped, scorned, occasionally hanged or beaten to death. There was little actual dismemberment, and that was mostly the cutting off of ears. At the same time, preachers and politicians of Boston managed to align themselves with the Devil; for the chief historical interests of the Devil have been sex and mutilation.

---

[4]A man named Robert Calef reported this in writing. Cotton and Increase called it slander. Increase had Calef arrested. When the case came to trial, the Mathers did not show up. The case was dismissed. Threats flashed back and forth. Somebody was sexually preoccupied, and to this day no one can be certain about who did what. A discussion is contained in David Levin, *Cotton Mather* (Harvard University Press, 1978), 240–49.

[5]The deal went this way: Love of God came first, but love of wife or husband, if it didn't get in the way of love of God, was (except for sex on Sundays) godly. One droll story comes about because of a preacherly belief that birth came, to the day, exactly nine months after conception. This belief faded pretty quickly after a preacher's wife gave birth on a Sunday afternoon.

Nor were the Quakers exempt. In two cases, women appeared in church or in the street as what in those days was called "a naked sign," denoting variously trust in God, or denial of authority.

There are at least three possible reasons why this happened. First, the women might have been as sexually preoccupied as the Puritans. Second, both women had suffered badly. Their families had been beaten, imprisoned, whipped. In these days, before anyone ever heard of autosuggestion, they might easily have heard a voice commanding them. They may have sunk into a level of madness and religious frenzy that sought some last, large statement.

As this was a generation of the guiltless, a third reason is not improbable. There actually *does* exist a peace that passes all understanding. What preachers have rarely said, although mystics do sometimes, is that such peace serves to illustrate the great culmination of religious life. Such peace offers the knowledge that one may be completely vulnerable without fear. In our Western culture, few conditions are more vulnerable than nakedness.

In Boston, which rapidly became encircled by Quakers, Puritans made their last stand. They had come to a new country with the avowed purpose of building a city on a hill, a city of God. They worked in the service of that God. They allowed a theocracy to become a dictatorship. When members of the churches fought back against the dictatorship, those members were fined and thrown from the community. Their property was confiscated.

As long as Puritan actions were confined to their own members, England did not bother them. When the hangings began, Quakers appealed to England and the king stopped the hangings.

The Puritans fought back with the Cart and Whip Act. People were tied naked to the back of carts during New England winters, and flogged as they were dragged from town to town. It proved a losing battle. Puritans failed to retain support from England. Businessmen among them knew the value of that support. The Puritan system crashed on the issues of brutality and practical business; and, it is a pleasure to add, because an awful lot of Puritans rebelled against the harshness of the theocracy.

## THE NEW IDEA

Most of all, Puritanism cracked because it could not deal with the idea of Original Possibility. In our national history, that idea would be the most enduring force bequeathed by the Quakers. They did not mean to do it. They meant to sow the seeds of their religion. Later, in Philadelphia, they would have their own theocracy. It was a far more gentle version—about like the one in present-day Salt Lake City—but it *was* a theocracy.

As a result of the development of Original Possibility, a great combination would enter American thought and the thought of America's writers. That combination is one of darkness and light. Later on, it turned into realism and romance, then into realism and social realism. From these combinations would rise two distinct currents that run through American literature.

From the Puritans came medieval night and the beginnings of realism. The darkness in our literature is not modern, but ancient. When Hawthorne wrote about sin, or Twain lampooned it, darkness rose. When Stephen Crane rebelled against romance, darkness hovered. Darkness in the work of Richard Wright is the darkness of history.

From the Puritans came discipline. Much later, when Victorian notions of "duty" held sway in our land, those notions sprouted from a carefully prepared seedbed. Duty, and its consequent attendant, honor, were as natural to the American character and the American writer as the obligation to fight against unjust authority.

From the Quakers came that fight: a fight in the spirit of Anne Hutchinson; a fight that variously expressed romance, naturalism, and social realism. The fight endures today and will endure for as long as American writers and artists remain honorable.

From the Quakers also came optimism. It was not lack of fear that produced the American Revolution or, later, the Oregon Trail. People were afraid, all right, but they had optimism greater than their fear. When the Romantic period broke against our shores, and the voice of William Cullen Bryant was part of the word stock of most households, the seedbed of optimism lay prepared and waiting.

One more great idea would enter the mind of America's writers. It was the idea of Original Good, and while it would be expressed variously in many parts of the new nation, the main wrestling match would once more happen in Boston. The idea introduced genuine fury into American thought and writing. It would also help produce the Civil War. That war, and its consequences, would fairly deal a deathblow to Americans' interest in theology. No single fact would be more important in producing the necessity for this nation to have strong writers, because literature and art would soon replace theology.

# THAT LONG, LONG TRAIL
# A-WINDING FROM
# ORIGINAL POSSIBILITY
# TO ORIGINAL GOOD

THE "INNIES" AND "outies" of early American thought are interesting because we see our country gradually break with seventeen centuries of European belief and custom. I say "gradually" because even today the American mind continues to develop idealism that derives from our early thought. America grows and, I am convinced, aspires to become more humane. In our own time, forces other than religions contribute to national understanding. That was mostly not true in our earliest days. We've seen, though, that the early situation could not last. Change flowed through the colonies. The Puritan/Quaker world was about to smash like broken crockery.

As the eighteenth century opened, conflict still came from contending religions, but a lot came because:

1. People of different cultures arrived in America at a time when the idea of toleration was nearly brand-new. Many of them could not handle toleration. In addition, the cultural differences were enough to cause problems. The main problems came when German and Eastern European cultures mixed with English, Irish, and Scots.

2. The frontier expanded with great rapidity. People on the frontier were enthusiastic, and often filled with optimism. Many (in some areas most) were also crude, rough, and generally unschooled. In addition, the northern frontier

around the Great Lakes, and along the southern-flowing rivers, had trouble with French and English battles, as well as Indians.

3. Scientific ideas about the nature of the universe, and the nature of God, circulated in the cities. Those ideas seemed in conflict with religious views. The universe was thought of as a giant machine, or a giant clock. Many believed it was possible to figure out exactly how the machine worked.

4. New political ideas began to enter the mainstream of American thought. These ideas denied the Divine Right of Kings. They gave justification for revolution.

## TWO RESULTS

One result of these new forces would be tremendous reaction from preachers all along the East Coast.[1] Religion was losing its power to control events. The preachers produced an evangelical movement known as the Great Awakening.

A second result would be unleashing of forces that caused the American Revolution.

## TOLERANCE

Let us consider these forces in some detail. We'll first look at tolerance/intolerance, because America was, is, and will be a land where questions of tolerance are of first importance. It could not be otherwise in this nation of immigrants. And naturally, from our country's beginnings to the present, tolerance/intolerance has been a main concern of American writers.

In the colonial years, problems of tolerance centered in Massachusetts, Connecticut, New York, Pennsylvania, Maryland, Virginia, New Jersey, and latterly, Georgia. Main players were Puritans, Episcopalians, Quakers, Moravians, Mennonites, Presbyterians, Anabaptists; and, as

---

[1] This was true only of the East Coast. On the West Coast, the Catholic missions were dominant and would remain so until after the Spanish-American War in the early nineteenth century. The nineteenth century would see Presbyterians and Methodists come into the Pacific Northwest and Alaska.

the century rolled along, Catholics, Jews, and Methodists.[2] Tolerance existed in a general way throughout many of the colonies, but fell apart in areas where religion bumped heads with political power structures. The greatest example of tolerance began in Pennsylvania. That example can serve as a rough model for what generally happened throughout most of the colonies.

## Tolerance and William Penn

The idea of tolerance became a main contributor to development of Original Possibility, and the eventual development of Original Good. William Penn's colony was a grand experiment open to all religions but tailored to protect Quakers.[3] The whole idea of tolerance proved earthshaking when actually put into practice because, for a while, it actually worked. However, confusion was inevitable.

Over the years, Episcopalians (Anglican) and Presbyterians moved to Pennsylvania. As their numbers increased, so did their influence. They eventually moved to the center of political power. One basis for their ascendancy came because Quakers would not engage in war. The Episcopals and Presbyterians looked at the French-Indian War and complained to England that the Quakers were not practical.

A second reason came because the Quakers gradually concluded that they could no longer abide slavery. This introduced a lot of conflict into the Pennsylvania/Maryland situation. All through the eighteenth

---

[2]Presbyterians were, more or less, Puritans with an elaborate system of church government. That system was set up with elders running spiritual matters, and deacons running temporal (business) matters. Presbyterian theology was about the same as that found in Puritan Massachusetts.

Moravians and Mennonites were Pietist religions from Germany and eastern Europe. Like the Anabaptists, they had strong and mixed beginnings, but by the time they got to America they were quiet, rather more thoughtful than most, and tended to mind their own business (although, of course, there were exceptions).

[3]The Dutch in New Amsterdam (New York) also presented themselves as tolerant, but their governments often did not come up to their presentation. Religious "radicals" were not hanged or beaten, but were fined or told to leave town.

Rhode Island, throughout the seventeenth century, had served as a haven for people who were persecuted because of religion.

Barbados in the British West Indies was the staging point for "heretic" religions during the seventeenth century. People sailed from England to Barbados, then to America. They sometimes fled to Barbados *from* America.

century, individual Quakers freed slaves. The Quaker meetings required that no one deal in slavery. They finally came to consensus and freed every slave in 1772.

A third reason came because pacifism and honesty do not work well when confronted by ambition, ego, and hunger for power. The question, metaphorically, that pacifist Quakers failed to answer was "What do you do when a lion is in your streets?" (Proverbs 26:13) Quakers who sought power, and Episcopals and Presbyterians who sought power, generally fitted the image of a lion.[4]

Other tensions rose because, while Penn treated fairly with Indian tribes, some other Quakers did not. Corruption ensued. Shady deals were cut. In addition, Penn unintentionally caused further confusion. He was a man so used to telling the truth he couldn't believe others would lie. In consequence, he managed to hire a succession of terrible administrators to run his colony. At least one of them was a thief. Penn's great experiment waxed, then waned.

In addition, Quaker meetings showed that there is "tolerance," and there is tolerance. The meetings tolerated many religions, but did what they could to keep their members from being infected with outside ideas.

Even so, from its founding in 1681 to 1756, Penn's colony represented something new under the sun of the Western world. At its height, it proved an enormous success. It showed that people with widely diverse opinions could not only get along with each other, but be fond of each other. This was an enormous discovery at a time when most everyone was new at the business of toleration.

## CULTURAL PRESSURES

German Mennonites from along the Rhine arrived in Pennsylvania.[5] Strain on the Pennsylvania system often proved not so much religious as cultural. By 1735, cultural conflict led to a teetering situation. People who were German viewed social and political control differently from people who were English, Scots, and Irish. In addition, for a while, the German and English languages seemed to be in competition. While no

---

[4]By 1756 the Quakers lost control. The government passed into utilitarian and certainly more warlike hands.

[5]Mennonites also settled in New York.

dependable figures are available, a fair estimate holds that Germans made up one-third of the Pennsylvania population.

Then Moravians, originally from Bohemia, thence by way of Saxony, ended up in Pennsylvania. They first landed in Georgia in 1735. Some stayed in Georgia. Some later migrated to North Carolina. Some traveled to Pennsylvania with an Episcopal (Church of England) preacher named George Whitefield. We'll look at Whitefield in a little while because he helped father an evangelical movement called the Great Awakening.

## TURMOIL

Change during the 1700s produced the French and Indian War along the upper Ohio River. The Pennsylvania rifle appeared.[6] Slave riots occurred in New York, and smallpox killed more than eight hundred in Boston, which by then had a population of a bit over ten thousand.[7] The British Parliament placed a heavy tax on colonial imports of sugar, molasses, and rum. These were essentials of colonial life, although the founders of Georgia thought otherwise. The brand-new Georgia colony outlawed slavery and rum. Both would later be legalized as plantations were established.

## THE FRONTIER

As the eighteenth century progressed, the main story centered on the expanding frontier. People cleared land, built farms, raised families, and gradually changed the face of the inhabited territories.

The frontier caused isolation, and isolation caused uncertainty. The frontier expanded so quickly that people became unsettled and lonely. By 1735, it may well be that there were 300,000 people in all of Penn-

---

[6]Also known as the Kentucky rifle because it was treasured on the frontier. The rifle had lansing grooves, and, in the hands of a skilled marksman, was deadly accurate. Firing of the earlier smoothbore weapons had been roughly as accurate as throwing rocks. Some historians hold that the Pennsylvania rifle was a main factor in winning the frontier. That may be an exaggeration, but only a slight one.

[7]Cotton Mather distinguished himself in defending smallpox inoculations given by a physician named Zabdiel Boylston. Mobs wanted to lynch the doctor.

sylvania.[8] While 100,000 were German, there were fewer than one hundred German-speaking ministers. One of the main symbols of order in those days, the preacher, was either missing or spread too thin. English preachers couldn't serve because they didn't speak German.

A second example of isolation may be found in the nature of settlement. There were few towns, a lot of forest, and a sufficiency of Indians. Insecurity, vigilance, and isolation are characteristics of the frontier.

## NEW IDEAS

A further cause of insecurity was reaction to a paradigm shift. In our contemporary world the term "paradigm shift" has become a buzzword. For that reason, let's get past the buzz and understand the real nature of a paradigm shift.

Such shifts have been especially relevant to scientific thinking. A new scientific theory or discovery will come along. The theory or discovery will require a new conceptualization of scientific fields. Let's view a modern example:

After Albert Einstein published the *General Theory of Relativity* in 1916, science had to develop a whole new way of looking at atomic structures. It was not a simple substitution of one set of rules for another. It demanded an entirely new view of the world.

When a paradigm shift occurs, it not only demands that people completely revise their views, it causes conservative reaction. In the case of the Theory of Relativity, even after the splitting of the atom, and five years after the use of the atomic bomb in World War II, some physics textbooks still taught that the atom was the smallest indivisible particle of matter. Those textbooks were not leftovers from an earlier time. The textbook writers simply could not bring themselves to acknowledge the truth of the Theory of Relativity.

People who have a lifetime of work invested in one assumption often go into wild reaction when told their assumption is wrong. They will defend the wrong assumption until their dying breath, and might defend it longer if anybody in a cemetery would listen.

That kind of reaction happened in 1735. The paradigm shift in those days saw science as a new way to understand both the world and the

---

[8]This figure comes from Moravian history. Quaker history gives a lower figure, a bit over 200,000.

mind of God. A main cause of the paradigm shift came from Isaac Newton's laws of motion and laws of gravitation published in 1687. Those laws suggested that scientific knowledge might be a substitute for faith. Newtonian laws also suggested that science might be able to explain the universe and its creation.

## REVOLUTIONARY IDEAS

The heart and soul of the American Revolution lay in the idea of Original Possibility, an idea demonstrated by William Penn's colony. Political ideas also came along and justified Original Possibility. Those ideas came from abroad. They were imported over a period of years.

It takes time for ideas to develop, be published, become widespread; and finally more time to be implemented. In the case of the American Revolution, it took from 1735 to approximately 1770 to move away from a Middle Ages way of thinking about government. Part of that change stemmed from two important English books, and one French book.

They were *Leviathan* (1651), by Thomas Hobbes, *Two Treatises of Government* (1689), by John Locke, and *The Social Contract* (1762), by Jean-Jacques Rousseau. Although often at odds, all three gave reasons to deny the Divine Right of Kings. Each postulated a social contract between the government and the governed. Hobbes and Locke agreed that as long as government keeps its contract, people are obliged to support the government (be it monarchy, dictatorship, or republic). When the government breaks its contract, the people are no longer obligated to obey. If the government threatens life (Hobbes) or life and property (Locke), there is justification for the citizen to overthrow the government.

To Hobbes and Locke, the right of revolution was inherent. Rousseau, a latecomer, was not a revolutionist, but a passionate thinker who understood the ideas of Original Possibility and Original Good from a social, rather than religious, point of view. His writings about society did more for thought that framed our Constitution than for actual revolution. He spoke for small communities and simple political structures.

These political and social philosophies, when combined with Original Possibility, and Newtonian science, formed the storming winds of the American Revolution. They also combined to cause a conservative reaction that was massive.

## THE GREAT AWAKENING

That already-mentioned preacher George Whitefield became a fiery spark in driest tinder. He first came into Georgia with a group of Moravians. Whitefield admired the Moravians and wanted their help to establish his influence in Pennsylvania. At Whitefield's behest, some of the Moravians accompanied him to Pennsylvania, where they built the town of Nazareth.

Then the Moravians and Whitefield disputed over Original Sin. (Whitefield loved it, while the Moravians had their doubts.) Whitefield lost his temper and tried to kick the Moravians out of Nazareth just as winter was coming on. The Moravians resorted to law, and a court allowed them to stay the winter because they had no other shelter. When spring arrived, they left Nazareth and built Bethlehem, Pennsylvania. The Moravians were well settled in themselves, but the conflict worked its will on Whitefield.

Whitefield then swung from an Episcopal view toward the view of Puritans and Presbyterians.[9] Then his friend John Wesley, who also came to Georgia in 1735 and dealt with Moravians, returned to England. Wesley credited Moravians for moving him away from Calvinism. He and Whitefield had been buddies in the Lord, but when Whitefield went straight Calvinist, the friendship was broken.

The break seemed to galvanize Whitefield, a man already galvanic.[10] He became one of the fathers of The Great Awakening.

All down the eastern seaboard, preachers rose to defend their "Middle Ages" way of thinking. While the most famous was George Whitefield, almost equally famous were Gilbert Tennent and Jonathan Edwards. Revivals rose and swept the colonies from Maine to Georgia.

---

[9]George Whitefield's difference as an Episcopal preacher was not so much theological as symbolic. The Church of England looked fundamentally Catholic, but with Protestant overtones. It was a hybrid with ornamental trappings, bishops, and a regular church hierarchy. American Puritan churches had far fewer trappings. They had more-rigid rules, and less church governance. Beliefs were not that much different.

[10]Meanwhile, John Wesley took what he learned from the Moravians and became the father of the Methodists. Methodists would later begin their own establishment in Connecticut.

The flow of religious preoccupation did not last for one summer, or one year. It lasted for ten.

These days, the Great Awakening would seem no more than a sidebar in history, but it marks a point where something new entered the American experience. Those religionists caused the first big American experience with galloping Evangelicalism, which was then, and continues today, as a gasp from the Middle Ages. Those religionists also caused the emergence of what would become an American type: the Spellbinder.[11]

The Great Awakening tried to contain the growing movement toward revolution in religious, social, and political thought. While it swept the colonies for ten years, it did not completely throttle voices of change. It lives in history as a way to help us understand our own time, as well as understand other times in the past.[12]

It also marks the first departure of the American mind from a religion asking for study and thought to a religion asking nothing but cant. It contrasts with the early years of our country, years run by religion, but religion that caused thought. Early America was harsh, often intolerant, but distinguished itself by thinking about its beliefs.

Fortunately, the Great Awakening did not control all events. In 1735–45, the American Revolution was not yet at hand, but was a-borning. When it finally arrived, it proved that it had only needed the flower of an emerging political philosophy, pollinated by the idea of Original Possibility.

Original Possibility did not start with Penn's colony, but Penn's colony was first to put the idea into institutional, theoretical, and physical practice. Almost exactly one hundred years after the Penn colony was established, its principles of tolerance combined with ideas of political revolution and produced a revolutionary religion called Deism.

---

[11]We have spellbinders with us today, and will probably always have them; men and women who can deliver the most inane kind of foolishness, make the foolishness sound profound, and get masses of people to follow the spellbinder's agenda. In addition to medical quacks who once ran medicine shows, and a certain variety of politician, we may add such twentieth-century ministers as Billy Sunday, Aimee Semple McPherson, and those unfortunate television creatures who, these days, preach a plumpest-God-the-preacher version of religion.

[12]The same kind of evangelical furor happened after the Civil War, and for similar reasons. It happened, equally ugly, in the 1920s and 1930s. After World War II, it became one trademark of the twentieth century.

Deism was the religion of many of the founding fathers. It was a set of simple and true beliefs, suitable for the task at hand. It served as prelude to the idea of Original Good, which we will examine in the next chapter.

# DEISM AND REVOLUTIONARY
# LEGACIES

I PAUSE FOR a moment to think well of some leaders in American history. I do so, because, of late, it has become popular to trash heroes. The trashing usually proceeds on grounds of Protestant prissiness mouthed by sensationalist media.

Examples abound. We are told that Amelia Earhart was a spy, that John Kennedy and Martin Luther King, Jr., are remarkable only because of their bedroom antics, that George Washington was the father of his country in a great many beds (people interested in others' beds, incidentally, have nothing going on in their own) . . . that Ben Franklin was a racist, that Booker T. Washington was an Uncle Tom, that Abraham Lincoln was a champion of slavery, that Franklin Roosevelt was in league with anti-Semites—about the only people who have not been attacked are Molly Pitcher and Dolley Madison—and I even hate to mention their names for fear that some media scamp will pounce.

Thus, I here assert that Thomas Paine,[1] Jefferson, Adams, Washington, Franklin, Madison, Morris, Jay, and others are worthy of being our heroes. Historical revisionists may manipulate, and special interests may whimper, but the record is clear. These men may have fought like alley

---

[1]No young American writer or artist can possibly go wrong by reading Paine's *The Age of Reason*. In addition, it pays to read Howard Fast's novel *Citizen Tom Paine*. It's also a matter of interest to know that *Common Sense* sold 500,000 copies when the colonial population stood at 2 million. Paine never received a cent for his work.

cats among themselves, but they bequeathed great legacies to both their nation and the world.

First, they bequeathed a revolution. It was something new under the sun. Let's think about that for a moment.

All through history people had risen covertly, or sometimes overtly, against churches and kings. As a result deals were cut and narrow principles announced: for example, the Magna Carta helped the English barons, but didn't help the peasantry.

In Europe, serfdom kept people down. No organized resistance could be mustered in sufficient strength to overthrow a reigning power. Churches preached the Divine Right of Kings because church and state were usually married to each other.

The American Revolution was the first time a people rose up, threw out an old government, and instituted one of their choice. The American Revolution led the way to revolutions in both Occident and Orient, from the French Revolution to the Chinese People's Revolution of Sun Yat-sen. Revolutionary doctrine now exists in the history of many nations. Because of this, tyrants may continue to beware.

A second legacy came when American revolutionaries bequeathed another half century of thought instead of cant. They did it by instituting separation of church and state, one of their greatest gifts to nation and world. That separation changed American thought. It worked this way:

Because of separation of church and state, religion in America would have to become competitive. From the American Revolution on, religion would have to sell its services, or falter when it failed to analyze its markets. For that reason, many religions for the next two hundred years would go for the lowest common denominator in order to appeal to great numbers of people.

Religion too often became simpleminded, and the result would be degradation of religious thought. That degradation, as we'll soon see, caused the nation to depend hardily on its artists and writers. American thought changed because people who were not simpleminded (and most are not) turned to other answers.

A third legacy of the founders was universal education. We can see its importance by contrasting it with education in England and Europe. Most Western nations failed to educate large numbers of their citizens. As late as the 1950s, for example, only 1 percent of the British population ever saw the inside of a university.

Universal education caused changes that propelled our nation's rise to world power. I won't trace all those changes, but will give one example.

Universal education changed economics. Classic economic theory held that wealth came from a combination of capital, labor, and resources. Economic theory did not see the spirit of an educated people as a resource. America demonstrated that classic theory was wrong. Our nation became a world power because of the spirit of an educated people. Those people combined universal education with the work ethic of Puritanism, and the optimism of Quakers. Our nation rose on the swift feet of universal education.

## DEISM

The sum total of deism is best expressed by Jefferson:

> The doctrines of Jesus are simple, and tend all to the happiness of man.
> 1. That there is one only God, and he all-perfect.
> 2. That there is a future state of rewards and punishments.
> 3. That to love God with all thy heart and thy neighbor as thyself is the sum of religion. These are the great points on which he [Christ] endeavored to reform the religion of the Jews.[2]

This doctrine changed American history. Deism turned the complications of religion into simple belief. That belief was so straightforward that it demanded a new view of the rights of religion, the rights of government, and the rights of individuals. It insisted that such rights be specified and guaranteed. Deism lies at the very heart of the First Amendment to the American Constitution.

The American Revolution, with its legacies, was not simply a revolution on one continent and in one country. It was a revolution establishing principles that would affect the world, and would, in fact, change much of the world. It was also a prelude to the Civil War, but

---

[2]From a letter to Benjamin Waterhouse, June 26, 1822, quoted from Norman Cousins, *"In God We Trust": The Religious Beliefs and Ideas of the American Founding Fathers* (Harper Bros., 1958).

that is another tale for another time, and must be told by someone else. At present, we are concerned with ideas leading to Original Good, and conditions that produced our artists and writers.

## UNITARIANISM

After the Revolution, and in Boston, New York, and Philadelphia, Deism became institutionalized. The institutional name is Unitarianism.

In 1785, Unitarianism raised its singular face, proclaiming the existence of one god. Unitarianism believed in human perfectibility. It believed in the powers of the rational mind. Unitarianism became the hottest item in Boston's inventory. It was born fast, came of age fast, and did not take too much time in dying. In the history of religious thought, few have managed to go to perdition quite as fast as Unitarianism.

At the end of the eighteenth century, though, Unitarianism conquered Boston, and had its way even where it failed; for those people who could not deal with old-time Puritanism, or with the hot surges of Unitarianism, sought other religions, some thoughtful.

By 1830, Unitarianism had gone downhill, and even developed its own complete dogma. The people of Boston became rich. Churches grew rich. History generally shows that when people and institutions become rich, they get in deep, deep need of dogma.

Wealth seemed likely to destroy the intellectual and cultural life of Boston. People prospered as merchants and seamen. Nothing seemed important except the steady flow of cash. For intellectual accomplishment, people turned to New York or Philadelphia. The enticements of wealth worked against any enticements of thought, and it seemed that Boston would soon become only a bastion of money. There was, however, a stalwart band of smart people, plus one genius, waiting in the wings.

## ENTER WILLIAM ELLERY CHANNING AND AMERICAN TRANSCENDENTALISM

Looking back on those days, it is easy to see the major figures as if arranged for a group portrait. The Unitarian minister William Ellery Channing was the Father; Ralph Waldo Emerson, the Son; Henry

David Thoreau, the great disciple; and the preacher Theodore Parker, the prophet of American Transcendentalism. Several other people might have taken the role of Holy Spirit, but all of them were at least a little flaky. Besides, it would be disproportionate to assign a trinity while discussing the greatest Unitarian of them all.

Channing gently celebrated the potential for goodness, even godliness, among humans. This absolutely flew in the face of Puritan, and even some Quaker, traditions.[3] Because of his nontraditional views, Channing became the subject of emotional attacks, many from Unitarians. The problem with attacking Channing was that the attacker could not win. Channing so valued active inquiry that any thoughtful attack was at least interesting. He had little affection for platitudes, and ritualists learned to give him lots of running room.

The idea of Original Good had kicked around the world for centuries, but no synthesist came forward to consolidate the idea and make it understandable. George Fox might have done so, because he certainly understood it, but in some ways Fox was narrow. The Quakers simply fumbled the idea of Original Good.

Channing was the genius who understood that the human condition need not be passive or defensive. Original Good meant celebrating the aggressive and hungry mind. Channing saw that human genius, when informed and unfettered, was the strongest moral and creative force ever known.

Channing launched his ideas beginning in 1819 with a sermon delivered in Baltimore. The fundamental goodness of this creature called "man" was cause for celebration. Channing did not say—although the inference is there—that God would be in pretty dire straits if it were not for humans. Humans define God. If they do not, it might well be that God could not exist.

Channing's ideas were just shucking every clam on the Puritan and Unitarian beaches. Look, for example, at what they do to this old and tired cliché:

"Every time I get troubled, I go out on a high hill and look at the stars and the universe. Before that kind of immense and inscrutable mystery, my troubles fade and take their proper proportion."

---

[3]In the third and fourth generations, many Quakers bought a wheyish version of original sin. Even the Quaker saint John Woolman could not quite believe he was not flawed.

That is straight Calvinist optimism. Now look at the same situation from Channing's point of view:

"When I've got troubles, I've got troubles. The universe does not show me a thing except that it is remorseless. I am different from the universe. Nothing the universe has ever shown me indicates the universe comprehends anything. Nothing the universe has ever shown me indicates that the human mind may not someday understand the universe."

In other words, and in contemporary terms, angels can sing their pretty little heads off out there among the stars, but *Rhapsody in Blue*, or a fierce and hungry jazz trumpet, amount to music.

No one gave better justification to Channing's ideas than had old-time Puritans.

Back in the days of the Hutchinson controversy, Puritan men and women stood up in behalf of Hutchinson and in opposition to the theocracy. In 1692, Salem men and women stepped forward to denounce the witch trials. They knew that they might be cried out against as witches, and might be hanged. About eighty years later, American revolutionaries would pledge their lives, their fortunes, and their sacred honor to a cause; but the lives and fortunes and sacred honor of Puritans in Boston had already been spent in behalf of justice. Thus, a tradition already existed in American history, and Channing brought it into the early nineteenth century, where its energy and integrity were needed.

Channing was able to make the idea of Original Good so easily understandable that people wondered why they had never voiced it themselves. Channing was one more great force in the struggle to preserve and make strong the American mind. He lighted the mind and imagination of Ralph Waldo Emerson.

## RALPH WALDO EMERSON

That fine man, that Emerson, originated and synthesized American Transcendentalism, a philosophy built on Original Good. He based his work on ideas from Channing, on areas of mysticism, and on the writings of the Scottish essayist and historian Thomas Carlyle. While the Unitarian preacher Theodore Parker twisted the whiskers of Boston by praying to "Our Father and Mother God," Emerson set out to synthesize the universe. Transcendentalism immodestly handles it, and handles it pretty well . . . of course, it's a rather large universe.

Emerson faced a tough audience. Because of wealth, the issue in Boston during the 1830s and 1840s was the same great issue that caused the Hutchinson controversy. It was the issue that caused the hanging of Quakers, and the crack-up of Puritanism. It is the great issue that sounds and resounds through American history. It was also the great issue that engaged American Transcendentalism:

*Will we be ruled by the dead hand of dogmatic law that is the creature of misplaced power, or will we be ruled by essential good; no matter whether that goodness rises from within ourselves, or is the expression of a loving and creative force that some call God?*

What was this Transcendentalism that set out on sudden conquest for the mind of a nation? For, like a reformation, Transcendentalism was not a flower blooming in one small area during the 1840s. In its many forms, whether philosophic or religious; and carried to speaker's platforms across the still-new nation, it appeared even beyond the Mississippi. It spread as far as there were listeners. The far West was wild frontier. The gold rush to California had not yet begun. Pioneers were into the Middle West, and the Conestogas to Oregon first departed in 1841. The great American adventure had just begun.

Transcendentalism is a philosophy, a religion, a song. It is the bold call of possibility, of hope, of optimism. It is as simple as ABC, and so complicated that the more it is explained, the more incomprehensible it becomes. It uses rationality as a tool, but is not rational in an arithmetic way; although geometrically it sometimes seems the most logical system on earth. Clutch it and it dies. Allow it to fly free and it becomes one of the strongest forces in the world.

From the point of view of theology, Transcendentalism may be described in this manner: There is a loving and creative force running in the universe, and this force, which some call God—and no doubt rightly—may be described as original creative energy.

Emerson called this force the Oversoul. When a human, in the full glory of his or her humanity, attains to the highest potential of mind, then that human connects with original creative energy, which may be compared to a constant flow of electricity. Occasionally our minds and arms reach far enough to allow us to plug into the current. Some people plug in and stay for a long time. Others barely reach a state of original creative energy, then falter.

Transcendental experience does not ask the individual to be a member of society, or even a member of the universe. It insists that society and the universe come to benevolent terms with the individual. It sees clearly that people do not act badly unless they are obstructed by fear (and its consequent hatred), or prejudice, or bum information, or custom. People are trained to be clods by the worlds they inhabit.

The important thing Transcendentalism recognizes is that many people break training. They refuse to be clods. They refuse to settle for some future Heaven, because they realize the worthiness of their own being in this particular present. This is revolutionary doctrine, and it is one main doctrine of American writers.

## The Oversoul

We can see examples of Emerson's ideas of the Oversoul all through our literature. While there are plenty of nineteenth-century examples, I'll choose a familiar example from this century because it's one most readers will have read: Steinbeck's *The Grapes of Wrath*.

"I knowed a fella. Brang 'im in while I was in the jail house. Been tryin' to start a union. Got one started. An' then them vigilantes bust it up. An' know what? Them very folks he been tryin' to help tossed him out. Wouldn' have nothin' to do with 'im. Scared they'd get saw in his comp'ny. Says, 'Git out. You're a danger on us.' Well, sir, it hurt his feelin's purty bad. But then he says, 'It ain't so bad if you know.' He says, 'French Revolution—all them fellas that figgered her out got their heads chopped off. Always that way,' he says, 'Jus' as natural as rain. You didn' do it for fun no way. Doin' it 'cause you have to. 'Cause it's you. Look a Washington,' he says. 'Fit the Revolution, an' after, them sons-a-bitches turned on him. An' Lincoln the same. Same folks yellin' to kill 'em. Natural as rain.' "

"Don't soun' like no fun," said Tom.

"No, it don't. This fella in jail, he says, 'Anyways, you do what you can. An',' he says, 'the on'y thing you got to look at is that ever' time they's a little step fo'ward, she may slip back a little, but she never slips clear back."

Steinbeck was not a Transcendentalist, or at least did not think of himself in that manner. He serves as illustration because, Transcendentalist, or not, he plugged into original creative energy when he brought a world to life in *The Grapes of Wrath*. He used every lick of talent he owned, and every technique he then owned; and he used no tricks. He was an extension of original creative energy.

This is dangerous business. It goes beyond possibility and opens the floodgates to original behavior, which in Steinbeck's case, produced one of the great novels in our literature. That book illustrates what Emerson talked about when he spoke of Transcendentalism; i.e., the universe has to come to terms with the book because the book will not bend its will to the universe.

No Puritan could ever conceive the potential force in Transcendentalism. Because he believed humans were born depraved, a Puritan would not be disappointed if humanity chose to push a peanut along the gutters with its collective nose. That is the sort of behavior every Puritan was raised to expect.

The Revolutionary Fathers, with ideas of Original Possibility, would be disappointed but not infuriated by lousy human behavior. After all, they would say, possibility dictates just what it says: It is possible to be great, and it is also possible to become wretched.

The Transcendentalists, with ideas of Original Good, were *infuriated* by lousy human behavior. In their day, a lot of ugly stuff was going on, so they had plenty of situations from which to choose.

# FROM TRANSCENDENTALISM
## TO WAR

AFTER THE ESTABLISHMENT of the United States as a nation in 1789, to 1861 when the Civil War erupted, issues of trade, national sovereignty, the frontier, and slavery occupied Americans; and, in the case of slavery, many other nations as well. The Western world may have broken chains of thought that bound it to the Middle Ages, but it still struggled to free itself from customs and institutions of the Middle Ages.

That struggle was especially harsh when it came to slavery, which, in one form or another, had existed in the West since at least the days of the Roman Empire. It seemed part of the natural order of things, as inevitable as the realities of the Divine Right of Kings, and rule by the Church. Then, as eighteenth-century revolutionary thought spread throughout the Western world, it became clear that slavery was not the creature of a predestining god. Slavery had to go.

Opposition to slavery had been around for a long time. Antislavery societies arose during the eighteenth century. The moral imperative to end slavery grew in America, and was shown when Quaker Pennsylvania released all its slaves before the American Revolution. In 1804, a revolution in Haiti freed all slaves and killed all whites who did not leave the country. In 1807, a bill forbidding trade in slaves passed in the English Parliament. Also in 1807, Thomas Jefferson pushed the

Importation of Slaves Bill through Congress. The bill prohibited any further imports of slaves.[1]

By the time American Transcendentalism arrived in the 1830s and 1840s, disputes over slavery had turned absolutist. On one side stood people called abolitionists. They were determined to end slavery by any, or all, means.

On the other side stood a way of life in much of the American South, where slavery was tied to economics. Slavery was also tied to customs surrounding the plantation system. In the American North, and in England, there was some silent support for Southern slavery. The plantation system supplied cotton for Northern and English mills. As Transcendentalists entered the fray, battle lines were well drawn.

Of all offenses rendered against Original Good, the Transcendentalists figured slavery had to be greatest; and they were doubtless correct since this was before the invention of napalm, which is, arguably, equal on any scale of violence.

When the Fugitive Slave Act came along, Emerson and Channing stated their refusal to obey publicly and clearly. Theodore Parker and Henry Thoreau, on the other hand, managed to cover themselves with inglorious behavior, and they had plenty of company.[2] The majority of abolitionists raved, while a minority of abolitionists turned maniacal because, like most movements, the abolition movement held some people who acted in behalf of their own ignorance, arrogance, and ego.

Like many others, Parker and Thoreau sometimes had that age-old problem of talking when they should have been listening. Rather than give an extended account of the tumult, I'll give one example that fairly stands for much of what went on:

A terrorist named John Brown was an abolitionist who believed in curing slavery by murdering people, which he did in Kansas and Virginia, while getting his own sons killed. He had originally studied to be a preacher, but got sidetracked into other occupations. He carried a Puritan firmness that was nigh maniacal; writing that he "had letters of marque [i.e., a commission] from God." Because he was against

---

[1]The trade was profitable. Some English and Yankee slave traders continued the illegal traffic in slaves.

[2]This is the same Fugitive Slave Act described in the earlier discussion of Daniel Webster on pp. 14–15.

slavery, many people thought him a hero. However, that does not blush the fact that he was a terrorist.

Thoreau, together with Parker and other Boston Transcendentalists, raised subscriptions for Brown and sent him money. They entertained Brown in Boston. They might have been more acute, because they missed an important point.

John Brown was not simply a zealot, but messianic. Unlike Christ's or Fox's, John Brown's message was one that could be carried by rifle and knifepoint, which is eventually the way it was carried. The Transcendentalists backed a dark messiah.

Even after Brown engaged in his massacres, plenty of Transcendentalists, including Parker, remained trapped. They got in the uncomfortable position of having to defend the idea that the end (abolition of slavery) justified any means (including the murder of children). In other words, they justified terrorism. In today's terms, it would amount to speaking favorably for killing children in the Sudan in order to get rid of slavery in the Sudan. Terrorism is the tool of the coward, and it almost never hits the people who are guilty of whatever offends the terrorist.

Actions and writings of the Transcendentalists simply stank. Thoreau defended Brown in a public address the night before Brown was executed. Thoreau's defense is usually reprinted under the title "A Plea for John Brown."

## THE MARCH TO WAR

Abolitionists and Transcendentalists had a great and pure cause, one that often demanded courage and sacrifice. It also demanded vilification of slavery. The mistake they made came because their cause did not justify vilification of the entire South. The South held a great variety of customs, as well as peoples who had little or nothing to do with slavery. In the mountain South, for example, lived people who had never even seen anyone except the descendants of Englishmen and Scots.

When war erupted, too much hatred stalked Northern and Southern minds because the noise level had risen to brutal proportions. Although abolitionists helped the nation, they also hurt the nation by riding the cheap feeling of power that comes from smearing someone else. They had exact counterparts in the South, where Southern politicians, preachers, and businessmen clamored about the noble institution of slavery, and the nobility of "states' Rights." The great horror and sadness of the Civil War walked across our history on waves of noise as mindless as the noise generated during the Great Awakening.

The idea of Original Good, as promoted by the Transcendentalists, and as it combined with the abolition movement, was a main factor in raising the noise level to the point where the Civil War became inevitable. If momentum to war was all that Transcendentalism accomplished, we would have every right to turn from it with all dispatch. The great accomplishment was the planting of Original Good in the American mind, and in the mind of America's writers. This nation would shortly need those writers. The United States was about to become an absolute pit of platitude. It happened, in large part, because of war.

## THE CIVIL WAR

The Civil War stands as the great catastrophe in American history. No other event, or series of events—the decimation of aboriginal populations, the Great Depression, the Vietnam War—ever affected so many people so deeply. That war stained the back half of the nineteenth century, and it destroyed people through most of the twentieth.[3] Action and reaction to the war set up conditions that literally forced Americans with some heritage in Africa to build a separate culture.

Five percent of our population died. Of the 360,000 Union soldiers killed, 37,000 were black, 323,000 white. We know of at least 127 women who disguised themselves as men, and fought.[4] Of the 130,000 Confederate soldiers who died, very few were black, although many black men were attendants to the army. Toward the end of the war, there was a proposal to promise freedom to any slave who fought for

---

[3]For some, that war is still not over. At Cave Hill Cemetery, in Louisville, the rows of Union dead lie on one side of a road, the rows of Confederate dead on the other. Many of the graves have markers reading "unknown." Even today, a new marker with a name appears occasionally. Someone has done research, or has given over to romance, or hope, or possibly anger; but at any rate has gone to the time and expense to commemorate a soldier now dead these 135 years.

[4]Based on research by Lauren Cook Burgess, as reported in *Smithsonian* (January 1994).

the South. The proposal was opposed on the grounds that it would invalidate the very principle the South thought itself defending.

## THE SOUTH

The South is a hot and fecund place. To this day it remains filled with passion and romance. While the abolitionist movement in the North became excessive, the emotional response in the South grew as bad or worse. The South not only convinced itself it could win a war, but equally convinced itself that the war was not only worthy, but noble. It could not have accomplished such a romantic job on itself had it not been produced by remarkable history.

From its very beginnings, the South remained essentially English. Early immigration into America settled largely in the North, while English and Scots and Irish made up the majority of the Southern pattern. Except in New Orleans, the South did not have the great mixture of people and languages enjoyed by the North. Indian and African languages either disappeared or went underground. To understand why a vast gulf existed between North and South, the following squib of early Southern history will help:

The Southern pattern began with a man named William Berkeley, who, in 1641 and for thirty years thereafter, recruited the younger sons of English noblemen to come to America. Because of primogeniture, these young men could not inherit land on English estates, but their fathers did send them to the New World with money. These cavaliers literally transplanted the aristocratic way of life they had known in southern England to the shores of Virginia. Many of their English values were admirable, as were values and actions of their descendants.

The Southern problem rose because the cavaliers lived in a style thought well suited to seventeenth-century England, but not suited for the long road through history that the style would travel. As plantations expanded, and as people with no aristocratic background mimicked the aristocratic pattern, that English-y aristocratic style became controlling. Then, because control meant power, the style became fixed. While the style rose from the fact of being English, the true Southern problem, as the nation rushed to war, came from being "only" English.[5]

---

[5]A complete presentation (and one from which my own presentation is condensed)

Thus, the lack of diverse immigration into the South caused a society with little volatility or change. Conditions were roughly the same as those that had troubled New England during the rule of Puritanism. At base, the problem rose because a society grew rigid and heavily styled.[6]

Problems leading to war rose partly because two highly contrasting societies lived side by side, yet depended on each other. Sectors of the industrial North relied on the South for raw materials. The South, heavily romantic, depended on Yankee practicality and Yankee manufacture far more than it would admit. Although slavery was the heralded issue of the Civil War, attendant issues were economic and cultural. While it would be the height of silliness to dismiss the national catastrophe of the Civil War as "growing pains," adolescent features certainly existed. A nation that claimed to be united had to go to war in order to actually become united.

And, in fact, although it tried to become united, the attempt has taken 135 years and uniting is not yet complete. It will not be complete, I think, until our society is sufficiently mature to consider itself one nation, and one people.

Politicians have not brought the United States into a true uniting, and religion has not; largely, I suspect, because both politics and religion often settle for easy answers. Pressure groups make their livings from dividing people, not uniting them. If the ugly legacy of the Civil War is ever completely erased, it will be because art, literature, science, and theology display our common humanity to the point where the society accepts and understands that American differences are completely superficial.

## AFTERMATH

The Civil War ended in 1865. The aftermath did not kill ideas of Original Sin, Original Possibility, and Original Good. But it did kill interest in theology and philosophy, and that interest would be dead for a long, long time.

---

is contained in David Hackett Fischer, *Albion's Seed* (Oxford University Press, 1989), pp. 207–418.

[6]The best single book about the South is *The Mind of the South*, by W. J. Cash (Alfred A. Knopf, 1941).

Between 1865 and 1940–literally, the space between the Civil War and World War II–few new ideas would enter American thought. During the progress of those seventy-five years, Mary Baker Eddy would introduce Christian Science. William James would introduce pragmatism, a philosophy rapidly misunderstood and misused. W. E. B. DuBois and Booker T. Washington wrote and spoke in behalf of understanding the problems of Reconstruction. President Woodrow Wilson put forth original thoughts about the obligation of government to its citizens, and Randolph Bourne gave brilliant insights into the nature of American history and society. For seventy-five years, the problem would not be that thinkers were not thinking. The problem existed because a nation's people felt in no manner ready to pay attention.

Reasons for inattention, beginning in 1865, were wealth, massive immigration, improving communications, expansion in the West, the growth of manufacturing, but especially, the aftermath of the Civil War.

Shock ran simple and deep. In addition to massive losses of life, a nation had fallen on itself. In the names of justice and humanity and honor, the nation performed enough degraded acts to place a sour taste eternally in the American mouth. Too many captured soldiers died of disease in prison camps. Too many women were raped. Too many towns and farms had been laid to waste. Too many people went hungry. Too many children died.

All of that was bad enough, but after the war, Reconstruction began. Reconstruction was an attempt by the North, and by the federal government, to rebuild the South and bring it back onto an equal footing in the Union. Oh, unhappy day.

Southerners thought (and some Southerners still think) of Reconstruction as exploitation so great even vengeance would be easier to take. It is still believed by many Southerners that the North literally tore the South apart with laws and rules and bureaucracy; with double-dealing by carpetbagger opportunists. What really tore the South apart was ineptness of Congress after the assassination of Lincoln.

As it turned out, no one except Lincoln had thought of a plan for reconstruction. While a lot of political grandstanding went on, the truth seems to be that at a time when leadership and imagination were wanted, little or none were available.

Exploitation of the South by some Northerners did occur. Shady land deals and legalized theft of property happened with great frequency. Congress neutered the Southern political system by restricting who could run for public office. Anyone who had served in the Confederate government, or been an officer in the Confederate army, could not hold office in state or local governments. This stripped the South of experienced leadership.

Most of the legislated discrimination directed against Americans identified as Negro in the late nineteenth century would occur as Southern response to actions by Congress. The response came from a culture so filled with romance, and stuffed with self-admiration, that it could not bear the thought it might be mistaken. The South did its level best to hang onto customs and attitudes surrounding slavery.

Both North and South could have done a better job, because what was done didn't work. Reconstruction was not nearly as neat and clean as the North believes, and it was not nearly as corrupt as the South remembers. It was one of those less-than-divine human situations in which pretty much everyone was wrong.

After the Civil War, original thought gave way to slogan. In the West, war continued among settlers and Indians. The nation also held a shabby foreign war, the Spanish-American (April–August, 1898), and slogans from "Remember the *Maine*" to "The only good Indian is a dead Indian" abounded.[7]

The big religious movement that followed is known to historians as the Second Great Awakening, circa 1890. It was as evangelical—and mindless—as the original Great Awakening. It gathered beneath its howling ignorance all of the insecurity of the times, plus all the guilt felt over the Civil War. People turned their faces toward preachers who carried rule books. Our people seemed to think if they followed the rules they would ease through insecurity and shock and guilt. Those became days when it was especially easy to follow the rules. Preachers rewrote the rule book to accommodate the desires and interests of any small-town, Middle West banker.

## AND NOW, WE BEGIN ANEW

This book now embarks on a brand-new course, because the post–Civil War period marks a time when the nation also set a new course. The

---

[7]We have General Philip Sheridan to thank for that one.

national life of that period turned topsy-turvy. Old and reliable forms of political and religious inquiry faded.

From 1620 until 1860, American life had never been far removed from ideas originating in religion. The history of those years tells of battle after battle between ideas, as America, and also Europe, shrugged off the Middle Ages.

Then, after the Civil War, our nation would gradually discover that it was no longer a regional power. It had become a player on the world stage. Our nation hugged itself in nervous self-admiration and called itself "modern" even as remnants of the Middle Ages survived in the culture. Americans became noisily proud, noisily insecure, and were convinced that they needed no further information from English, European, or American thinkers; because, it was believed, America "knew it all."[8]

Religion in America became a sustaining force for many people, but it was no longer an *originating* force. The evangelical movement could not handle new information, especially ideas about evolution and psychology. Evangelicals got into roughly the same position as had been occupied by Puritan preachers of early New England—i.e., they had to defend a point of view that became more and more ridiculous as new information arrived.

This failure of religion would have a greater impact on the twentieth century than is generally believed. The whole business of morality (not moralism), and integrity, would be handed over to our artists and writers.

From the Civil War to the present, but especially from 1865 to 1940, characters in our art and literature would be constantly concerned with moral questions. The fundamentals of the Puritan and Quaker spirits run all through the paintings of Winslow Homer, Mary Cassatt, Thomas Eakins, and most of the rest. Sin is central to much of the written work, and is a preoccupation in some of the work. Our writers wrestled in behalf of characters who fought against a growing and ugly American tradition of mindlessness.

Briefly: Puritanism passed in America, but puritanical behavior did not.

---

[8]Even while believing this, Americans would buy the opportunistic speculations of the English philosopher Herbert Spencer. Consistency is seldom a big feature of the popular mind.

The great flaw of the puritanical mind is that it is intolerant and, at its depths, will kill. In the first half of the twentieth century it engaged in lynching in the name of its god. It currently will bomb abortion clinics in the name of that same god. It will ban books, raid libraries, try to pack school boards, and dictate curriculum. It will also trash the Constitution in behalf of liberal causes, because puritanical behavior is not limited to religious conservatives.

In the name of more-temporal gods, such as money or power, it will blame all of society's problems on welfare mothers, or black men, or white men, or homosexuals, or "men" or "women." The puritanical mind operates in a closed circle. It feeds itself with dogmatic proclamations of "right," and those proclamations are then thought of as fully true, and thus are justification for even greater bigotry.

This is not to say that all religion should be equated with puritanical behavior, or that religion has had only destructive results. Religion serves in many ways. I think there is probably no single organized religion that has not produced at least a few saintly people. Individuals, and individual congregations, cause strong forces of goodness and even grace in their communities.

Thus, the point of the argument is not that religion is good or bad, but that religion in all of its shapes has played a far larger part in the conscious and subconscious mind of the American people than has been generally acknowledged.

Religion has played such a big part because, as we've seen, for the first 240 years following colonial settlement, religious thought contributed great forces to the development of the American mind. A nation does not get rid of such a heritage (even if it wished) in one generation, or two, or three.[9]

After the Civil War, churches became places offering security, not risk taking. As a sustaining force, religion worked for a great number of people, and does to this day. Religion supplies a sense of security. Over the past 130 years, religion has helped bring people through economic depressions, wars, and technological change.

However, for those who see the function of religion as a method of search, rather than a bastion of belief, organized religion seems an easy

---

[9]For example: in Russia's twentieth-century experience, seventy years of totalitarianism could not erase the Russian church.

answer, and not a little silly. Into that group of those who search, we may include writers and artists, be they religious or not.

After the Civil War, the American writer faced a time of doctrinaire babel. The American mind was being told to place itself on ice. The American writer would not, and did not, put up with being iced.

Our writers were mad with carrying messages against the staid, terrible platitudes of those days. Our writers were beautiful. They were fabulous. Together with the arts, they carried the burden of thought for this nation, and would carry it from the end of the Civil War to the beginning of World War II.

With interest in theology and philosophy dead, the American writer replaced theology and philosophy with literature.

# PART II

# A Word About Literature
# and a Meeting with
# Four Old Friends

As WE APPROACH the American writer at work from 1865 to 1940, I want to suggest wider definitions of literature, and, in the following chapter, a definition of terms. I do so for two reasons: As this book continues, we will be looking with deserved admiration at some writers whose work has been set aside as "unliterary," although it was work of great value at the time it was published. The second reason comes because I remember, as a young writer, the confusion of trying to deal with material while not understanding how writing/reading/and writing about literature fit together. I thought writing in the twentieth century could emulate work from the nineteenth century; a belief only partly true, because different times require different kinds of wizardry in language. I thought reading was reading, that everyone did it the same way and for the same reasons. Worse, I thought everyone, except me, understood the exact meaning of words describing literature.

We'll approach definition of the writer's position by considering hazards and strengths we receive from literature teachers.

Sometimes I'm a literature teacher. When I wear my literature-teacher hat, I care about meaning in a story, and whether it has symbolic, ethical, or historical application in the lives of students. I care that it fits an acknowledged stream of American literature, whether that stream is presently favored, or not. I need the streams as context. A teacher can't just stand before a class, hold a book in his hand, and pant.

When I wear my writing-teacher hat, I couldn't care less for symbol, and care nothing at all for greater meaning, so long as meaning contains no cheap shots. I care for complete honesty from the writer, and complete respect for the material. The writing teacher is more demanding than the literature teacher, but both sets of standards are firm.

From the writer's viewpoint, fiction deals with the truth of a character or characters in a particular situation(s). A story can be a love story, science fiction, a cowboy story, or humor. A love story does not have to descend to the level of bodice rippers just because it's a love story. It can be so well written that it becomes a lasting part of a nation's literature—for example, *Portrait of Jenny*, by Robert Nathan. Science fiction and fantasy stories attain to the condition of art in such stories as *The Illustrated Man*, by Ray Bradbury, and "Professor Gottesman and the Indian Rhinoceros," by Peter S. Beagle. A cowboy story rises into literature in *The Oxbow Incident*, by Walter Van Tilberg Clark, and no one, I think, would deny the value of humor by Robert Benchley and James Thurber.

All of these are wonderful books because they are honest. Yet, plenty of honest books never receive much recognition. They appear for a season, are treasured by hundreds or thousands, then pass into history with the shadow of a backward wave. They stand outside of what is known as the canon. Long after they pass from view, they stand on writers' and readers' bookshelves, treasured because they are sustaining voices of the culture, and because they are loved.

## THE CANON

The canon is made up of books deemed worthy by the current crop of English teachers. The canon changes over years because English teachers change, and usually change with their times. At present, for example, few of them teach Longfellow, although Longfellow certainly helped keep the American mind glued together back when worlds seemed falling apart. Longfellow is presently deemed "too romantic." Such judgments often tell us more about literature teachers than they tell about Longfellow, who was only "too romantic" sometimes.

Literature teachers have a problem that increases with years. Writers keep writing books, and those books add up. It is impossible for students to read even 2 percent of the work one feels they really should read. A fellow teacher says about the class "Survey of American Literature," "You can teach it twenty times and fail twenty times," and, of course, he's correct.

No surprise, then, that good and honest books do not enter the canon. While the canon comprises only a tiny bit of the nation's literature, it sets standards. Thousands of books meet and often exceed those standards, even when not included in the canon. It is also well to remember that honest books are written for readers, not for English teachers.

## LITERATURE TEACHERS

Worthy books not in the canon often function in ways beyond the scope of literature teachers, especially as they function in lives of young writers. For that reason, a young writer can really get messed up by a literature teacher, even though the teacher tries to help. Here are four ways:

1. Literature teachers tend to either lionize writers or completely dismiss them. It is not true, for example, that Herman Melville never wrote a bad line. He wrote some wonderful stuff, and he wrote some drivel. It is important for young writers to have heroes, but we learn from our heroes' mistakes as well as their successes.

2. Literature teachers tend to view bestselling authors as simple entertainers, of no interest to "sensitive minds." Yet, the usual run of genre fiction, and popular fiction, reflects the demands of a large audience. If nothing else, the popularity of such books says something concrete about the state of the society. In addition, the idea that a popular novel must necessarily be of little interest is unsound. The majority of books in the canon sold very well in their day.

3. Literature teachers forget to tell young writers that great writers usually went through hell, and that art will serve up a predictable amount of hell. Teachers too often romanticize the lone soul starving in a garret while producing a great novel. There's nothing romantic about it. Hungry is hungry, and cold is cold. Be prepared.

4. Finally, literature teachers approach books with one or

another critical bias. The absolute *last* thing any writer needs is heavy exposure to lit-crit. Literary criticism places an invisible critic on a writer's shoulders. The writer becomes self-conscious. When that happens, writers stop taking chances and start writing for critics. They would be better off in cold garrets.

## THE FLIP SIDE

On the flip side, literature teachers have a lot to give. They validate stories and storytelling in a world now mad for easy entertainment.

Literature teachers stand as the first bulwark against the saturating cheapness of popular culture (and popular culture has usually been cheap, but only with the rise of communications technology has it become saturating).

Literature teachers are not simply curators of literary museums, although they are stewards with an obligation to preserve work. Their enthusiasm sustains us, and I love to hear one of them go breathless in an attempt to show poet James Russell Lowell as a fine young madman making a stalwart fight over ill-defined ground. I love to hear one of them adoring Lowell's cousin Amy for being a hard-writing bad girl in a time when women were not allowed such voices.

Finally, writers and literature teachers conspire in behalf of the American mind. While historians make comprehensible the events of the past, writers and literature teachers bring that past to life. They are active historians, people who impart feeling as well as facts about history.

## STANDARDS IN WRITING

In order to get a sound look at writerly attitudes, let's look at four writers of the Transcendentalist period who were not Transcendentalists, but who bequeathed important standards. There were others, but these four are well known.

Nathaniel Hawthorne, Herman Melville, and Edgar Allan Poe combined romance with realism, two mainstreams in our literature. These writers were joined by Louisa May Alcott, who, while engaged with other matters, did for children, and did for history, what no Transcendentalist, and no other storyteller of her time, could pull off. She is properly included with the Transcendentalist period since, by birth and most often by inclination, she felt obliged to be kind to both children and Transcendentalists.[1] While she published a good bit before the Civil War, she did not begin serious publication until 1864.[2]

## Nathaniel Hawthorne

When one of my writer friends first read Hawthorne's "Rappaccini's Daughter," she insisted Hawthorne was a woman, because, as she said, "The story forgives Eve." What she did not say, because she assumed I already knew, is that Nathaniel Hawthorne set a standard for American writers.

Since writing bequeaths moral and ethical standards to a nation, it follows that one or more writers had to set the deal up in the first place. Hawthorne's standard insists on full portrayal of character. Thus, my friend figured Hawthorne as a woman (while knowing he was not) because he dealt with Beatrice Rappaccini as a full human being, and not a social or literary cliché.

As a writer, I view "Rappaccini's Daughter" in a way different from the way I view the story as an English teacher. The English teacher says the story is a different take on the Garden of Eden and the Fall from Grace. It is also a caution against the sin of pride. The writing teacher says that "Rappaccini's Daughter" is a standard I must meet in dealing with characters of both genders, but especially women.

Hawthorne set this standard over and over. He did it with Hester Prynne in *The Scarlet Letter* and with Hebzibah Pyncheon in *The House of the Seven Gables*. These women exist as fully human in the context of their times and places.

It follows that one question important for writers, and especially for American writers who must deal with great matters of conscience, asks: does the male writer handle female characters as well as he handles male characters, and does the female writer handle male characters as well as she handles female characters? This is often not of great im-

---

[1]She was the daughter of Bronson Alcott, who may be charitably described as an ineffective man, although a Transcendentalist. If one wishes to be less than charitable, Bronson may be described as a Transcendental deadbeat.

[2]Her prewar publications were in the form of pulp, mostly horror. See *Behind a Mask (the Unknown Thrillers of Louisa May Alcott)*, Madeleine Stern, ed. (William Morrow and Company, Inc., 1975).

portance to literature teachers, who are generally more interested in meaning than in characterization.

The question is important to writers because writers understand that the story is not an imitation of life. It *is* life.

Exceptions exist. A few books succeed when they portray flimsy characters. Those few do so because characters are in such a limiting situation that the situation becomes the story. Examples are *U.S.A.*, a trilogy by John Dos Passos, and *Catch-22*, by Joseph Heller.

Writers before Hawthorne were true to their characters, but none more obviously true. From his standard rises concentration on the importance of the individual in our literature, an importance different from the notion of the American individualist. The first is real, the second a fond hope; or quite possibly a memory.

## Herman Melville

Herman Melville introduced a palette of anguish into the literature. His personal pain translates straight across to the story and displays itself as torment. Such torment succeeds because it lives beyond the writer's ego. It would wish well for the entire world, and would suffer the world's pain in order to relieve that pain. Melville is the first of our writers to say, metaphorically, to other writers: "It is all right to be crazy, to be stark, staring nuts, if you can hold onto artistic control and make something out of it. It is all right to rifle the language for the imagery of the poet, and to use poetic forms in prose."

In other words, it's okay to walk naked down Main Street in the middle of the day if that's what it takes to get the story honestly told.

Melville's legacy is remarkable if we consider that he sat in starchy and glum New England during the shank of the Victorian period with its lace, formality, stuffiness; and, while sitting there, lionized Hawthorne, a man not known for rant.

## Edgar Allan Poe

Great writers often embarrass people. Melville certainly did, and Poe did it even better, because he turned over polished stones to reveal grim undersides.

Poe bequeathed a strain in American literature that acknowledges things weird. The large majority of writers we value have written at least one weird story, even literary types. William Dean Howells, as respectable a gent as America can offer, wrote ghost novels, including *The Seen and Unseen at Stratford-on-Avon*. Henry James, equally respectable, wrote *The Turn of the Screw*. It is pretty hard to find an American writer who has not fooled around with something weird at some point in his or her career.

There are reasons, and they are fascinating:

As our history shows, this has traditionally been a Protestant nation. Protestants traditionally read their Bibles, and weirdness is part of the Judeo-Christian tradition. In proof (and Poe would enjoy this): these days there is an element of storytelling called "magical realism." Such stories occur in normal worlds, in which exist one or more magical events or objects. The form is originally said to have started in South America, where it handled political statements.

If you pick up the Protestant Bible, and turn to the Book of Mark, you'll find magical realism on the hoof. Forget it's the Bible. Just read the story.

Then review our literature. The whole business of magical realism has been there all along. With Puritans and other early people, realism contained magic. It was dark magic, true; generally satanic.

Quakers, who didn't even have the combination of words to describe themselves accurately, were practical mystics. They operated on mystical terms in a day-to-day and often-dangerous world. Their mystical experience constantly exposed them to danger through action. For example, many of them went unarmed among the Indians at a time when such action seemed (and sometimes proved) unwise.

The Revolutionary Fathers, the most rational of men, acted rationally on matters of sheer faith. What, for instance, are inalienable rights? Rights get alienated all the time.

Jefferson, a Deist, believed wholly in the message of Christ; a belief in lovely but unprovable assertions. Our nation's founders also believed in the social contract as espoused by Thomas Hobbes in the already-mentioned *Leviathan*; even though Hobbes could not prove (although he manfully tried to do so) a logical basis for the social contract, only a utilitarian basis.

Our nation, religious or nonreligious, was built on articles of faith. Such faith certainly believed in magic (called miracles), and faith constantly skated on the ice of the surreal. At the time the Constitution was written, there existed no concrete reason for the framers to believe it would last as many as fifty years. Ben Franklin, among others, believed it would not. Representative government was a less-than-real idea.

In addition, there is a long-standing tradition of rebellion in our Western world. From at least the thirteenth century, the Devil performed as a rebellious figure. Devil worship circled through the nights, a secret revolt against economic and religious systems. Weirdness is as much a part of the Euro-American, Judeo-Christian tradition as logic ever was.

That European tradition would combine in America with traditions from Africa, Asia, and the American Indian. Looked at as a wonderful mixture, it is surreal, beautiful, and carries truth so fantastic that ordinary realism sometimes pales.

Poe validated the dark side of the American consciousness. He made manifest the awful fact that there are monsters in the closet and under the bed; echoes of guilt, storm, and fire.

## Louisa May Alcott

Literature changes lives. If it did not change lives, we would have very few writers and no English majors. Alcott changed the lives of children, as well as lives of families. Whereas Hawthorne, Melville, and Poe sought combinations of realism, the fantastic, and romance, Alcott worked on that everyday road we all travel. In order to understand her importance, it's necessary to take a look at one function of literature too often ignored. It changes the lives of children, and children grow to be adults.[3]

Take, for example, the children's book *Black Beauty*. It is about a horse who started life well, then suffered. If an adult reads the story, it is rapidly seen as sentimental, emotionally sloppy, and preachy. However, it wasn't written for adults. If a ten-year-old reads *Black Beauty* and if, in reading, becomes acquainted with feelings of compassion and

---

[3]I have often wondered at those writers and intellectuals who regard writing for children as suspect, second-class, or uninteresting. Where in the world do they believe readers come from? Readers do not hop from television tubes. They appear in the children's rooms of libraries, or seated beside a parent who reads to them. A book equally as long as this could be written about writers-for-children; and who did what for whom. My own debt is to a writer named Charles Major, whose *The Bears of Blue River* showed a young boy the power of stories.

outrage at wrongness occurring in the world, then even that awfully sentimental story functions as literature. The child grows and may forget the story, but will not forget the feelings. *Black Beauty,* however, serves us only as an example. It has nothing to do with Alcott, who wrote with honesty and power.

Alcott, in such novels as *Little Women* and *Little Men,* took stories that formed children and placed them on the page. Always before, such stories existed largely in little morality tales, or in family history in an oral tradition.

Alcott lived in a stylistically formal time, the Victorian era, when it was not easy to be either a child or an adult. Because of an inept father, she knew about making money to support the family. She knew about caring for children.

Alcott deals in the realism of the Victorian family. She does not butter problems over with euphemisms, as did so many Victorian writers. She tells her stories of little women and little men precisely as her characters were supposed to exist in the context of their time. People are allowed to acknowledge anger, and learn that it must be controlled. Her books are extremely moral, without being moralistic. There are no "little walks and talks" with the author. Her stories show a correct way of "being" among a number of characters. The reader is then allowed to make up her mind for herself. Among other contributions, Alcott's books are the perfect blueprint for raising children in Victorian America.[4]

She shows another function of literature. She shows what Emerson called the Mind of the Past. The Mind of the Past comes to us from honest literature, because literature, as we see by reading Alcott, is a special kind of history.

Regular historians record and combine facts. Historians explain forces leading to wars, revolutions, social change, and even changes in the way different peoples view the world at different times. Storytellers record the "feel" of history, because each generation feels and experiences the world in somewhat different manners. We might read histories of the Victorian period late into the night without learning as much about the "feel" of the Victorian home as we find in *Little Women.*

---

[4] A discussion of this is contained in Stanley Coben, *Rebellion Against Victorianism, The Impetus for Cultural Change in 1920s America* (Oxford University Press, 1991).

In addition to values, literature is a record of ideas and dreams, whether or not those ideas and dreams were implemented by a society. The United States, for example, still advertises itself as a Christian nation. Its religion, as practiced by the majority, has nothing to do with Christianity, or, if it does, then Christianity has nothing to do with Christ. That does not mean the purity of founding ideas does not echo through the centuries. Those founding ideas were expressions of dreams.

Literature, in addition to its many other virtues, is the record of the dreams of a people. Without dreams, there would have been no American Revolution. Without dreams, there would have been no formative work by Hawthorne, Melville, Poe, and Alcott. Without dreams, there would not have been—or be today—anger by American writers when offenses are rendered against the dream.

# Defining Our Terms

Dreams and anger were fit subjects for the American writer after the Civil War. From forces of darkness and light bequeathed by our beginnings grew other forces. I call them *romance, sentimentality, realism, social realism, naturalism,* and *the fantastic.* I define terms because literary people spin these terms into many different fabrics. What I call realism is known as naturalism (sort of) in some crowds. I also define terms so young writers can be clear about approaches to their tasks.

## Romance

ROMANCE has a history dating, at least, to the Crusades. A case could be made that it dates as far back as the *Odyssey.*[1] The romantic tradition includes love, but also includes adventure, ghosts and other spectral matters, tragedy, farce, religion, and chivalry.

Early American writers, William Cullen Bryant, Washington Irving, and the Transcendentalists experienced romance in connection with nature. The theory said that you should immerse yourself in the benevolent bosom of fields, streams, cows, and small varmints, together with sun and moon and stars and weather. You should carefully remain

---

[1]The poet Kenneth Rexroth makes a case for the *Odyssey* being the first cowboy story, at least in spirit since it happened a good while before the appearance of cowboys. At any rate, the *Odyssey* is a romance.

wide-open to the influences of the Whole (the wholeness of creation, of which you become a part). In doing this, you transcend, entering into the living soul of the world, or of the universe.

In other words, Romantics and Transcendentalists theorized to a point of nearly understanding what probably 90 percent of American Indians learned from the day they were born. The Indian, having nowhere else to live but in nature, accepted the world in mystical terms. One of the great spiritual losses of the nineteenth century is that the white population failed to learn much of what the Indian knew.

Romance may or may not include nature. What it always includes is heightened awareness, and/or sensitivity, in important situations.

It's easy to get confused about romance, and confusion can happen to any writer. For example, in the twentieth century, Hemingway believed himself a realist of the first order, but was often romantic. He could write about the aftermath of battle as a "garden of death," which, of course, in a realist, is the silliest kind of pap. Like every other writer willing to take chances, Hemingway scored successes. He also wrote a few things that should have melted the page. Hemingway deserves to be one of our heroes. He was a great writer.

When we mess with romance, we take awful chances, which, of course, is exactly why we should mess with it. The main danger comes because it is easy for romance to change into sentimentality. Because such danger exists, and because young writers are at an age subject to sentimentality, a caution is probably warranted.

## SENTIMENTALITY

SENTIMENTALITY amounts to a cheap shot. It pretends that things not true, are true. Here's how it works:

Let us take a ten-year-old boy standing before a rack of greeting cards for Father's Day. A card shows the picture of a guy in full hunting dress, in a field bordered by woods, and accompanied by a gorgeous Irish setter. The guy points a shotgun at a fleeing quail. Inside the card is a message reading "To the best Dad in the world."

The father of this ten-year-old is a marginal alcoholic who screams at his wife and kid. The father scales 25 percent overweight, and his idea of being an outdoorsman is to walk off the porch for the newspaper when the paperboy misses the porch. This father once noticed his son. He said something like "Hey, kid, tell those punk friends of yours to play in somebody else's yard." This father would not know what to with an Irish setter if he had one. The only tool he really knows is a beer glass, so keep him away from a shotgun. A live quail would frighten him gaga.

There is no card reading "To a Dad whom I wish would Sober Up." This ten-year-old picks up the card "To the best Dad in the world." Sentimentality occurs because the kid tries to fool himself into believing the message is true. Or, at least he's unconsciously thinking that if he pretends hard enough, maybe the loser he's stuck with actually will change into the best dad in the world; "because actually, sort-of, he's a pretty good old dad."

Illusion. Nothing is going to happen. The writer of the card helps the kid lie to himself, and the lie in this case is sentimentality.

Nor is the greeting-card writer excused because there might actually be, somewhere, one dad who *is* the best dad in the world, and who blows away quail with great abandon whilst gathering the admiration of an Irish setter; but who somehow forgets to take his kid along and teach the kid how to hunt. Writers who deal in sentimentality, and people who run the greeting-card industry, will deservedly be reincarnated as bows of pink ribbon.

If we move from greeting cards to literature, we can see sentimentality in phrases, and in denial of evidence; for example: "Granny's wrinkled face shone cheery as a dried apple, and her voice sounded in gentle whispers instead of her once-hearty laugh. It was true, her family thought, that Granny showed her age, but goodness-gracious, Granny was sturdy and would live forever."

For those who write this sort of drivel it is useless to point out that dried apples do not shine, that dried apples are not cheery, and dried apples are often shaped to imitate faces; not the other way around. Granny's voice is failing because her voice box is shot, and, because she's failing, she isn't going to live forever. She's dying in front of her family's eyes.

## REALISM

REALISM denied the romantic view of nature. It saw nature as indifferent—not nice, and not intentionally cruel. Nature was alien to the hopes and plans of humans. The best-known story dealing with this is "The Open Boat," by Stephen Crane. Following shipwreck, four men are adrift. After the story gets us intimately acquainted with them, they come ashore in surf. One dies. The sea doesn't give a wavelet, or even think about it. The surviving men are left with that responsibility.

Realism portrays life as it engages with the known world. One might compare realism to representational art in painting. It is in realism, and in the fantastic, that we are most likely to meet American preoccupation with sin.

## SOCIAL REALISM

SOCIAL REALISM: Stephen Crane also dealt with social realism, which sees people as subject to forces or prejudices in society. When he was little more than a kid, he wrote *Maggie: A Girl of the Streets.*[2] Maggie is a slum girl who hopes and dreams, and who is destroyed by life around her. She is betrayed by a loser of a boyfriend, a piggish family, an entire society; and everyone gets to feel sorry for himself—and feel guiltless—when the combined forces kill her. When Crane wrote *Maggie,* the streets of big cities killed kids with great indifference. It was even worse than today. Crane's story is ill formed, clumsy, an ugly duckling.[3] Still, his youthful anger over injustice makes the reader pay attention.

Social realism is not new in literature. Shakespeare wrote what might be called early social realism when he wrote *The Merchant of Venice,* a man bludgeoned by "decent folk" because he was a Jew. Arthur Miller would later do an equal or better job in *Death of a Salesman.* In that play, assumptions of a society that buys its morals from the dimestore combine in the character Willy Loman's mind and force his death.

This approach to writing holds up a mirror. The writer says to the society: "This is what you are doing. I can't stop you from doing it. I can't even stop you from *liking* it; but I can blamed well show it. Let your actions be your own accuser." This is the art of storytelling practiced at a very high stage of development. Because of its power, it need

---

[2] His war novel, *The Red Badge of Courage,* was published two years later (1895).

[3] As a young writer you will probably publish work that, later on, will seem embarrassing. You need never apologize for any work that was the best you could do at the time it was written. If you remained true to your material, and took no shortcuts or cheap shots, no apologies are necessary.

not always use literal realism. Shirley Jackson, for example, would use the fantastic in "The Lottery," a story that holds up a mirror.

## NATURALISM

NATURALISM, as used here, refers to the American love of land, and the American frontier. It tells rural stories, from the harshness of Frank Norris to the celebrations of Willa Cather to the sometimes-wistful longings of Steinbeck. Naturalism is at the base of some tremendously strong Western novels, Frank Spearman's *Whispering Smith*, or *Somewhere South in Sonora*, by Will Comfort.

The difference between naturalism and the romantic view of nature is the difference of action and experience. Both the Romantic and the Transcendentalist could love the land by walking through forests and across pastures. The sons and daughters of naturalism, however, loved the land in a different way. They grubbed out tree stumps to plant crops, cut firewood to get through the winters, and felt the buck and kick of a bull-tongue plow over rocky ground. They lived on the land and, when they died, were buried in it.

## THE FANTASTIC

THE FANTASTIC, as used here, means anything weird that aids a tale, but which is not the tale. The fantastic can range from a character who is slightly clairvoyant all the way up to witches and warlocks riding brooms. It can include spaceships, time warps, characters with funny ears, trolls, fairies, talking bears, Santa Claus, and the Easter bunny. However, in order to qualify as the fantastic, and not a cartoon, the fantastic element needs to allow change, or deeper understanding, in the lives of characters and readers.

# AFTER BATTLE

HAVING LOOKED AT four writers who set high standards early in our
history, and having defined our terms, we may now look at America
at the tumultuous end of the Civil War. Americans and American writers saw a mixed bag of problems, influences, and opportunities; and
they reacted.

As we've seen, our nation was founded on great ideas, not simply
big ideas. The post–Civil War period was a time when ideas were
merely big.

Our nation was also founded in a battle between gods, not godlets.
This was a time of godlets.

More divinities came alive in the public mind than existed in ancient
Rome. A few things worshiped were Science, Nationalism, International
Trade, Capitalism, Expansion, Industry, Evolution (both biological and
social), Psychology, Communications, and, by the turn of the century,
Bicycles.

If none of the above seem particularly holy, it may pay to consider
the proposition that humans create their own gods. Then, propitiating
those gods, the gods become real. Whether this is true in essence, we
can't determine. Whether it's true in the way people act is a matter of
record. The religion of America from 1865 to 1929 became acquisition,
pure and simple.

## ACQUISITION

As ideas died in the wake of the Civil War, the nation fell into a period of change. People called it "Progress." An entire national economy reshaped from the traditional farm economy to an emerging industrial economy, although the farm would remain one of the strongest forces for good and ill through half of the coming twentieth century.

Expansion into the West, and conquest (in some areas extermination) of the American Indian, seemed to hold agriculture as a main goal. That is only partly true. Expansion also had to do with capturing resources claimed by the federal government.

During this period, most valued resources were tangible: iron ore, lumber, copper, gold, silver, fisheries, coal, and oil. A group of awfully exciting men stepped forward, if, in fact, one enjoys excitement liberally mixed with greed, arrogance, vulgarity, duplicity, contempt, wastefulness, and the absolute determination to capture anything worth a nickel, whether nailed down or not.

We can look back and see a who's who of economic creatures who divided the spoils: John D. Rockefeller, Jay Gould, Andrew Carnegie, James Hill, John Pillsbury, Leland Stanford, Cornelius Vanderbilt; and political types: "Boss" Tweed, James G. Blaine . . . a thousand such polecats, give or take one or two evil perfumes.

## IMMIGRATION

In addition to tangible resources, much of the economic adventurers' successes depended on exploiting people who arrived in massive waves of immigration. Immigrants supplied a workforce that could be manipulated, and population figures suggest the ease in finding workers. The U.S. Census shows 14,215,989 people entering the country between 1860 and 1900. In 1860, the national population stood at a little under 31.5 million. By 1900, it had more than doubled to just under 76 million. One-third of that increase came from immigration.

During the change from an agrarian economy to a manufacturing economy, and because of a plentiful supply of workers, ugly practices occurred. Many of those practices were not then regarded as abuse, but would be so regarded today. Children, and women, and men, died of overwork, squalor, malnutrition, disease, and hazards rising from operating machinery with no safeguards.

## ABUSE

Standards of the Industrial Revolution, as practiced in America, produced an extension of slavery, called "wage slavery." Treatment of children was cruel beyond belief. Child prostitution became dirt-common in cities, especially New York. Children were as expendable as chaff. In New York City, for example, the price of a living human baby ranged from $10 to $25.[1]

In industry and mercantile employment, in 1880, only nine states limited child labor to ten hours a day. Dakota Territory had an eight-hour law. The rest of the states and territories had no law. Only one state, Maine, had a law limiting child labor to ten-hour days in all areas of labor. In the rest of the states, you could work a twelve-year-old to death, and not pay for the funeral; and you may be sure twelve-year-olds and younger children lay dead because of "Progress."

By 1900, laws had improved very little. Nineteen states and/or territories had ten-hour laws for children, one had a twelve-hour law, but the rest had none.

Women's work laws followed similar patterns: one eight-hour state in 1890, one nine-hour state, twenty ten-hour states/territories, and no law in the rest.

In 1890, four states allowed men's contracts to be written for eight-hour days, four states had ten-hour laws, and the rest had no law. In the steel industry, Irish workers revolted against twelve-hour days and were replaced by immigrant Slavs and Hungarians.

Real wages (the relation of wages to the cost of food and housing) for industrial workers in the 1890s were $10.73 a week, and declined by 1900. With such conditions, every member of a family had to work. If people became sick, they either got well or died, because they could not afford a doctor. If they were injured at work, and disabled, the

---

[1]Hard to believe. Yet, the price of babies is documented by Brooke Kroeger in her biography of one of our first investigative journalists. *Nellie Bly* (Random House, 1994).

A picture of New York City during this period can be found in two beautifully researched novels by Caleb Carr: *The Alienist* (Random House, 1994) and *The Angel of Darkness* (Random House, 1997).

attitude of industry was "How sad. He should have been a bit more careful." The period is not the finest hour in the history of American capitalism.

## PROGRESS

If this was all that was going on, the nation might not have survived. It did, however, stumble back toward some hope of continuity after the Civil War. While misery lived among an exploited immigrant population, and while the black population of the South waited for education and a leader, and while the last of the Indian wars died not with war whoops but with whimpers, an optimistic nation built railroads and homesteads. The smell and feel of Progress filled the air. Robber barons were more often praised than criticized, because it seemed to most Americans that toil, grit, and mother wit would soon make everybody rich.

## EXPANSION

This was an age of colonial expansion. Western nations pressed economic and missionary values in places where the resident population lived fairly content with what it had. England, for example, built a colonial empire so large that the brag "The sun never sets on the British empire" was true. The American empire extended into experiments in China, and to the Philippines. For our purposes, American expansion existed largely as a conquest of the West. Some of that conquest was as brutal as any happening anywhere else in the world.

## EFFECTS OF CONQUEST

These days, it is popular to condemn colonialism, and pretend that only evil came from expansion. Such claims are adolescent. Colonialism meant change, and change caused the evils of death and disruption in social and cultural systems. In America, the aboriginal cultures were either wrecked or destroyed.

However, colonialism also caused better sanitation, longer life expectancy for future generations, the setting up of economic foundations that would produce an indigenous middle class, and, eventually, schools, roads, and the gadgets of Western civilization, from bottle openers to engines. Before universally damning all colonial effort, it may be well to ask residents of a nation if they would prefer the way of life existing before colonialism. You can bet the residents of Hong Kong did not want the English to leave as Hong Kong returned to China. That, however, is an example so obvious perhaps it does not serve the argument.

The American Indian, among the most badly used of any people in history, would, as a people, probably not wish to return to the life their nations led before European settlement. Birth rates were low, life expectancy hovered beneath forty years, and in large areas of the country, many died of cold during winters. War flared fairly constant.[2] The social fabric varied. In the Southeast, men and women dealt more or less equally in the societies. Among some western tribes, women were treated worse than were the dogs. In other words, the American Indian was a human being first, and thus subject to successes and mistakes that characterize humans. Colonization destroyed a lot of people, and injured a lot of cultures. Despite remembered sorrow and indignation, the descendants of those people would probably not wish to get rid of the gains that came from change. When winter hits twenty below zero, with the wind blowing, propane heat beats buffalo chips.

## VICTORIANISM

In the midst of the turmoil of conquest and expansion, Victorian style arose in manner bold. It was a manner of life and thought imported from England, and adapted to America. The broad, overall picture looks like this:

Victorianism rose from the Romantic period in England. The Romantic period had risen as a reaction to the regulated poetic meters, and mechanical philosophic thought, of the eighteenth century. The eighteenth century, called the Age of Reason, had been a reaction to the lingering taste of the Middle Ages. That reaction came about because of the growth of science, the growth of cities, the massive problems of plague, power, religion, and politics; which, of course, was a reaction. . . . and so on. (I do not mean to treat human thought, desire,

---

[2]Warfare was mostly a matter of raiding. It was not the massive, all-out effort we presently associate with the word "war."

dreams, or suffering lightly here. I only point out that no element of history exists in a vacuum, nor, as writers, do we.)

At first, Victorianism contained much that was admirable, and it contributed positive forces during a time filled with shabby shapes of greed. Victorians believed in family. The home was sacred. Like lots of political and economic people of today, many Victorians did not particularly concern themselves with other people's homes. Too often these days, when a politician says he is interested in the American family, and American children, he means his own family and children, not yours. And so it was with the Victorians.

Victorians salvaged their attitude by a strong belief in duty. Generally speaking, it became the duty of men to fund charitable societies for the rehabilitation of the fallen, the drunks, the orphans, the unwed mothers; and it was the duty of women to run the societies.

This belief in duty ran all through Victorian life. We owe them quite a debt, because, at their best, they bequeathed a mighty legacy to the back half of the twentieth century. They bequeathed a memory of order. Their important idea is that society can be ordered by the self-disciplined behavior of individuals.

While most people today think of Victorians (when they think of them at all) as fuddy-duddies, the fact remains that our contemporary world hungers for order. A need for order is the main reason why an overzealous political right wraps itself in the guise of religion. It's the reason why cowards and goons stockpile weapons, dress in brown shirts, and decorate their worlds with swastikas.

The Victorian legacy, on the other hand, validates order without necessity for weapons and raised fists. Instead, it suggests that social order may come from a firm sense of duty, honor, courage, and charity in a broad, not narrow, sense.

This does not mean that cops of the Victorian period would not bust skulls, and it does not mean that the emerging labor-union movement in those days would not suffer many deaths. The Victorian idea of order is the statement of an ideal. We, sitting at the turn of another century, may be devoutly grateful. Victorian styles have mostly passed, but some sound shapes of Victorian thought remain.

## STYLE

The Victorian world went sour through exaggerated style, and style was one issue that would drive American writers to fury. Style is something people and society lean on when they have no genuine sense of self. The false appeal of style generally drives writers and artists to the bare edge of sanity.

Victorian style insisted on the purity and the frailty of women. A woman might be tough as a buggy whip, but was required to grow faint in the presence of anything vulgar or alarming. In another age, she might have been a mountain climber, but the myth of frailty restricted her to strolls through a variety of gardens.[3] A myth of purity kept her in her own home, or outside that home only when with an escort.

Imagine yourself a woman with time on your hands, and restricted to the world of your house. Discourse with servants about anything other than domestic duties is frowned upon. You have no electricity, thus no phonograph, radio, television, or other electronic trinket. You do have a piano, and can beat the dickens out of that, and you do have a massive library, so there is always something to read. You can write letters, keep a diary, supervise the gardener; all useful occupations, no doubt, but all more-or-less private. You can also have children, but the servants change the nappies.

The philosopher Lewis Mumford, I recall, observed that men create society and women create culture. Traditionally, this seems more-or-less true. The human being will create. If the human is blocked from creation, as Victorian women certainly were, that human will still create something, even if that something is Hell on earth.

The Victorian woman seems to have said, "Okay, if that's the game I'm in, I'll show the world how to play." The culture grew from a base of firmness to a flaunting of style that, by the time it collapsed in the 1920s, became utterly ridiculous.

---

[3]There was some justification for the idea that women were frail. Antiseptic was not discovered until the Civil War, and not widely adapted for at least ten years after the war. Sanitary conditions ranged, in our terms, from unacceptable to awful. Women suffered the same rampant diseases suffered by men. In addition, death rates of women were high because of childbirth. Without antiseptic, women died of "milk fever," postpartum infection of the uterus. It was not uncommon for a man to lose two, or even three, wives in a lifetime.

Examples:

*Duty* required that a person always be prepared. In photographs of Victorians going afield for a day of bird watching, the ladies wear long skirts, jackets, carry parasols. They have lunch baskets provisioned to feed an army. They wear sturdy shoes, have huge hats to broaden the shade of the parasols (because a lady could never, never be exposed to the elements). They have a bird book, tablecloth, china, and a steadfast appearance.

The men wear wool suits, vests, heavy boots, and carry at least two pairs of binoculars, a telescope, a shooting stick, a pocket pistol (in the event, one supposes, that they encounter a particularly delicious-looking bird), a tent, matches, hatchet—enough equipment, in fact, to sustain the party in the field for two weeks. Overabundance became a token of preparation, as preparation had become a token of duty.

*Purity.* Books of instruction for the training of young ladies include advice such as "When a gentleman offers you his chair, you must demur, because the chair will still be warm from the gentleman's person." Books of instruction about marriage gave stern advice: A married couple should never see each other naked. Victorians put skirts on their pianos so no one would have to look at piano legs. Young women demanded prenuptial agreements requiring that their husbands-to-be not consummate marriage. There was even a movement among very serious people to clothe the "private parts of animals"; horses, cattle, and dogs thus attaining an "ample modesty."[4]

The problem with style is that people who value it actually come to believe it of first importance, whereas its importance is almost always secondary or nil. Victorians actually told themselves that sex was one of those inconvenient acts associated with marriage, and only marginally associated with great and romantic love. Sex was also viewed as an unfortunate but necessary element that maintained male health. (Women, of course, were pure, thus already healthy, though naturally also frail.) If one reads Freud's conclusions about sex in the context of the Victorian period, and not the context of the present, they make sense.[5]

Since creativity can be blocked, but not stopped, Victorian women created an exaggerated culture. Men helped, of course, but men had

---

[4]This kind of dazed thinking lasted for a very long time. As a child in the 1930s, I recall hearing the idea discussed (and cussed) more than once.

[5]A full discussion of this is contained in "The Freud Revolution," Si. Fullinwider, in *History Today*, April 1992, 42:23(7).

their own problems. Somehow they had to square ideas of nobility and duty with what they saw of industrial excesses. They also came to have a genuine problem with sex. Women were supposed to be pure. Men were, at best, ambivalent. This, plus economic necessity occasioned by mass immigration, accounts for the great numbers of prostitutes in large cities. The immigrant women, and kids on the street, had to make a living, somehow.

Victorian men and women shared another problem, one many of us would like to have: how to kill time. Settled Victorians had so much time on their hands as to die of boredom. Immigration supplied a workforce bought for little money. Scandinavian servant girls, for example, often worked a six- or a six-and-a-half-day week. They received room and board, and sometimes 50 cents. It was not uncommon for a Victorian home to employ eight or ten servants.

## CREATING DEATH

If people have time on their hands, and are denying fundamental impulses such as sex, they make do by substitution. Sublimating sex, Victorians became preoccupied with death. Customs surrounding death produced a death industry that any Madison Avenue hypester of today would envy. Photos of dead guys formally dressed, sitting in chairs, and surrounded by live and sober friends give only a tiny suggestion of how crazy the style became. Manuals for mourning were everywhere. They told how to dress, and for how long. If you were second cousin to the dear departed, you could get by with a black armband for a year. If married to the dear departed, rules applied even to your underwear, which had to be black. Coffins were ornate. Mausoleums rose like little castles. Cemeteries groaned beneath the weight of monuments: concrete angels, marble angels, sculpted lambs above the graves of children.

The entire culture seems one of lace and pastel and ebony. While evangelical religion raged among the working elements, Victorians dismissed the idea of Hell and brimstone. Their children were raised believing that death had no call to be proud, and the end of life would see the family reunited in the realms of paradise. It could have been worse. It was better than scaring the kids into conniptions, which is what Puritans once did, and what the evangelicals were doing.

In fairness, the Victorian man contributed a sense of steadfastness and duty to the society, a sense that may have since diminished, but has not departed. The Victorian woman's touch gave a flavor of goodness to our culture during an extremely sour era, a goodness we still encounter daily through courtesy, or care of one for another. The Victorian man was admirable in manly duties. The Victorian woman was no spoiled kitten. She was, in fact, tougher than the whalebone stays in her corset. She gave form to our basic human yearning for solid families.

This, then, gives a rapid sketch of a society the American writer faced. A lot of other shenanigans went on, but this is probably enough for context.

# Toward a New Mythology

New myths were needed. The nation looked at issues that would extend from 1865 to—and through—the entire twentieth century. Of major concern to writers and artists were:

The farm
The woman question
The American Indian
A definition of citizenship for freed slaves, and the treatment
    of minority populations
Greed, especially as the greed of industry exploited labor
The absurdities of style
Changing social and economic forms

In later years, some of these concerns would combine. For example, in the second half of the twentieth century, minority concerns would include women. At the time, though, these concerns were seen separately.

Because all of these issues were at least loosely knitted, a new mythology was needed, one that would support the new world forming. America's situation was about the same then as it is at the end of the twentieth century. Change asked for different myths so that Americans could understand America.

Mythology before the Civil War dealt largely with stories, songs, and art that came in the wake of the American Revolution. Our nation did not yet have a mythology of cowboys and Indians, of railroad building, or of empire. Thus, much of the way the American twentieth century would develop came from stories told after 1865. Our writers tried to figure out what in the world was happening. They would do three things:

Build new myths
Attack old myths
Offer original ways of thinking about the nation's situation.

Let us begin by looking at how our writers handled problems of the land. These days, the American land asks us to think of conservation and preservation. In those days, issues concerning land were every bit as pressing, but were completely different.

## THE FARM

The happy farmer, with his happy cows and lambs and stalwart shocks of corn, had been part of the main inventory of early-nineteenth-century Romantics. They could get into a transcendental tiz just thinking of the delights of rural life. In literature, this mode is termed "pastoral." It's easy to think of a farm in this manner if one has never spent time on a farm; agriculture being to romance what erasers are to pencils.

In the late nineteenth century, romance about the land faltered. Mythology of the farm had been mostly based on East Coast experience, where the farms of New England, New York, and Pennsylvania were generally small, prosperous, and staid. They owned pride in self-sufficiency and stories of the American Revolution.

The revolutionary stories didn't work for what was happening in the West. Hunger for land brought settlers and immigrants, and there were tons of them. Land remained cheap. New immigrants supplied extra labor at low cost in busy seasons. Transportation for crops to market became available as railways rapidly webbed the nation. Farms would remain small for many years, there being a limit to how much land a man and his family could cultivate with horse-drawn equipment. The people rapidly turned from being pioneers and became dirt farmers.

Small towns rose along the routes of railroads. Those small towns shone about as romantic as the farms; and the farms, sad to say, were about as romantic as what fell from the rear of the horse. Life was not as bad as life in the earliest colonies, but not much better. In treeless regions of short-grass prairie, people lived in sod houses. They could barely travel farther than farm to town and return, the trip taking the entire day, and town little better than the farm. Life for many remained tedious, exhausting, and provincial.

One job of the writer is to define situations and show reality. If there existed a new romance in the land, and romance in the small towns, it could be discovered only if the reality was stated first. American writers would deal with the farm, the small town, and the love of land until at least the 1950s. We'll encounter twentieth-century writers later on, but let's look at where farm mythology of the twentieth century began. Here is a writer dealing in realism:

## Edward Watson Howe

This excerpt is from a strange and haunted novel of the period, published in 1883. It is *The Story of a Country Town,* by Edgar Watson Howe, a journalist whose other novels were wooden. This novel, however, was greatly admired by Mark Twain and many others. Howe writes about the region called Fairview in Kansas:[1]

In the dusty tramp of civilization westward—which seems to have always been justified by a tradition that men grow up by reason of it—our section was not a favorite, and remained new and unsettled after counties and states farther west had grown old. Everyone who came there seemed favorably impressed with the steady fertility of the soil, and expressed surprise that the lands were not all occupied; but no one in the great outside world talked about it, and no one wrote about it, so that those who were looking for homes went to the West or the North, where the others were going.

There were cheap lands farther on, where the people raised a crop one year, and were supported by charity the next; where towns sprang up on credit, and farms were opened with bor-

---

[1]This novel is also notable because it contains the most despicable character in all of American literature. Jo is a self-centered destroyer. The book is worth reading to see just how miserable a human can become.

rowed money; where the people were apparently content, for our locality did not seem to be far enough west, nor far enough north, to suit them; where no sooner was one stranger's money exhausted than another arrived to take his place; where men mortgaged their possessions at full value, and thought themselves rich, notwithstanding, so great was their faith in the country; where he who was deepest in debt was the leading citizen, and where bankruptcy caught them all at last. On these lands the dusty travelers settled, where there were churches, schoolhouses, and bridges—but little rain—and railroads to carry out the crops should any be raised; and when anyone stopped in our neighborhood, he was too poor and tired to follow the others.

I became early impressed with the fact that our people seemed to be miserable and discontented, and frequently wondered that they did not load their effects on wagons again, and move away from a place which made all the men surly and rough, and the women pale and fretful. . . .

The narrator of *The Story of a Country Town* then moves from the countryside to the town of Twin Mounds:

Most of the citizens of Twin Mounds came from the surrounding country, and a favorite way of increasing the population was to elect the county officers from the country, but after their terms expired a new set moved in, for it was thought they became so corrupt by a two year residence that they could not be trusted to a reelection. The town increased in size a little in this manner, for none of these men ever went back to their farms again, though they speedily lost standing after they retired from their positions. . . .

There was the usual number of merchants, professional men, mechanics, etc., who got along well enough, but I never knew how at least one half the inhabitants lived. Some of them owned teams, and farmed in the immediate vicinity; others "hauled," and others did whatever offered, but they were all poor, and were constantly changing from one house to another. These men usually had great families of boys, who grew up in the same indifferent fashion, and drifted off in time nobody knew where, coming back occasionally, after a long absence, well dressed, and with money to rattle in their pockets. But none of them ever came back who had business of sufficient importance elsewhere to call them away again, for they usually remained until their good clothes wore out, the delusion of their respectability was broken, and they became town loafers again, or engaged in the hard pursuits of their fathers. The only resident of Twin Mounds who ever distinguished himself ran away with a circus and never came back. . . .

While the frontier owned a myth of "growing up with the country," the farm had nothing. Settlement negated romance. Those small farms caused people to grow down.

I cannot say how long this way of life lasted in country towns, but can attest that it lasted in one Indiana town, and one Kentucky town, until World War II, and survives in each (in somewhat diluted form) until this very day. I can also attest that one Midwest town seems to me very like another.

Yet, the countryside held hopes and dreams of humans, and as writers we need always be respectful of dreams, even, or perhaps, especially, of ones that probably won't work. It may well be that the "meaning of life"—at least, the meaning of human life—is that we dream.

The dreams of a great many people centered on land. One of the great American stories would turn into a tale of quiet passion. The land itself became a character in stories. Even today, among families that have lived in urban areas for three generations, there is still a sense of the living land as part of a heritage stemming all the way back to American aboriginal cultures. The American Indian was the first to feel one with the land, and to adore it with no concept in his language of owning. Many modern urban dwellers still feel a vague understanding of that adoration. The great majority of conservationists live, I'm convinced, in cities.

The American writer became what writers often become: a voice for the voiceless. In behalf of that passion for land our writers were asked to affirm what, about the land, was true.

## Willa Cather

Judge for yourself. Here are words from *O Pioneers!*, by Willa Cather, who is one of our best. She does not hide or cloud the hardness of pioneering farm life in the 1880s, when her character John Bergson lived, but she defines in perfect terms the love of land about which others were inarticulate:

> It is sixteen years since John Bergson died. His wife now lies beside him, and the white shaft that marks their graves gleams across the wheat-fields. Could he rise from beneath it, he would not know the country under which he has been asleep. The shaggy coat of the prairie, which they lifted to make him a bed, has vanished forever. From the Norwegian graveyard one looks out over a vast checker-board, marked off in squares of wheat and corn; light and dark, dark and light. Telephone wires hum along the white roads, which always run at right angles. From the graveyard gate one can count a dozen gayly painted farm-houses; the gilded weather-vanes on the big red barns wink at each other across the green and brown and yellow fields. The light steel windmills tremble throughout their frames and tug at their moorings, as they vibrate in the wind that often blows from one week's end to another across that high, active, reso-lute stretch of country.
>
> The Divide is now thickly populated. The rich soil yields heavy harvests; the dry, bracing climate and the smoothness of the land make labor easy for men and beasts. There are few scenes more gratifying than a spring plowing in that country, where the furrows of a single field often lie a mile in length, and the brown earth, with such a strong, clean smell, and such a power of growth and fertility in it, yields itself eagerly to the plow; rolls away from the shear, not even dimming the bright-ness of the metal, with a soft, deep sigh of happiness. The wheat-cutting sometimes goes on all night as well as all day, and in good seasons there are scarcely men and horses enough to do the harvesting. The grain is so heavy that it bends toward the blade and cuts like velvet.

This is as young and impassioned as the hearts that yearned for land. If written today, we might think it a tad sentimental; but it was written by a child of the Victorian period, and its power would bring tears to the eyes of a statue. If the land needed a valid myth of romance—and the land did—the land found it here. Cather published this in 1912. *O*

*Pioneers!* is a story of immigrants into Nebraska in the 1880s. When your heart is sad with pessimism, and you need a lift, read Cather's *My Antonia.*

We can see our writers holding a mirror that acknowledged and praised romance of the land, while pointing to the destruction of humanity on those farms. Here is an example of love of land, and cruelty of the farm. It's an exercise in realism.

## Hamlin Garland

Garland grew up in Wisconsin, South Dakota, and Iowa as farmers struggled through Midwestern mud, ice, and summer heat waves. He traveled East as a young man, lived a sparse life as he attended school in Boston. His best-known story is "Under the Lion's Paw." The following excerpt is from his story "Up the Coulé," 1893.

The sun had set, and the Coulé was getting dark when Howard got out of McTurg's carriage, and set off up the winding lane toward his brother's house. He walked slowly to absorb the coolness and fragrance and color of the hour. The katydids sang a rhythmic song of welcome to him. Fireflies were in the grass. A whippoorwill in the deep of the wood was calling weirdly, and an occasional nighthawk, flying high gave his grating shriek, or hollow boom, suggestive and resounding. . . .

It was humble enough—a small white house, story-and-a-half structure, with a wing, set in the midst of a few locust-trees; a small drab-colored barn, with a sagging ridge-pole; a barnyard full of mud, in which a few cows were standing, fighting the flies and waiting to be milked. An old man was pumping water at the well; the pigs were squealing from a pen near by; a child was crying.

Instantly the beautiful, peaceful valley was forgotten. A sickening chill struck into Howard's soul as he looked at it all. In the dim light he could see a figure milking a cow. Leaving his valise at the gate, he entered, and walked up to the old man, who had finished pumping and was about to go to feed the hogs.

(There occurs a brief conversation with the old man. Howard decides to wait for his brother, until his brother gets done milking.) The scene continues:

> As he waited he could hear a woman's fretful voice, and the impatient jerk and jar of kitchen things, indicative of ill-temper or worry. The longer he stood absorbing this farm-scene, with all its sordidness, dullness, triviality, and its endless drudgeries, the lower his heart sank. All of the joy of the home-coming was gone, when the figure arose from the cow and approached the gate, and put the pail of milk down on the platform by the pump.

When given all the facts, humans have the opportunity to change their own lives, and the life of the nation. As the pastoral version of romance died before real romance, and real romance combined with realism, new results could be expected. One of those results, in the second and third generations, amounted to people fleeing the farms as fast as trains could chuff.

The other result was the creation of a myth that carried the American farm through two big economic depressions, two world wars, and into the second half of the twentieth century.

The myth claimed that the farmer was the backbone of the nation—morally, economically, ethically, and actually. The farmer was the last independent businessman. He relied on the weather, and trusted God to handle the weather. His love for the land was so deep, and his love for the nation so great, no mere city dweller could ever equal either. The farmer plowed a straight furrow and took no sass from nobody, no-time. He was the only true American.

Egos, being what they are, put up with a lot of hardship because of this myth. The farm endured, remained, and continued as a stable presence in the life of the nation. I am quite sure the myth was not what our writers thought they were talking about, but it's what came, and they created it. Or, rather, they provided the basic myth. Rural newspapers and farm magazines adapted the myth and sold it to the farmer. In fact, rural newspapers and farm magazines are still selling the same myth. We can be grateful for the sales job because our nation benefited. This is how it works:

The American farm has been the source of rigid morality and ethics for a hundred years. Farmers still do not get to town often, and to the city but very seldom. A lot of the force of the farm derives from that original myth that validates staying at home, because home is the seat of everything that is good, and is also "the garden spot of the nation."[2]

Thus, the morality, and the ethics, of the farm are often narrow, sometimes mean, and usually not adaptable to city life. They exist, though, as certainly as we know the clapboard church will be painted white. Because of the narrowness of views, the farms exhibit considerable intolerance, or, at best, misunderstanding, about the ways and problems of people in cities. To this day, there are places in the Middle West where people watch television's city scenes in the same manner that a cynic might view the Emerald City of Oz.

We cannot, though, dismiss the farm as antiquated or irrelevant. It maintained itself, through myth, for the entire twentieth century. In doing so, it served as a savings account for the country, a sort of "morals bank" instead of a land bank. The nation has been making regular withdrawals for the entire century, although the withdrawals lessen as the farm population decreases.

This is what happens: People raised in the towns and farms of the Middle West are generally imbued with the remnants of Victorian moralism, and with the loud gasps of a stricken evangelical movement that began in the nineteenth century. Because of the mythology, they also know themselves as individualists. They also know they are just naturally more moral and "right" than anyone else.

Those Americans (of whom I am a walking, talking, itching, and scratching example) bring that old-time baggage with them when they migrate to cities. They may spend years thinking about that baggage, and adapting it to their present conditions, but it is unlikely they will ever completely dismiss moral concerns. In this way, the countryside exports far more morality to the cities than the cities ever offered the countryside. And all because of a myth.

The myth proved strong enough to serve as a true resource for the nation.[3] It wasn't the best myth. But it has served.

---

[2]There is no area of the Middle West that does not know itself as "the garden spot of the nation." I doubt if there is a single rural newspaper that has not used the term. The term has gone beyond a cliché and become an article of faith.

[3]It wasn't the only resource. Cities create moral structures; for example, the ideal of the honest cop.

## KEEPING OR THROWING AWAY

Some writers were called to remind the nation that not all of the past was worthless. They asked: What was good in the past, and how may it be recorded, or celebrated, so that its spirit will endure as a creative myth? What is worth preserving for the next generation? What, in the midst of change, is worth affirming, and what must be denied?

Obviously, a civilization that colonized a continent, created a culture, a democracy, a powerful body of art, an ascending literature; a nation that got rid of slavery, that worked toward enfranchisement of women—and both of the latter at a time when those issues hung in doubt in much of the world (and in many places in the world still hang in doubt)—that nation must have something worth protecting. In the case of American traditions about small towns and land, as well as early American culture, a great number of writers puzzled to themselves. Some writers went beyond Victorian assumptions. I am especially fond of two:

## Sarah Orne Jewett

Sarah Orne Jewett portrayed Maine, and latterly, New England. She was never an apologist for Yankee hypocrisy, but she worked truly in behalf of showing her New England world. Maine was, and remains, tough territory. (Alaskans feel comfortable in Maine, and Maine folk feel comfortable in Alaska.) The harsh winters, the rocky soil, and the bountiful sea produce a people inventive and capable. They have a reputation for reticence, but not amongst themselves.

Jewett caught all this, and one of her best pieces of work is a small book you can read in an evening, and one that will stay with you for the rest of your life. *The Country of the Pointed Firs* preserves the best of Maine, and thus, early America: land, people, and sea. Her characters live so simply, and are so strong, they become quietly elegant. The book is filled with people you love to meet. I promise you that when you lay the book down, you will feel lonesome.

## Ellen Glasgow

Before the Civil War, and certainly afterward, the standard Northern rap on the South went: "It's all the same. There's a bunch of snotty guys down there who ride horses and women and black folk, and who shoot cannons. Everybody else is a redneck."

So far as it went, that standard rap was true, but it didn't go very far. The South was—and remains—a fantastic place filled with mists and heat and ghosts. It has at least seven separate regions, and those regions resemble each other as much as a cat resembles a turnip. Among them was the Tidewater South, whose customs derived from English aristocracy. Given the social structure, the customs were not all bad. For example: The Southern gentleman was duty bound to protect the weak: women, children, and slaves. The Southern system was in many ways insulting, and certainly dreadful; but, imagine what it would have been without that gentlemanly ethic.[4]

Ellen Glasgow did with Virginia what Jewett did with Maine. She wrote with the knowledge that the Old Dominion would soon become an echo in the history books. She attempted to capture that entire world, because, if it was going to disappear, at least she could record it as memory. She tells stories that become history as they hit the page. Part of that history is a record of Southern self-consciousness, and, as a writer, she owns part of that self-consciousness. She is not shy in being critical of the South, but she loves the South; a characteristic of most Southern writers. Two early novels, *Virginia* (1913) and *The Deliverance* (1904), are worth any writer's attention.

The mythology of land, small town, and place gave America a foundation in the midst of change. The economy might go crazy, Congress might become as corrupt as Congress has ever been, and Victorian prudes might manipulate entire populations in behalf of profit; but, by heaven, the great writings about land allowed the nation to feel that the country remained basically sound. Some of this would alter in the next century, as we'll later see. Between 1865, and even as late as 1920, the mythology of land was a main force in preserving the sanity of a nation undergoing changes that were mighty.

---

[4]There's actually no need to imagine. Read just about any work concerning Mississippi or Alabama.

# Breaking Down Old Myths
# and Creating New Ones

THREE GREAT ISSUES would come together in the twentieth century and would seem inseparable: feminism, race, and what was then called Socialism. All three would demand action, art, and philosophy. Back in the nineteenth century, though, the three issues seemed separate. The earlier history of feminism is easily defined.

## THE WOMAN QUESTION

The best single history of the feminist movement is doubtless Eleanor Flexner's *Century of Struggle*, which documents the actions of leading feminists, and feminist movements, from their beginnings to the adoption of the Nineteenth Amendment in August 1920. It is a history, not a philosophy, of feminism. For philosophy it pays to read *The Female Imagination*, by Patricia Meyer Spacks. Such books are useful for background, and even for contemporary views of women's place in society.

## And Now, a Caution

If one is a feminist more than a writer, it's possible to stay with such books and be content. They are well thought-out and present strong positions. If one is a writer more than a feminist, caution is advised. We've already seen how a literature teacher, with the best intent, can cause trouble for a writer. The same is true in the case of historians, philosophers, and leaders of causes. The very nature of their work asks that they take a position, and then present that position as 100 percent correct—and, in the case of leaders of causes, 100 percent wholesome.[1]

One other caution before we proceed: It is always easy to see the human condition as the result of a plot or conspiracy. Conspiracy theories generally arise from inexperience, fear, or insecurity. They may designate anyone as an enemy. (I must even suppose that somewhere, there is someone who believes an international cabal of vegetarians is about to take over the world.)

Stuff like this can be fun. It can give a sense of self-importance, and a sense of belonging, for those who agree on the truth of such assertions. It is, however, not the way history works. For one thing, humans are not that well organized.

## BASIC ASSUMPTIONS

If you are first of all a writer, you will need to understand the worlds women face or have faced. The reason we seek to understand the situations of women, or men, is because our essential human beings—our characters—will have been formed by experience. Part of that experience will have to do with gender.

We've already seen that writers who best portray female characters may be female, or they may be male. It follows that the best portrayals of characters come from writers who hold the deepest respect for all people. Nathaniel Hawthorne, as we've seen, does a far better job of showing the position of women in Puritan America than do any number of essays on the Puritans, or any number of novels written by Victorian women.

## THE VICTORIAN WOMAN'S WORLD

It is difficult for the modern feminist, or writer, to view with clear eye the world of the nineteenth and early-twentieth-century woman. If the

---

[1] In the case of elderly writers who write books offering information to young artists and writers, matters are a bit different. Having seen a lot of history, and read a lot more, I know the things I write are true. I also know they are only part of the truth, and that it is impossible to know everything that goes on in a given time or place.

woman of those times was a settled Victorian, she lived under one set of difficulties. If she lived on a farm, the difficulties were different. If she was an immigrant, crowded into slums and working in factories, she had other difficulties. And it makes no difference that men had equally difficult situations. Two wrongs do not make a right, and one set of problems does not negate another set.

Almost every woman, however, shared these problems:

She was dependent on a man.

She would, if married, almost certainly have children.

She would, in running a household, be nibbled to death by constant association with people. She would have no privacy.

Her creativity was either channeled into the making of utilitarian goods, or raising children, or was blocked.

Her society left major decisions to the man because the man supported the family. Or, in the case of immigrants, because of Old World custom and New World necessity. Even if the entire family worked, the man's pay was generally highest. Recall that these are broad truths. There are probably a million contradictions.

She had few legal rights. Women could vote in no state, but could vote in four of the territories. They could vote in school elections in about half of the nation. In general, they could not contract independently. Legally, financially, and politically, married women were virtually helpless.

This combination would be enough to drive most people insane. Add to it the pressures of Victorianism and/or fundamentalist religion. No wonder late-nineteenth-century society went loony.

Historically, much of "the woman question" arose because the world began to get smarter, and urban. Back when the majority of people lived on small farms, necessity fairly dictated roles. If one lives on a farm, is barely literate, and society is structured in such a way that one is never going to get off that farm, it's easy to see that choices are limited. People, knowing they are going nowhere, finally cannot even *imagine* going anywhere.

The feminist movement grew over more than two centuries as versatile people brought about great change. It grew most powerfully in America because, in America, the myth of the American individualist came to life after the Civil War. It also grew in America through principles going all the way back to Anne Hutchinson and the Quakers.[2]

It arose because revolutionary men, and revolutionary women, ran around hollering about the Rights of Man; and after the hollering was done, wrote a Constitution. The movement did not grow equally in any other nation, and has not to this very day.

# Kate Chopin

The American writer, at work in the turbulent years of the late-nineteenth and early-twentieth centuries, faced a main question. The great issue was not "Do women have souls?" but "Having souls, do women have a right to express themselves, intellectually and socially?" Since writers always search, we may begin with one of the best searchers, Kate Chopin. She questioned the controls of society. She also explored a human situation that affects a lot of people, no matter their gender. The situation can wear the headline *"Trapped by Life."*

Chopin's most renowned book is the novel *The Awakening* (1899). The book is about Edna Pontellier, who feels trapped by family and society. She loves her husband and kids. She is amused by her society. Nevertheless, something is missing. She asks unsettling questions.

Those questions, as examined in *The Awakening*, certainly unsettled the minds of Victorian readers. Polite ladies and polite gentlemen did not flee screaming. That would be unmannerly. They fled tsk-ing.

To superficial understandings it was (blush) a sex book. Edna Pontellier not only "did it" with her husband, she "did it" with somebody else. And, she not only "did it" with somebody else, but the "somebody" was a cad and she did not care for him. This—and because it was a mainstay of Victorian creed that women, being pure, had no sex drive whatever—caused a tortured "Oh, dear."

This corseted reaction was typical of Victorian society. Toss in the extra glitz and phoniness of New Orleans, the locale of the novel, and where much tsk-ing took place; and the tsks are really vulgar. New Orleans is the city that, until the secretary of the Navy closed the

---

[2]The Quaker assumption of "That of God within each person" did not separate male and female. Granted the assumption, everyone was equal.

whorehouses in 1917, was the most wide-open city in the world, Paris not excluded.[3]

The "oh, dear" ladies and gentlemen of New Orleans, who could not handle one teeny case of adultery, actually lived off of trade in a city that specialized in vice. In the annals of the human race this is termed hypocrisy. It wasn't new to New Orleans, but New Orleans dusted it off and gave it a bright new coat of red paint. And, of course, reaction was not confined to New Orleans. The book caused sniffs and snorts across the entire nation.

If adultery was not enough to condemn her, the superficial view held that Edna Pontellier was not the Earth Mother. She liked her children well enough, but she had other things to think about. Her lack of interest in each detail of her children's lives condemned her among Victorian women. After all, the Victorian role of the woman was not only Mistress of the Domestic Domain, but, within her domain, goddesslike. When a proper woman did not respect that role, disrespect amounted to an attack on all women who lived Victorian lives. When a real character in a real book decided to go her own way, and when that way did not build a holy shrine to the great goddess "Victorian Mother," the world lay strewn with gasping female Victorians.

Gasping male Victorians secretly admired the sexy stuff—it was all in their imaginations; there's nothing graphic in the book—but what really made them gasp was the idea that a woman could have a mind of her own. She could originate ideas and points of view.

Fortunately for the superficial reader, at the end of the book, Edna strips naked and walks into the sea. It is not the answer I hoped for her, but it's what she decided. And, it sure made the day happier for prudes.

*The Awakening* was not nearly as sexy as really sexy stuff published in those days. That sexy stuff, though, was without characterization. Without fully drawn characters, the subject of sex, or anything else, is

---

[3]Louis Armstrong reported that prostitutes lived all through the city, and came down to the cribs and houses of Storyville just like anyone else going to work. Jelly Roll Morton reports: "Some were dope fiends as follows: opium, heroin, cocaine, laudanum, morphine, et cetera. I was personally sent to Chinatown many times with a sealed note and a small amount of money and would bring back several cards of hop. There was no slipping or dodging. All you had to do was walk in to be served. . . ." From *Hear Me Talkin' to Ya*, by Nat Shapiro and Nat Hentoff (Rinehart & Co., 1955).

only so much tinsel. (These days, we call it television.) Chopin's novel was threatening because sex was not the point of the book, or the point of Edna Pontellier's life.

We may now look beyond those superficial views by people who could not live without style, and ask why the book is so important.

First, it put the Victorian ideal of duty to the test. At one point in the book, when questioned about her children, Edna replies: "I would give up the unessential; I would give my money, I would give my life for my children; but I wouldn't give myself. I can't make it more clear; it's only something which I am beginning to comprehend, which is revealing itself to me."

Edna kills herself because of her children. It's the only answer she has to preserve them in the society. She will give her life, not herself. This is a tough concept for superficial minds to handle.

Second, the book forces Victorian society to accuse itself. Most decisions about marriage were made at a young age, at least for women.[4] *The Awakening* asked Victorians—and especially young Victorian women—if they were happy. Many were not. The corollary to unhappiness is the question "If you're not happy, is it possible your assumptions are incorrect?"

Third, a character told a society that her understanding of herself was more important than the society. It is the same question that began with Anne Hutchinson. It is the great American question: Will we be ruled by dead hands of dogma, or will we become our own creative and originating force?

On its publication, *The Awakening* was denounced. The book lay in the dustbin of literature through most of the twentieth century, but its ideas gathered strength. For every action, there is reaction. When a book like *The Awakening* comes along, the very act of denunciation has a way of validating its ideas.

Hawthorne, followed by Chopin, set the stage for female characters in our fiction, and in our worlds. No American writer who hopes to be taken seriously can now dismiss a female character by using clichés.

---

[4] Men tended to marry later. They were expected to be settled in as good providers before marriage.

## TWO OTHER TAKES ON THE WOMAN QUESTION

A nation grew physically but struggled intellectually. Artists, musicians, thinkers, and storytellers felt the changing times. They faced problems because they wrote of change. Change frightened their audience.

Then, as now, some of the strongest opponents against a changing role for women were women. Many Victorian women, having never been trained to the idea of work beyond the home, pursed their lips and settled into the casement of "family."

Victorian men probably shivered most beneath winds of change. They were, after all, closer to the void.

Writers whose stories held fully drawn female characters could expect to be condemned, sniffed at, or regarded as criminals. It's a sad question that asks, "Given two evil choices, would you rather have your work ignored, or hated?" At the turn of the century, those were largely the choices.

## Charlotte Perkins Gilman and Theodore Dreiser

Charlotte Perkins Gilman and Theodore Dreiser represent a great number of writers from the late-nineteenth and early-twentieth centuries. Whereas Hawthorne and Chopin dealt with women defining their own lives, Gilman and Dreiser faced the equally important proposition that, like it or lump it, society would have to accept new roles for women, economically, sexually, and politically.

Dreiser used social realism to write of characters in struggle against urban, industrial society. Gilman used realism, plus something we might call psychological realism, plus the fantastic. From a rationalist point of view, Gilman ran far ahead of Dreiser.[5] From debunking the standard Victorian and romantic view, Dreiser proved even more hardheaded than Gilman. Dreiser used an older form of "author intrusion" to make some points that might have been better made by showing character.[6] Gilman was usually out-and-out political. Any considera-

---

[5]Gilman compares favorably with another brilliant writer on women's issues, Harriet Martineau. Martineau was an Englishwoman whose *Society in America* was published in 1837.

tion of either brings up another one of those pesky digressions, this one concerning a question the young writer will eventually have to answer.

## DIGRESSION

Two traditional views deal with writers as they engage with social or political causes. Both views are valid, I suppose, but one is not exactly lovely. Both have holes wide enough to accommodate a gaggle of elephants. Both have posted strong records of performance.

The first view—and one that persuades me—says the storyteller should avoid politics and social movements when writing. That doesn't mean the writer cannot be engaged with such matters when not writing. If the writer wishes to stand on a street corner and demonstrate against social or political abuse, that's good. It does take time away from work but it gives experience. It's easier to write about being in jail once you've been there.

When actually writing, however, it's best to forget politics and social causes. The problem with joining a cause is that it forces you to take sides. This not only restricts your point of view, but restricts your sympathies. That tends to oversimplify issues in your story. It is possible, then, for a woman to blame all her problems on men, or a man to blame all his problems on women; or characters may blame all their problems on economic systems, the military-industrial complex, the Holy Roman Empire, or, as the current saying goes, "whatever."

If you restrict your point of view, it is impossible to discover the truth of the material. This is not a clarion call of "art for art's sake." The idea that the writer should not deal in causes when writing assumes, as truth, something you probably already suspect. The idea assumes that the world runs on lies, even when it doesn't mean to, or

---

⁶Author intrusion occurs when the writer tries to tell the reader what to think. It was one of those less-than-charming techniques Victorians loved. The third paragraph of *Sister Carrie* begins: "When a girl leaves her home at eighteen, she does one of two things. Either she falls into saving hands and becomes better, or she rapidly assumes the cosmopolitan standard of virtue and becomes worse."

This, of course, is dumb. It assumes absolute standards of "better" and "worse." When a girl leaves home, she may do many things, both better *and* worse. However, Victorians loved such observations. It allowed them to look at each other, nod their heads over the profundity, and whisper, "Oh, how true. Oh, *how* like life."

want. I won't even work at demonstrating that proposition. Just look around you.

Thus, when you discover the truth in the material of your story, and discover it in a world that lives on lies, you engage in a revolutionary act. This is precisely what Chopin did in *The Awakening*.

The other view holds that the writer should actively team up with causes. There's a long tradition dating back to political doggerel and songs of the American Revolution. The best-known example came later: *Uncle Tom's Cabin*, by Harriet Beecher Stowe. Abraham Lincoln once greeted Stowe as "the little woman who wrote the book that made this great war."

In a way, Lincoln had a point. More, even, than the New England Transcendentalists, *Uncle Tom's Cabin* influenced the popular mind of the North.

And, perhaps this is the main argument against political activism in storytelling. The story does not build a myth on which a people can rely. Instead, it supposes a universal truth that can be reduced to slogans. The main flaw of political stances in storytelling, then, is that they appeal to people who prefer to vibrate, rather than think.

On the other hand, a main strength of political stories is that they cause noise. A loud and obnoxious, widely proclaimed general *Truth* in the form of a story serves to announce that a real issue walks the streets. End of digression.

## THEODORE DREISER

In *Sister Carrie* Dreiser tells of Carrie Meeber, who leaves the small-town Middle West and heads for Chicago. Carrie is young and inexperienced. Nothing in her background suggests she is above average; just another pretty girl. She does, however, know where babies come from, and why, and how; and that's more than a lot of young city girls knew in the 1890s.

She meets a traveling salesman on the train. He takes her address. She is mildly smitten. She gets off the train and moves in with her sister, and her sister's husband. These people are hardworking, acquisitive, humorless. Carrie gets a job at $4.50 a week. She punches holes in leather uppers for shoes. Ten-hour days. Her room and board costs $4.00 a week. The 50 cents left over is not enough for carfare. She has to walk to work. Something's gotta give.

The salesman from the train comes by. She ends up living with him. Then a really romantic man comes along. She ends up falling for him. His wife divorces him. He steals money from his employer. He kidnaps Carrie. They flee. Carrie doesn't fight being kidnapped, or at least doesn't fight all that much. They go to Canada, then to New York.

The rest of the book traces the downward spiral of the man's fortunes as it traces the upward spiral of Carrie's. She goes on the stage and becomes a solid success. He turns on the gas in a rented room and breathes deeply. He dies realizing mistakes have been made.[7]

It was whispered that Dreiser was a "sex writer." He was said to be a socialist, and against "progress." He was degenerate, a pervert. In some places his books were banned.

This, despite the fact that there is not a single sexual reference in *Sister Carrie*. She lives with a couple of guys. Her choice in men may not be the best, but is better than what a lot of other women had, including her married sister. She may not be the best actress in the world, but she's better than average. She does what artists often do— i.e., take advantage of any situation in order to get the work out.

Dreiser hammered away. In 1926, he was still at it. In "Typhoon," a young girl is so restricted by Victorian parents that she develops no social skills. She has few defenses. A handsome young man arrives. She gets pregnant, is betrayed by the young man, and becomes so desperate she shoots him. Then, after being acquitted by a sympathetic court, she has the baby. She then walks into a lake where she and the young man used to ride on a boat.

Cotton Mather would have said she suffered the wages of sin. Dreiser would have said, "We'll quit our own sinning when we teach our kids how to handle themselves."

Between 1900 and 1926 Dreiser wrote fourteen other books. Not all are about women, but when women appear they are real humans with real problems. They are not Victorian paper-doll cutouts.

---

[7]There are similarities to Gustave Flaubert's novel *Madame Bovary* (1857). "French novels" were a Victorian pastime, and were considered pretty "fast." Still, French writers could get by with material that American writers were scarcely allowed to touch.

## CHARLOTTE PERKINS GILMAN

Gilman is more political; but, unlike most crusaders, she has a wicked sense of humor. Her novel *Herland* tells of three young Victorian gents who have a flying machine. They go exploring, and arrive in a society of women who reproduce by parthenogenesis. Everybody is a mother, or soon will be, and all children are girls. The young guys are placed in confinement. They learn the local language. There is great swapping of information about the culture of Herland, as opposed to the culture of late-nineteenth-century America. You can guess, of course, which civilization comes out on top.

The women of Herland decide to give men a try, so there are three marriages. The marriages don't work out, although the narrator (a young man) very much loves his wife. Herland, a nigh-perfect society, regretfully kicks the guys out. *Herland* is a utopian novel, and it has a sense of humor rare among utopians.

Much of Gilman's reputation rests on nonfiction and feminist writing. Her best story is titled "The Yellow Wallpaper" and it has entered the feminist bible as a book equal to The Acts of the Apostles, which it should. The story goes beyond causes. It examines the madness of a woman driven crazy by people who wish to help her become sane.

Except, she isn't crazy to begin with. What makes her crazy is a loving husband who is a doctor, and who exercises husbandly, doctorly control to keep her confined in a room with awful wallpaper that was once a children's nursery. The doctor is no psychiatrist.

The story will break your heart as you realize how the Victorian woman was subject to enormous external controls. In a manner of speaking, it was society that was crazy. Men believed women were weak and fluttery. Too many women, being told they were weak and fluttery from the day they were born, came to believe it. Then they raised their sons and daughters to believe that women were weak and fluttery.

No wonder that, as the twentieth century opened, the feminist movement put such tremendous importance on universal suffrage. Those women felt powerless. Politically and economically, they *were* powerless, although culturally they exercised amazing influence.

# THE GATHERING STORM

THESE DAYS, THE subject of race, especially among Americans who trace some heritage to Africa, is mighty tender business. Equally sensitive is the subject of gender. In the same manner that American writers worked with gender from 1865 to 1900, so also did they work with race; as they also do today. They fought against misconceptions then, as writers fight against misconceptions now.

Before looking at the race situation after the Civil War, it will pay to examine a writer's view of race. That view will throw one whale of a lot of other people into fits of denunciation, but that's the price they pay for their prejudice. As writers, the price we pay is the work it takes to discover the truth of our material.

While American writers are generally writers first, and members of groups second, many other people are not so lucky. A changing society causes people to feel insecure. They then identify themselves as members of groups separated by skin color or gender. It allows them to feel special and less lonely. Some then turn around, and viewing skin of another color, or a different gender, take an unhappy hop into bigotry. As a writer you'll be fighting against prejudice, and in behalf of humanity, for the rest of your life. Welcome to the battle.

## GENETICS

Back in the nineteenth century, sociologists, anthropologists, and psychologists embarked on a search. They wanted to see if differences between races caused differences in intelligence and physical ability. The studies went slowly because the social sciences were young and awkward. Social scientists made the obvious, if mistaken, assumption that separate races existed. After all, people displayed a range of skin colors, shapes of skull, slight differences in structure of bones in the forearm, and other minor features such as eye color. Barring evidence to the contrary, the notion of vast differences was a reasonable basis for inquiry.

These days, with the aid of studies in genetics, scientists and social scientists have learned it is time to throw those original assumptions into the history books. Race, as an actual genetic presence, does not exist. Every apparent "difference" between human beings is actually superficial. Genetics has shown that there is only one race; human.

## THE SOCIAL CONCEPT

Race, then, is a social concept, and in America the concept has caused separate cultures to rise within the main culture. Race has formed people into camps. This reaction was understandable in light of where the nation and the world came from. After all, less than two hundred years ago, the Western world was just shaking itself free from the mind of the Middle Ages. Our world had a long way to travel.

# The Social Notion of Racial Purity

The whole notion of a *pure* race is a fraud, as is the notion of a pure ethnic group. There is no pure Caucasian, Mongol, or Negro. Even isolated peoples—pygmies, Australian aboriginals, or Eskimos—are not genetically exclusive. The concept is mathematically impossible. As philosopher Guy Murchie demonstrates in *The Seven Mysteries of Life*, no one is pure *anything*.

If you punch a few numbers into your pocket calculator, you can prove it. You have two parents. They each had two parents, which means that you have four grandparents. You have eight great-grandparents, and sixteen great-great-grandparents. The numbers double with each generation. If you run the numbers back twelve generations (approximately 1620 to present), you have 4,096 ancestors, and each of your ancestors over twelve generations had 4,096 ancestors (total 16,777,216).[1] Since the numbers continue to double to infinity, and since traffic between peoples around the world has been going on for upward of sixty centuries (or, in the Orient, for two hundred centuries), there isn't one chance in infinity that you are pure anything.

For these reasons, the whole subject of race is, at present, a leftover from the nineteenth and early-twentieth century. As a social concept it is mainly useful for maintaining current power structures. If a nation can be divided into camps, and camps played off against each other, people are easier to control. God help, then, the politician who faces a united electorate, and God help the corporation that faces a united workforce, and God help the ideologue who faces good sense as he depends on racial issues for personal power. Division of people is different from division of opinion, which is often useful.

## HISTORY OF THE TERM *RACE*

Concepts of race change through the centuries. In the nineteenth century, people of both genders were likely to speak of the "female race," the "male race," the "Irish race," and so on. Sometimes races were mooshed together by occupation: the race of cowboys (both white and black) or the race of frontiersmen (black, white, and Indian). The term was often used honestly by people who attempted to understand what seemed fundamental differences.

And that, of course, is the problem. Looks deceive. Customs deceive. The whole idea of race—and for that matter, gender—seems based on the human capacity to suspect people who are deemed "different."

The young writer will quickly learn there is no essential race, and no essential gender, when it comes to storytelling. There is only the *essential* human being.

---

[1]This, of course, is not a pure number. Because of geographic isolation among some groups, there's bound to be a certain amount of inbreeding.

## CONTEMPORARY FOIBLES

Nothing characterizes the legacy of Puritanism, and Original Sin, so well as the indiscriminate spreading of guilt. It is plain silly to blame the ills of the present on someone who had absolutely nothing to do with the past. This opportunistic way of viewing history is usually done by people who wish to rewrite it. If they can rewrite history, they do not have to take responsibility for their own lives. Such people are dangerous, and that is especially true when they are in positions of power.

For example: One of my feminist friends, a woman old enough to know better, and a teacher, still blames all of her troubles on Moses. She blames Moses for being born into a patriarchal society, as if Moses could help when and where he was born. She is absolutely sure that, had someone of the caliber of Germaine Greer led the Hebrews to the Promised Land across a wilderness, then her own car would run better, more people would really be fond of her, her television reception would be perfect, and she would not endure sleepless nights.

This teacher then makes an emotional jump into the position that every male in her class (and, for that matter, every male in the world) owes every female a great debt because Moses was a patriarch. In addition, every male in the world is said to be guilty of abusing females.

My friend does not have problems because of Moses, or because she is female. She has problems because, being unhappy, she will go to any length to find someone to blame. That, of course, is her business.

However, when she faces classroom after classroom, while expressing these doctrinaire views, she retards the lives of her students—especially her female students. She tells them that they have been victims from the very cradle. The subconscious message says that, as a victim, the student hasn't a chance for success. She doesn't even realize that her message says, "Kiddo, you're an automatic loser."

She is not alone, of course. Her equal can be found in every ethnic and racial group.

## RESPONSIBILITY

Puritanical guilt-tripping is a mark of adolescence. It obscures our true obligation to each other. It does no one a whisker of good. Rather, it perpetuates problems the society might have solved long ago.

We are responsible for our own actions, not the actions of history in which we did not participate, and in which we would not engage. Thus, if your great-great-great-grandfather roughed up some Irishman, let the dedicated Irish complain to your great-great-great-grandfather. If your great-great-great-grandfather was a slave, praise him for his tenacity and ability to hope. Don't blame him because he didn't start a revolution. Equally, don't blame your fellow writer for the existence of ancient cotton fields. Or, if your great-great-great-grandfather, a Union soldier, died in a war he believed was fought to end slavery, give him the credit. Don't blame him for not understanding that a major basis for the war was economic.

We do not read history in order to feel guilty, or spread guilt about matters over which we had no control. We read history in order to understand forces of good that we try to carry forward, as well as to understand forces of wrong against which we fight.

## REVISING HISTORY

An additional point is appropriate: A person cannot be held accountable for an idea, if that idea is not in the world during the time the person lived. Examples:

*It is* ignorant to think less of Martin Luther or John Calvin, or other sixteenth-century people, because they believed in witches. The state of knowledge at that time was such that little or no evidence could be marshaled to prove otherwise.

*It is* plainly infantile to hold a man or woman of the mid-Victorian period responsible for views originated by modern psychology and genetics. Thus, people who denounce Freud as "sexist" use a term not known in Freud's time, and they demonstrate absolute ignorance of the Victorian period.

*It is* nigh unbelievable that some people regard Booker T. Washington as an Uncle Tom. They demonstrate that they haven't the foggiest notion of the problems Washington faced, or how brilliantly he solved them.

## LANGUAGE

People who insist that language of the past be consistent with current usage demonstrate unswerving devotion to the belief that nothing ever changes. As illustration, we may examine the word "nigger," which these days has one main usage.[2] But in the eighteenth and nineteenth centuries, it had a variety of usages and connotations. For example, on the late-eighteenth and early-nineteenth-century frontier, white men used to refer to themselves, or Indians, or to each other, as "niggers." The connotation was approximately the same as the one we currently associate with the word "guy"; as in "that guy drives a Plymouth."

In the twentieth century, it's never been a pretty word, and these days it damns itself. At the same time, we should look at how current usage can destroy our perceptions of the past. We'll do so by looking at the flak surrounding a great American novel that has been roundly denounced because of that word.

## ADVENTURES OF HUCKLEBERRY FINN

*Huckleberry Finn* is an even harsher indictment of slavery than was *Uncle Tom's Cabin. Huck* aspires to the condition of art, while Stowe's book, for all its virtues, reads like a religious and political tract. *Huckleberry Finn* ran into trouble because it uses the word "nigger"—as does *Uncle Tom's Cabin.*

Opportunistic people prove they have never learned to read, except superficially, when they denounce *Huck.* They fail to see that the book is written in the first person, and thus Twain has no option in using that word. Stowe's book is written in the omniscient, so she has the option of letting her bad guy say "nigger" and her narrator say "Negro."

The mistake the ignorant make with *Huck* is to believe the writer speaks, when it is really Huck who speaks; and, as you'll recall, Huck is the kid who believed in Hell, and was willing to go to Hell in order to free Nigger Jim.

---

[2]It has secondary usage. It is still used indiscriminately in big-city ghettos.

The second mistake is to believe that the word always and only accused itself. When Aunt Polly asks Tom if anyone was hurt in a steamboat explosion, and Tom replies, "No, mam, killed a nigger," the usage accuses the entire society. This is known in some circles as satire, and in more serious circles as irony (and, in the case of Twain, total sarcasm).

In the case of *Huck Finn,* modern usage and political correctness are brought forward in an attempt to damn the most powerful antislavery novel in the world's literature.

## CONTEXT

A final point: Language is understood in context. Without context, words in and of themselves are meaningless. Thus, those folk who have scrapped over what we name each other these past few years miss the mark. It is possible, for example, to say the words "black" or "white" or "Indian" with the greatest respect and reverence. It is also possible to use the terms "African-American" or "Asian-American" or "Native-American" or "Euro-American" and make them sound like sweepings from a gutter. Meaning rises from context and delivery of a word. This fuss about which words are "nice" and which words are "bad-bad-bad" is childish.

We might, for example, designate a group of people as "so-goods," and it wouldn't tell a thing about them. They might be called "so-goods" because they were good, or they could be called "so-goods" because, although the nastiest creatures afoot, they believed themselves "so good."

The point is: we could only understand the "so-goods" if we spoke of what they believed, and how they followed their dreams.

The reasons just given show why America, which has always needed alert and honest writers, needs them now as much as ever. Writers are great suppliers of context and great transmitters of dreams. We do so today, and our fellow writers did the same between 1865 and 1900, a period to which we now turn.

# DEALING WITH RACE AND ETHNICITY

RIGHT AFTER THE Civil War, our writers looked at different situations from those we see in the late-twentieth century. Generally speaking, these were the problems of our nation's regions:

*In the West,* Indian nations faded before disease, tribal wars, and wars waged on behalf of U.S. national and territorial governments. Some Indian nations disappeared completely. Both white and black mythology concerning Indians held them as savages intent on destroying everyone in their paths. The facts rarely fitted the case, although raids and battles were certainly savage. Mythology, however, requires few, or no, facts.[1]

While pulp writing of the period was equal, in its way, to those slander sheets that these days are sold in grocery stores, good writing about Indians was available. It existed mostly in the form of journals. Three of the best now available are *Tough Trip Across Paradise,* by Andrew Garcia, *My Army Life and the Fort Phil Kearny Massacre,* by Frances C. Carrington, and *The Adventures of Bigfoot Wallace,* as reported by John C. Duval. The great novel is *Ramona* (1884), which was so important in the Victorian period that we'll see it in a separate chapter.

---

[1]This ability of myth to arise from vague foundations is the reason why we, as writers, make certain to keep essential truth alive in our stories. We may alter a fact to fit the story, but we never alter a fact in such a way that it violates the truth of our material.

It was written by Helen Hunt Jackson. She also wrote in behalf of Western tribes in her *A Century of Dishonor*.

*In the East,* and through the upper Middle West, other ugly mythology developed. Immigrants from southern Europe flooded into cities. The mythology concerning immigrants held that they were different from "normal" people. They were thought to be oxlike, strong, but not sensitive. They were said not to suffer under persecution in the manner that "decent folk" might.

*In the South,* the mythology of slavery insisted the "Negro race" was either inferior, or not human. As such, the "race" could not be expected to contribute anything but chaos. It became necessary to define former slaves, not only as Americans, but as human beings. It became equally necessary to validate them as creative, contributing members of society.

Half a million people were freed into a society of 44 million, with little or no provision made for them.[2] Many—perhaps the majority—of freed people pretty much stayed on or around plantations where they'd lived. This was especially true of older people. In contrast to some already-free people throughout the South, and the literate, and often-wealthy, folk of New Orleans, most newly freed people could not read or write.[3] They had never had opportunity to learn of the world beyond the plantation, thus easily fell victim to the first con artist who came along; and plenty of con artists did.[4] For this reason, education became a priority for the nation, although a lot of national leaders were not swayed.

These freed Americans had only provisional identity. They owned their mythology, an oral tradition rising from both Africa and slavery.

---

[2] The 1870 U.S. Census total of all Americans was 44,034,312.

[3] The South had free Negroes in every state, sometimes more than 1,000 per county; although some counties were unsettled or had none. The largest concentrations of free people were scattered through Virginia, the Carolinas, the tip of Florida, and New Orleans.

[4] One scam went this way: A man wearing a suit would come among freed people and tell them that the government was going to give each man five acres, or forty acres (depending on the size of the scam) plus a mule. In order to get the land and mule, each man had to help the government get straightened out. He could do this by paying 25 cents or 50 cents a week (depending on what the traffic would bear). For people who had nothing, this false hope was exceedingly cruel. In addition, 25 cents a week was quite a bit when a man might work a twelve-hour day for little more than that.

They had a raw but often-vibrant religion based in Christianity, but spiced with influences from Africa, and from the American Indian.

They faced other assumptions both North and South. Many of those assumptions were gentle, even well intended, but stupid. For example, it has been a cliché throughout two centuries that the "Negro race" produces the best dancers and singers and musicians; that there is an inherent rhythm in the genes. This is largely nonsense. During slave days, all creative effort was blocked *except for* music and religion. Creativity ran in channels where it was allowed. Some of our greatest musicians rose from a culture that survived principally by the expression of religion and music. The present is really but an echo of history, and that is true in all art and religion and science.

What else, besides education, was needed for freed Americans? The answer: pretty much everything.

Who stepped forward? A little of this, a little of that, plus some notables:

The main players were Booker T. Washington, educator, scholar, founder of the Tuskegee Institute, and peacemaker; W. E. B. DuBois, rationalist and political activist; and Charles Sumner, leader of the Senate, who during the war and on other matters had been a pain in the neck for Lincoln, but who was now perfervid in his call for education and equal opportunity. He was joined by Senator Thaddeus Stevens, who did not want Southern states readmitted to equal status until they attained universal male suffrage. Sumner and Stevens were sincere.[5] They were also political. If the South came in without universal suffrage, the region seemed forever lost to the Republican party.

Congress faltered, fouled up royal, but did get relief into the South through the offices of the Freedmen's Bureau. Private help moved south, while Frederick Douglass, newspaperman and orator, traveled about the nation providing some unity for those concerned with Southern causes. Douglass, who had been a leading abolitionist, took up the slack until Booker T. Washington matured and stepped onstage. Teachers, social reformers, and medical folk went south to help. Philanthropists built schools. A good picture of the push and shove is given in Catherine Pomeroy Stewart's beautifully researched novel *Three Roads to Valhalla*.

---

[5]Stevens was white; his wife was black. He was a much finer man than Sumner, who, despite a just cause, was a nasty little man.

## PRESERVATION

The first great task facing our writers in all three regions was one of preservation, because many stories from the tribes, from immigrants, and from former slaves were not written down. They were part of the American scene that also contained tall tales, white and black and tribal legends, and spirituals. These traditions were oral because, in the case of Indians, none but the Cherokee had a written language. In the case of blacks, before emancipation, custom and law had prevented the education of slaves. Except for Charles W. Chesnutt and James Weldon Johnson (whom we'll look at shortly), written storytelling from Americans of African ancestry would arrive in the generation born after the war.

Because oral traditions are certain to change, and also tend to die as older generations disappear, we may thank a couple of people who had more foresight than historians generally expect to find.

## John Wesley Powell

John Wesley Powell was not a storyteller, but he deserves to be our hero, and the hero of pretty nearly everyone else. He lost an arm in the Civil War, then, after the war, was first to explore the Grand Canyon. He was an adventurer, an ethnologist, an intellectual, and a guy who could use politicians the way politicians wished they could use each other.

Powell was responsible for establishing the Bureau of American Ethnology, and was its director. He sent ethnologists all across the United States to collect the mythology of those American Indian tribes that still existed. Ethnology was a brand-new discipline in those days, yet those early ethnologists did the variety of respectful work that marks all fine ethnologists and anthropologists. Most stories of the Indian nations would be lost were it not for Powell and his ethnologists. You can find complete sets in large libraries under the listing *Annual Reports of the Bureau of American Ethnology to the Secretary of the Smithsonian Institution*.

## Joel Chandler Harris

Joel Chandler Harris was a newspaperman, but one with an ear for nuance and language. He was also a storyteller worth any writer's time. His story "Free Joe and the Rest of the World" tells of a freed slave during slave times, who, because he is free, becomes an outcast. White folk see him as a threat. Slaves exclude him from their company. His wife is owned by a man named "Spite" Calderwood, who sells her. Joe and his dog sit just beyond Calderwood's property every night. Joe waits for his wife, who can never return. The dog goes to look for her and is killed by Calderwood's dogs. Joe waits, night after night after night, until he dies.

Harris wrote powerfully about the South, specifically the small town of Hillsborough, Georgia. A second important story is "Little Compton," a tale of honor between a Northerner and a Southerner, in which both save each other and the town. In "Aunt Fountain's Prisoner," a slave saves a Northerner, who then saves a plantation and a family from depredations by Northerners. He protects for life the freedwoman who saved him.

Harris's best-known works are the Uncle Remus stories, folktales told by former slaves. Harris used the figure of a kindly old man, an "uncle," as the teller of the tales, and Harris had perfect pitch for dialect. Several collections were published from 1880 to 1906, and many of the stories would have been lost had he not written them down. Other serious work in collecting these folktales seems not to have started until the 1920s.

## The Contributions

Powell contributed essential work at a time when, in Victorian society, the American Indian would soon become romanticized (as we'll shortly see in *Ramona*), thus unreal. The Indian would be held up as noble and good and wise and beautiful, and, because of being Indian, never did a wrong thing in his/her life. In other words, the Indian would be placed on a shelf in much the same way the Victorian woman had been placed on the shelf. Victorian society peddled this, even as the Western tribes were being decimated in the Indian wars.

Obviously, some Indians were noble, and some were wise. Some

Victorians, for that matter, were noble and wise. That does not mean, however, that all Victorians or Indians glowed with beatitude and charm. Some were dumb, some were mean as a mink, and many possessed the same imagination as a doorknob. The mythology of the American Indian, as collected by Powell and company, made the American Indian into a real person. Victorian glamorization, or Victorian brutality, could no longer get by with easy answers.

The same is true of the stories collected by Harris. After the Civil War, a myth rose in the South (and was well purchased in the North) that slavery had been a good thing for everybody, especially slaves. Sentimental ribbons decorated the figures of black mammies raising and loving the white chilluns as well as they loved their own. Gray-haired "uncles" sat around telling fond tales of days when they went a-coon huntin' with ol' massa. Sentimentality tried to smooth over all of the complexities that had existed, and still did. Since we're talking about human beings here, you may be sure many people of both races were fond of each other, or loved each other. Because of the system, though, we may also be sure the large majority had different experiences.

The other myth was that the Negro was a primitive brute who must be contained. There is no end to the garbage people can come up with when they choose to think with their mouths and not with their brains.

Uncle Remus stood against the falsity of both myths. In the Uncle Remus stories, weak creatures sometimes lose to stronger creatures (Brer Rabbit does get nailed by the fox, and possibly becomes lunch). But in many other stories, the weak creature wins. These are tales of revolution, cloaked in the fantastic. The Indian storytellers, and those Southern storytellers, worked against false mythologies by substituting true ones.

## James Weldon Johnson and Charles Waddell Chesnutt

Two able writers of those early days were James Weldon Johnson (1871–1938) and Charles Waddell Chesnutt. Johnson, born in Florida, apparently went north before age thirty. Chesnutt lived in North Carolina from age eight to twenty-six. Both, however, reflect Northern attitudes, especially relating to economics.

The difference between these men, when compared to later writers like Richard Wright and William Faulkner, is twofold. Chesnutt and

Johnson had serious college educations. Both were driven toward many accomplishments besides writing. That drive kept Johnson from writing as much as we might wish, and it exposed Chesnutt to enough turmoil that he turned to other ways of making a living. Johnson spent time in show business, the NAACP, and foreign service in South Am erica. Chesnutt held a law degree and ran a law clerk's business. It would be Johnson who would take on what, at the time, was an unspeakable subject.

## "PASSING"

"Passing," the ability of light-skinned people to cross from a lower social/racial group to a higher-status one, is deep in our literature. In part, it is a fantasy. For those who pass or passed, fantasy became reality. The first novel dealing with "passing" is William Wells Brown's *Clotel* (1853).[6] The best-known novel is *The Autobiography of an Ex-Colored Man*, by Johnson. It is fantasy turned real. At the time it was written, and for decades afterward, anyone with so much as a teaspoon of black blood was considered black. Perhaps there are still people who think this sort of thing worth believing, but mostly these days (at least in my neck of the woods) it seems few really care. It's with mild amusement that I watch some people now trying to "pass" in the other direction.

It's the old story of the grass being greener on the other side. When a person is poor, for example, almost anyone with a good job looks rich. When a person suffers discrimination, almost anyone who is part of the mainstream seems successful. Imitation is a natural result. The fantasy of "passing" was simply the fantasy of being respectable in a society that claimed complexion told more about a person than actions or brains.

There's an old saying: "Be careful what you wish for. You may get it."

---

[6]Brown was an escaped slave and an abolitionist. *Clotel, or The President's Daughter*, is an abolitionist tract that contains the old bromide about Thomas Jefferson siring children by his slaves. The book is a mixture of sincerity, insincerity, and downright plagiarism. It doesn't amount to much as a novel, but is well worth reading in order to gauge the height of passions in the abolitionist movement. The book was published in four versions. My conclusions are drawn from the first version, reprinted by Carol Publishing Group (1995), with scholarly introduction and notes by William Edward Farrison.

In Johnson's book about a man who passed, married, had children, this unhappy paragraph appears toward the end:

> Several years ago I attended a great meeting in the interest of Hampton Institute at Carnegie Hall. The Hampton students sang the old songs and awoke memories that left me sad. Among the speakers were R. C. Ogden, ex-Ambassador Choate, and Mark Twain; but the greatest interest of the audience was centered in Booker T. Washington, and not because he so much surpassed the others in eloquence, but because of what he represented with so much earnestness and faith. And it is this that all of that small but gallant band of coloured men who are publicly fighting the cause of their race have left behind them. Even those who oppose them know that these men have the eternal principles of right on their side, and they will be victors even though they should go down in defeat. Beside them I feel small and selfish. I am an ordinarily successful white man who has made a little money. They are men who are making history and a race. I, too, might have taken part in a work so glorious. . . .

## CHARLES WADDELL CHESNUTT

Chesnutt wrote at a time when the generation of Americans who had known slavery lived side by side with the generation born free. He came from small-town North Carolina and had perfect pitch for what went on in the South, where a region defined a new "place" for freedmen. That place was roughly the same as during days of slavery. One main difference was that former slaves no longer had economic value. They were, in many ways, more vulnerable to abuse. Including lynching.

Chesnutt became something of a literary lion in the publication of three books: *The Conjure Woman, The Wife of His Youth and Other Stories of the Color Line,* and *The House Behind the Cedars.* He was regarded as the first great Negro American writer. He found himself consulted about literary matters. His books were so well received that he appeared destined to join the literary mainstream and make a good living as a writer. It was not until he published *The Marrow of Tradition* (1901) that his career pointed downward, and he went back to making a living as a lawyer.

*The Marrow of Tradition* arose because of a race riot in Wilmington. Chesnutt took off the gloves. Because he was both angry and truthful, *The Marrow of Tradition* broke the back of white enthusiasm for Chesnutt's work, and it broke the back of black enthusiasm as well.

White people didn't really want to hear about white mobs and white incendiaries and white newspaper publishers promoting white supremacy. Black people didn't really want to hear about wildly successful black people (at a time when most black people were not), or about black people who were cowardly. In other words, Americans wanted to live content with racial clichés while avoiding a complete picture of the small-town South. *The Marrow of Tradition* is a book tortured with honesty. It carries a few lectures about slavery and the aftermath of slavery, but mostly it tells a story in which only one former slave is noble, and everybody else ranges from slightly seamy to revolting. If Chesnutt had been a lesser writer, he could have pulled off a bestseller that would have made his fortune. Instead, he was an American writer in the great tradition of our writers, a tradition that requires us to show the full truth of what we see.

*The Marrow of Tradition* is a book that should be avoided by those who want easy history. For those who want to know what really went on, the book comes as near as one can ever get to a complete picture of Southern small-town custom, prejudice, and violence. Such matters would pretty much remain that way for decades, until 1965, when Jesse Hill Ford, a badly neglected writer, published *The Liberation of Lord Byron Jones,* and then *The Raider* (1971). Other writers would give strong, hurtful pictures, but not complete pictures of the Southern small town.

## Another Situation at the Turn of the Century

These days, the early work validating the humanity of a freed population makes it seem like our writers strained to prove the obvious. In those days, though, it was a strong issue. The issue surrounded former slaves, and it surrounded others. What follows is a quote from E. A. Ross, a sociologist of that period:

To the practised eye, the physiognomy of certain groups unmistakably proclaims inferiority of type. I have seen gatherings of the __ in which narrow and sloping foreheads were the rule. The shortness and smallness of the crania were very noticeable. There was much facial asymmetry. Among the women, beauty, aside from the fleeting, epidermal bloom of girlhood, was quite lacking. In every face there was something wrong—lips thick, mouth coarse, upper lip too long, cheek-bones too high, chin poorly formed, the bridge of the nose hollowed, the base of the nose tilted, or else the whole face prognathous. There were so many sugarloaf heads, moon-faces, slit mouths, lantern-jaws, and goose-bill noses that one might imagine a malicious jinn had amused himself by casting human beings in a set of skew-molds discarded by the Creator.

I left the word "immigrants" out of the quote. In doing so, I allowed your imagination to picture a group of people. This quote came from a college professor who was, otherwise, a very good social theorist. The passage was not about Americans, but about immigrants to America from southern Europe and the Balkans.

At the time this was written the discipline of sociology was still finding itself.[7] American sociology appeared in the 1880s. Thus, Ross, writing as late as 1914, did not have a whole lot of information to go on, although one wishes he had been more acute.[8]

At the turn of the century, there were far more people around who sincerely believed in the inequality of "races" (the term included immigrants) than there were people who imagined that equality existed. Psychological testing on people of different nationalities had not been done. No adjustments were made for social and cultural backgrounds.[9]

---

[7]Sociology dates from August Comte's *Course of Positive Philosophy* (1830–42), Emile Durkeim's *The Rules of Sociological Method* and *Le Suicide* (1895 and 1897), and Herbert Spencer's *First Principles* (1862). Comte and Durkheim were French, while Spencer was English; the greatest of them, Comte.

[8]It is also possible that he was opportunistic, because when he wrote the above he taught at the University of Wisconsin, and played to an audience whose roots lay in northern Europe.

[9]The great sociologist who would finally pull it all together from a social-sciences point of view would be William Isaac Thomas, writing *The Polish Peasant in Europe and America* in the late 1930s.

It would be our writers who would do the most telling early work against the myth of inequality. They did it by showing their characters as fully human. In the case of immigrants, the best storytelling would come from American writers with Jewish backgrounds; writers whom we'll see in a later context because most of them belong to the twentieth century.

Two of the most important novels, though, came from a writer working in both centuries: *Yekl: A Tale of the New York Ghetto* (1896), and *The Rise of David Levinsky* (1917), by Abraham Cahan. A third, but later, book is *Call It Sleep* (1934), by Henry Roth. More than any other writer, we look to Roth for understanding of the immigrant experience. We'll take a brief look at *Call It Sleep* in a later chapter.

At present, I'll close this chapter with a quote from one of the greatest storytellers of all time, and I mean all the way back to the Book of Ruth. This is Eudora Welty writing in the preface to her collected stories, and affirming the attitudes of every American writer who has been mentioned in this chapter, and every honest American writer from the last two centuries:

> I have been told, both in approval and in accusation, that I seem to love all my characters. What I do in writing of any character is to try to enter into the mind, heart, and skin of a human being who is not myself. Whether this happens to be a man or a woman, old or young, with skin black or white, the primary challenge lies in making the jump itself. It is the act of a writer's imagination that I set most high.

# RAMONA AND OTHER
# INDIAN NOVELS

ONE OF THE most popular Victorian novels is *Ramona,* by Helen Hunt Jackson. The publisher's note in my faded copy tells that the book appeared in 135 editions, three movies, plus stage plays.[1] The copy at my local library, in a town of eight thousand, has been checked out seventeen times in the last twenty years; not bad for a popular book published in 1884. As a kid, I hummed the hit song "Ramona." In antique stores, even today, one can still find prints by artists who rendered idealized characters and settings from the book. *Ramona* takes on a lot of questions, of which two are dominant among writers and readers who value America's aboriginal cultures: How does a person live in two worlds? While living in two worlds, how does a person decide how much weight to give each?

In American storytelling, both white and tribal characters fall, or are forced, into traps of having to choose one culture or the other. They always lose a part of themselves, even when they choose well. Situations are further complicated because the majority of Americans—at least, the majority of those whose families have been in this nation for four or more generations—carry Indian blood. We have become so intermixed that an accurate, hyphenated description of a fourth-generation American might well read: African-Native-Anglo-Hebrew-American with bar sinister, and a crest displaying varmints rampant.

---

[1]It is still in print in paperback.

Even our mythology supports that picture. For example, in America, it's popular to be Irish on St. Patrick's Day (even if you ain't) and an Indian at Thanksgiving. I don't know if the majority of Americans claim Indian blood, but a lot of them do; and every blessed claimant will brag about an ancestor who was a tribal chief.[2]

Into this quagmire stepped Helen (Fiske) Hunt Jackson, a beloved and lifelong friend of Emily Dickinson. Jackson went through hell in her early years. Her husband, Major Edward Hunt, was killed in 1863 by a submarine gun he invented. She had already lost one of her children at birth. The second died in 1865. At age thirty-five, her life seemed over.

She moved to Newport and met an editor named Thomas Wentworth Higginson, who convinced her that the path away from grief lay in writing. She started publishing poems of such literary quality that Ralph Waldo Emerson carried copies around in his pockets. Her life turned to revolt against a strict Calvinist upbringing. She wrote passionately, and generously. She turned to writing articles, then to romantic (even sentimental) books directed to Victorian girls. In 1872 she went to California, in 1873 to Colorado; and married William Jackson, a Quaker, in 1875. She became novelist, reformer, and advocate for the American Indian.

Jackson's first attempt at advocacy was nonfiction, titled *A Century of Dishonor*. At her own expense, she circulated copies to every member of Congress. There was far too much money to be made in stealing Indian lands. Thus, Congress yawned.

In 1882, she gained appointment as one of two special commissioners to investigate the plight of mission Indians. Her report, in 1883, hit the congressional round file. This tough and brilliant writer turned to storytelling. She wanted to write a book that would do for Indians what *Uncle Tom's Cabin* had done for slaves.

Instead, she produced what on the surface seems a classic Victorian novel. Looked at with a bit more intensity, though, it's easy to see that *Ramona* is a main bridge between Victorian romance and modern realism.

Ramona is half-Spanish, half-Indian, and she falls in love with a mission-educated Indian. She abandons the Spanish world to be with him, and the hammers of hell begin pounding.

---

[2]Such brags are wishful thinking. Many tribes did not have chiefs. They had men or women who knew customs, traditions, stories, and who understood the great wheel of the seasons. Such people were leaders, but with little or no formal recognition. The "chief," as someone with dictatorial powers, is a white notion that most American Indians were not likely to understand.

All Victorian components are intact: a great and romantic love, the death of a beloved, the plight of another character who loves from afar, the loyalty of family (in this case a brother), the evil relative (an aunt who raises Ramona), and an ending mixed with joy and sorrow.

The magic of the book is the magic of Place. The old Spanish homes in and around San Luis Rey and Los Angeles served as Jackson's models: specifically, Guajome Rancho four miles east of San Luis Rey Mission, and Camulos Rancho sixty miles northwest of Los Angeles. Jackson does not discuss the cruelty of early Spanish history in the area. Hers is a contemporary report of Spanish customs showing warmth, formality, sometimes elegance: when dawn breaks, for example, the first person to see the sun begins to sing. Then the entire household joins the song.

Mixed with the love story, and the romance of place, lives an indictment of the American takeover of California after the Mexican War.

All land claims by Indians, Spanish missions, and Spanish citizens become invalid. Whites move in. Indians die, or flee. The Spanish gradually return to Mexico. Missions fall into decay. Greed, murder, ignorance, and inhumanity crowd against the main story, and defeat romance.

No other writer of the period proved better at showing inhumanity directed toward the American Indian. Helen Hunt Jackson, who believed that *A Century of Dishonor* was her best book, died of stomach cancer in 1885, the year after *Ramona* was published. She did not see *Ramona* catch the engaged interest of a nation and serve as a main force in validating the American Indian as fully human, capable of love and dreams. She also did not see her book serve as a basis for romance about the Indian, rather than indignation over murder and land grabs. As so often happens to books with planned messages, *Ramona* wrought well, but not as its author hoped.

Jackson was buried in a cairn on the top of Cheyenne Mountain near Colorado Springs. The body was later moved to a cemetery because of vandalism by tourists and curiosity seekers.

## EDWIN CORLE

Two later books merit mentioning in connection with *Ramona*. Both were written in the first half of the twentieth century, but both are nearer in spirit to the nineteenth. They are *Fig Tree John*, by Edwin

Corle, and *Crazy Weather,* by Charles Longstreth McNichols. Both deal with place—in this case, the American Southwest.

Tales of Indians in the Southwest hold but a minor place in the American canon, or at least that is true of work before World War II. As with areas of the South, and with Maine, and the Northwest, much early writing is dismissed by the literary establishment as "regional." I've never quite understood the term. Writers write what they know, and when they are true to their characters, those characters will be partially formed by place. In that sense, all stories are regional.

*Fig Tree John* (1935), by Edwin Corle, tells the story of Agocho Koh Tli-chu (Red Fire Bird), a White River Apache from Arizona. In 1906 he and Kai-a, the youngest of his three wives, ride into the California desert. Kai-a is about to have a baby. The two discover the Salton Sea, a great salt lake that resulted from a mistake by white men who tried to divert the Colorado River for irrigation. They camp. Kai-a gives birth to a son. Agocho decides that the Gods have determined that he is to have this place. He builds a hut, plants fig-tree cuttings, and plans to live the life of an Apache; he will hunt, watch his son grow, and he will deal with the Gods.

He goes to town to trade baskets Kai-a has made. Two white renegades stumble on the camp, rape and kill Kai-a, and steal horses. By the time Agocho returns the murderers have a long head start. Agocho trails and nearly catches them. The two hop a train. Agocho returns to camp, goes through the four-day burial ceremony for Kai-a. He settles down to wait, confident the Gods will someday bring the men back so that he can kill them.

The rest of the book tells of the great division between father and son as the son grows and is enticed by the white world. The son marries a Mexican woman, works on a ranch, buys a Ford. Agocho, now known in the neighborhood as Fig Tree John, cannot understand the depth of offense that his son causes him to feel. He finally comes to a point where he stabs his son's wife. She flees. Father and son live side by side until a message comes for the son; his wife will have a baby. He prepares to leave. Agocho opposes him. They fight, and the son kills the father. The son then performs the Apache burial ceremony. As he leaves to rejoin his wife, this passage appears:

Johnny was white now. He had thought it all out very carefully as he sat out there in the greasewood. The Apache Gods would hate him. He had defied them; he had killed his father. That was unpardonable, but what made it a heinous crime was that he had killed his father when his father had been fighting for what was right. The Gods knew that; and Agocho knew that. Neither the Gods nor Agocho's spirit would ever forgive him. He was forever a pariah. He was white. He would never dare think of Ste-na-tlih-a again. But he could pray to Virgin Mary. He had her. He had something. Yes, but he had more than that. He had himself. He had Johnny Mack. . . .

## CHARLES LONGSTRETH McNICHOLS

Longstreth McNichols's *Crazy Weather* carries echoes of *Penrod, Tom Sawyer, Huckleberry Finn,* and *Peck's Bad Boy.* The book tells the story of South Boy, a white fourteen-year-old raised on a ranch in Mojave territory. His father occasionally teaches him arithmetic and double-entry bookkeeping. His mother, when not ill, is hell-bent on "Cultural Advancement and Christian Instruction." She claims to live surrounded by two worlds: the Rough World of the White Man, and the Heathen World of the Indian, and the poor woman is not all that far from wrong.

The book is a mixture of tribes, whites, issues of power, and adventure. It displays the mixing of cultures in a manner not often accomplished by even the best writers. One white man, The Mormonhater, is undoubtably crazy, but is undoubtably wise in Indian ways. He has power no normal white man could ever have because he has learned more from Indians than from whites.

South Boy, armed with a mail-order pocket pistol, heads off to war with the Piutes. He is accompanied by his Mojave friend Havek. Before the frolic is over, they actually engage a renegade Piute, a witch, and manage to get three arrows into him. The Piute flees downriver, but they figure him for a dead man because he has nothing to seal his wounds. Flies will deposit eggs and maggots will grow. At this point the story departs from worlds of folk like Tom Sawyer and Penrod, and heads more toward Huck Finn. Life-and-death issues are decided. So are issues of identity. South Boy turns back toward the white world, but just barely.

# Money, Money, Everywhere,
## and Not a Cent to Spend

LET US LOOK at the third issue in that nineteenth-century triptych of Feminism, Race, and Economics.

At the back half of the nineteenth century, and through the early twentieth, the flat-out cruelty of the economic system spurred great numbers of our writers to action. The economic system not only corrupted society and religion with its low assumptions, it destroyed massive numbers of people.

Nothing can be more obscene than taking a child through systematic destruction. Remember yourself at age ten. Recall your fairly short attention span. Your physical ability was not large because you were not large. You could jump around, and play, then suddenly burn out. The idea of doing *anything* for twelve hours straight would be inconceivable.

Having imagined yourself at age ten, now imagine that someone has placed you at the mouth of a coal mine. Coal is hauled from the mine and dumped at the mouth. Your job is to pick pieces of slate and rock from the coal. You do this from sunrise to sunset. Your hands bleed. Coal dust works its way beneath your skin, and your eyes constantly feel crusty. Try to take a nap, or cry, and you are beaten.

This is your life. You wake in the dark, have a bowl of mush, and work. At sunset you will go back to an orphanage and will be given a piece of bread and a bowl of soup. You will do this six days a week until you die. If you begin at age ten, you will probably be dead by age twelve—sooner, if you're lucky. And even then you will not have suffered quite as many beatings as children working the streets. You will not, as a ten-year-old boy or girl, die a prostitute.

This sort of treatment of children is a part of the record of the Industrial Revolution in England. If we largely substitute cotton mills for coal mines, it is part of the Industrial Revolution in America.

Violence did not happen to a few children, it happened to thousands. It happened to women. It happened to men. In terms of violence, it became worse than slavery. Slaves had cost money and thus had at least minimal protection. Workers didn't cost anything. If a thousand were ground down and died, a thousand more needed jobs and were fit for grinding. The great economic metaphor of the Victorian Age was The Machine. Workers were subject to the metaphor. Workers were treated like machines.

If you mention this to friends, they may say: "Surely you exaggerate. My papa is a banker, my uncle is head of an oil company, and my momma runs an ad agency. They tell me those stories are nothing but 'communist' lies."

You may accurately reply that there are, indeed, apologists for the Industrial Revolution. These folk will tell you that people did not live well before industry changed the world, and they'll be correct. They will point out that from the eighteenth century on, the Industrial Revolution was experimental, changing, growing. The inferences will be that working people were victims of an indifferent force, and that human responsibility in the matter remained nil.

You may also accurately reply that some people believe the Holocaust did not happen. And some people have been sold the Brooklyn Bridge. And some people believe in the Tooth Fairy.

## ECONOMIC THEORIES

Industrial abuses caused the rise of "communism" and "socialism." These words resemble the words "God," "democracy," and "satisfaction," in that they can mean whatever the speaker likes; thus, they are virtually useless as tools of communication. Since they've been so twisted by speakers you've heard, a brief description of each is appropriate:

# Communism

Communistic ideas have existed for centuries. As a working theory, though, communism rose in the nineteenth century from the writings of Karl Marx, a German philosopher who comes down to us as an economic determinist.[1]

Marx believed "the whole man" was "the economic man." Every human problem was tied to the production and distribution of goods. He did much of his work in the British Museum at a time when the Industrial Revolution in England reached the depths of depravity. Marx made unwarranted assumptions, chief of them: the human condition depends entirely on economics.

There is reason, though, to see why he felt that way. All around him, people were turned into wreckage. Marx witnessed prolonged murder.

*Communism,* as understood at the end of the nineteenth century, descended from a Marxist theory called Dialectical Materialism.

Marx assumed there were three social classes. The aristocratic class could be largely ignored, since it already lay among the sweepings of history. The bourgeoisie class owned money and machinery; in other words, it owned the means of production. The proletariat, a third class, owned only its ability to work.

The two social classes were in continual struggle for money. The bourgeoisie tried to pay as little as possible for labor, and the proletariat tried to get as much as possible for its labor. Because of the machines, the proletariat could produce more than the value of the products consumed. The difference was called profit. The bourgeoisie controlled the profit. It could thus buy governments and police forces and armies in order to keep the proletariat in subjugation. This was the "materialism" side of the equation.

The "dialectical" side of the equation claimed that every economic

---

[1]A determinist, in this context, is someone who believes that human behavior is dictated by a single force. In the sixteenth century, John Calvin was a religious determinist. In the nineteenth century, and in the twentieth, we've had quite a few of these types. The oddest may well have been a psychologist named B. F. Skinner (1904–1990), whose psychology was a mixed-up run-through of the eighteenth-century concept "the blank slate." The smartest was Thomas Henry Buckle, a nineteenth-century historian who felt that geographic location determined the shape of society; which, in part, it does. Eskimos, for example, never invented surfboards.

system held the seed of its own destruction. Marx went to great lengths to show how the seed of a rising middle class destroyed feudal society in the French Revolution. That revolution transferred power from the aristocracy to the middle class, and the middle class became the bourgeoisie.

In the case of the Industrial Revolution, Marx claimed that oppression by the bourgeoisie would become so great that there would be a "revolution of the proletariat" (working class). The proles (social shorthand for proletariat) would overthrow the system and take charge of the means of production.

There would then arise a transitional government called "the Dictatorship of the Proletariat." That government would organize production, and get goods distributed equally across society. When everything was up and running, and when everyone became deliriously happy, the State—i.e., the dictatorship—would wither away. True communism would arrive.

The process did not work as Marx proposed. In Russia, dictatorship came not from the proletariat, but from a bunch of intellectuals who created a totalitarian government. That government held power for most of the twentieth century. In America, the Marxist revolution never happened. It got blunted by a lot of things, including labor unions, the moral structure of the people, awareness by our writers, the myth of individualism, and socialism.

## Socialism

*Socialism,* before it descended from Marx, ties to any number of religious and social theories predating the eighteenth century. In 1647, for example, the Diggers and Levelers in England represented early socialistic and communist views. The Diggers were socialistic, concerned with the English land, and with the rights of citizens to share in the use of the land. The Levelers were early communists. They wished to eliminate differences in social classes. By the late nineteenth and through much of the twentieth century in America, the terms "socialist" and "communist" became interchangeable.

## THE SEED OF DESTRUCTION

Socialism would become the seed of destruction for Marxist theory because it exerted enough strength and control to water down the worst excesses of industry. Socialism, like competitive religion (which, in fact, it was), showed a multitude of faces. Its main idea held that government needed to play a part in the economic structure of the nation. Some socialists contented themselves by saying that government should own public utilities and transportation. More-radical socialists wanted government to own the means of production—i.e., the factories and mines. Other socialists wanted government to regulate industries. The key to various forms of socialism was that each wanted government to have a say in how the economic system functioned.

Socialism also reacted against a "philosophy" of American business called laissez-faire. This notion originated in England and France. It means "hands off" and it began as an individualist reaction against monarchy. By the time it got to America, it came to mean that government was established to help business. If it couldn't offer help, government was supposed to butt out.

The result? Americans in the late nineteenth century faced an economic world that sent the message "Root hog or die." If a man failed in business, woe betide. Or, if he died, his family had virtually no resources unless the man had put together a successful business, or laid aside a pot of money. If he failed to do so, the woman, and children, took any sort of work to pay for rent and food. Earnings for one person might be as little as $1 a week. Rent for a room could be as little as $4 a month, but the room would not be a place where you would want to raise chickens or fish-worms, let alone children. It is no wonder, under such circumstances, that men were in constant battle to succeed. They fought each other for success, claw and fang.[2]

---

[2]The "claw and fang" metaphor fits the times. The nineteenth-century sociologist Herbert Spencer sold the Western world, and subsequently the United States Supreme Court, on the notion of "social evolution," in which the fittest survived. In the popular mind, this meant the toughest and meanest, not the most adaptable. Mill and factory owners sometimes thought it sad that so many of their employees hit the graveyard, but they assuaged their sadness with the knowledge that "natural selection" had selected those poor creatures for extinction.

Three other theorists contributed to the common wisdom of the factory owners. In

Nor is it a wonder that unmarried women looked over the field of available suitors with an eye to future earnings. If a woman made a bad choice, she and her future family were in trouble.

Welfare, food stamps, unemployment insurance, rent subsidies, public housing, social security, and surplus commodities did not exist. Some charitable organizations fought against the tides of misery, as did some churches. Despite the caterwauling of the evangelicals, there were honest churchmen and churchwomen, as well as philanthropists, who battled against truly insurmountable problems.

"Real Americans," by which was meant white people who were not recent immigrants, got a better shake, but not much better. Most counties had something called a "poorhouse," where lived destitute old people, and an occasional orphan. Cities had orphanages, always filled. Beyond the orphanages, stray children were treated as expendable.[3]

In the early twentieth century, the main form of social and economic support came from what is called "the extended family." In a nation still made up mostly of farms and small towns, it was not unusual for everyone in a given county to be related to everyone else. Grandparents and parents, children, cousins, sometimes aunts or uncles, all might live under the same roof. Or, they lived in a nearby town, or on a neighboring farm. Families took care of their members. In farm communities, neighbors helped out on large problems; for example, rebuilding a burned barn. Two famous lines from Robert Frost's poem "The Death of the Hired Man" read: "Home is the place where, when you have to go there, / They have to take you in."

This suggests that not everyone was in trouble, and that is true. The nation built rapidly. Optimism ran rampant. So did fear. As we've seen, the settled population was either in good shape or had reasonable hope

---

1776, Adam Smith had published *An Inquiry into the Nature and Causes of the Wealth of Nations,* which effectively threw out former economic theories. Smith held that wealth depends only on a combination of capital, resources, and a labor pool; a mechanistic view suitable to his day.

In 1798, Thomas Malthus published *An Essay on the Principle of Population,* which postulated that population could not grow beyond the food supply.

In 1817 David Ricardo published *Principle of Economics and Taxation.* His Iron Law of Wages claimed that wages could not rise above the lowest level for subsistence.

[3]This attitude toward "expendable children" remains at the end of the twentieth century. Corporations and government have yet to learn that children, economically, are a resource, not a deficit.

of progress. Grindstones of industry rode largely on the backs of immigrants.

Early union movements fought back. Trade unions were started by true believers, and with all the fervency of new religions. It's possible to get a notion of conditions and ideals by looking at a couple of articles from the constitution of the Industrial Brotherhood (1874):

*Article Eleven:* The prohibition of the employment of children in workshops, mines, and factories before attaining their fourteenth year.

*Article Thirteen:* To secure for both sexes equal pay for equal work.

These, together with an eight-hour day, were what the union hoped to achieve. You can guess conditions simply by looking at what the union thought was a good deal. A lot of unions started up and were immediately knocked in the head.[4] When industry went too far, as in the Pullman railroad strike of 1877, workers walked out, although they were unorganized.

Then, in 1878, the Organization of the Knights of Labor, under Terence Powderly, won in negotiations with Jay Gould, a captain of industry. This was the first time that a robber baron like Gould dealt with unions by any other method than calling the police.

After ten years of struggle, labor leader Samuel Gompers saw the American Federation of Labor (the AFL) come into being in 1886.

The Haymarket Riot in Chicago also occurred in 1886. A man named Bonfield, a head cop at the Des Plaines Street Station, countermanded orders of Chicago's mayor. He marched 176 policemen to a union meeting in Haymarket Square. As the police approached, someone, probably an anarchist, threw a bomb. Police opened fire and shot a bunch of people, including each other. Results? Eight policemen dead, and over sixty more policemen wounded. Without any evidence to connect them with the bombing, eight unionists were tried as anarchists, which they were not. They were convicted, and five, including Albert Parsons, were hanged. Albert Parsons was husband of the revolutionist Lucy Parsons. Both of them had survived for years while being reviled by cops, newspapers, factory owners, and solid citizens. The two were reviled because they held sincere belief in the

---

[4]Some movements lasted for quite a while. A group of Irish terrorists called the Molly Maguires kept the coal mines of Pennsylvania shuddering for about ten years, ending in 1877.

equality of all people. They had previously been run out of Texas because Albert was white, Lucy black.

Next, in 1905, and mostly in the West, arose an outfit called the Industrial Workers of the World (the IWW, or Wobblies). In the West, where I live, they are still either loved or hated. They were brave and sometimes foolhardy men who took power in the union movement and held it until World War I.

Meantime, other forces were in operation. An anarchist named Lewis Masquerier, in 1877, published *Sociology: or, The Reconstruction of Society, Government, and Property*. His vision would abolish all organized government and religion. He paved the way for Emma Goldman, an anarchist who also espoused feminist issues.

In the midst of all this, the American writer performed with both good sense and fury; and in a manner soon to become a tradition. Before or during the Civil War, our writers had shown how business or institutions beat down people who worked for them, or how poverty, rising from inadequate wages, destroys the human spirit. The earliest work is John Woolman's *A Plea for the Poor* (1763). The best-known early novel is Herman Melville's *White Jacket* (1850), and the second-best-known is Rebecca Harding Davis's long narrative *Life in the Iron Mills* (*Atlantic Monthly* 1861). William Austin published *Martha Gardner*[5] in the 1820s. He dealt with the rights of labor. George Lippard, best remembered for *The Man with the Mask*, published *The Quaker City*[6] (1844), in which he exposed vice and corruption in Philadelphia. In later life, he also started an organization called Brotherhood of the Union, which was his own brand of socialism.

After the Civil War, Mark Twain and Charles Dudley Warner published *The Gilded Age* (1873), and Edward Bellamy published *Looking Backward 2000–1877* in 1878. Alice French (pseudonym Octave Thanet) published *A Slave to Duty and Other Women* in 1898 and *The Lion's Share* in 1907. Stephen Crane published *Maggie: A Girl of the Streets* in 1893. Frank Norris published *The Octopus* in 1901. Upton Sinclair published *The Jungle* in 1906. Jack London published *The Iron*

---

[5]He is best remembered these days for his story *Peter Rugg, The Missing Man* (1820). It is one of the first written (as opposed to oral) American stories dealing with the Fantastic.

[6]Originally published under the title *The Monks of Monk Hall*.

*Heel* in 1907. Theodore Dreiser's *Sister Carrie,* having been suppressed after its publication in 1900, was reissued in 1907, and Dreiser embarked on a career of social annoyance that would ruffle the fur of fat cats until World War II.

These writers would be followed, in the next generation, by Michael Gold's *Jews Without Money* (1930), Albert Maltz's *Man on a Road* (1935), John Dos Passos's *U.S.A.* (1930–1936), Richard Wright's *Native Son* (1940), and two of the strongest novels you will ever read: John Steinbeck's *In Dubious Battle* (1936), and Meridel Le Sueur's *The Girl* (1939). Our writers drilled at the public consciousness. They would mostly do so without sentimentality or romance. Political parties might advertise "the worker" as a brand of pure hero, but our writers showed the worker as a valuable human trapped in a dreadful situation. No more, no less.

We are now prepared to understand how socialism, feminism, and the "race" movement combined by looking at three books from two generations.

# THREE BOOKS, THREE ISSUES:
## FEMINISM/SOCIALISM/RACE

DREAMS OF UTOPIA go all the way back to Plato's *Republic*, but for our purposes, they begin with a book titled *Utopia*, by Sir Thomas More in the sixteenth century. That book envisioned a perfect society, and it caused writers in the next three centuries to build utopias of their own. While the American writer Edward Bellamy fought against a destructive economic system and wrote *Looking Backward*, companion novels were published in England. The best English book is *A Dream of John Ball*, by William Morris. It is short and beautifully crafted. Both Bellamy and Morris used the fantastic. Both were socialists. They had little else in common. Bellamy liked to lecture at length, and included a love story appropriate to the period. His book eventually sold a million copies; this in a nation of 86 million.

## LOOKING BACKWARD 2000–1877

This novel is about Julian West, a thirty-year-old rich man who has trouble sleeping. He hires a mesmerist, a self-styled "professor of animal magnetism," to put him into a trance. West's manservant has been taught how to wake him from the trance. The mesmerist puts West in a trance, then leaves town. West's house burns. The manservant is presumed dead in the fire, thereby failing in his task. West is left, sound asleep, in his concrete-vaulted underground bedchamber.

West went into trance in 1887. When finally waked by one Dr.

Leete, it is the year 2000. He has slept 113 years, three months, and eleven days. Unlike Rip Van Winkle, he has not aged.

The rest of the novel, except for the part about falling in love, explains the background that produced socialism, and the perfect world wrought by socialism. It also tells how socialism, throughout the twentieth century, evolved peacefully from the rack and ruin of nineteenth-century economics. In the last chapter, in order to get in one more lecture, Bellamy wakes Julian who, oh, Big Surprise! has been sleeping and dreaming all along.[1]

Why was the book so popular? A lot of nerves vibrated in those days, and this book plucked at them.

It dealt with the woman question. It did so in Victorian romantic terms, but it dealt with it. Here is a quote describing society in the year 2000:

> "Our girls are as full of ambition for their careers as our boys. Marriage, when it comes, does not mean incarceration for them, nor does it separate them in any way from the larger interests of society, the bustling life of the world. Only when maternity fills a woman's mind with new interests does she withdraw from the world for a time. Afterwards, and at any time, she may return to her place among her comrades, nor need she ever lose touch with them. Women are a very happy race nowadays, as compared with what they were before in the world's history, and their power of giving happiness to men has been of course increased in proportion."

Pretty cute. It is not a passage to please radical feminists at the end of the twentieth century, but then, it wasn't written for them. It was written for the Victorian woman of 1888, and she loved it.

Racial groups and immigrants, in the year 2000, are included through extensive statements of human equality, and the need to educate everyone. Education was not pointed toward making money, but required so all workers might lead happy and productive lives.

*Looking Backward* offered options to everyone, even the rich. In the late nineteenth century rich men could not count on remaining secure.

---

[1] In terms of propaganda, such an ending works. In terms of art, it's a cheap shot. Bellamy was an excellent propagandist.

These were days of business combines called trusts. Trusts caused fear even among the wealthy.

There were two kinds: A vertical trust controlled a product through every process on its way to market. We still see this in oil companies, which drill, pump, process, store, transport, wholesale, and retail their product. This would constitute a vertical trust, if there was only one oil company.

A horizontal trust was an interlocking of related businesses. For example: A railroad might own a steel mill while also interlocking with grain companies, grain storage, and even bakeries to make bread. That railroad could control the price of steel rail it charged itself, could control the price of grain, grain storage, grain transport, and even determine in which areas of the country a farmer would be allowed to stay in business.

Thus, moderately rich men could not count on staying rich, because a trust could make or break other businesses. A rich man's wealth would fade if he made one bad mistake in investments.

A man who was only in the middle class perched precariously. Labor problems could easily break the middle-class businessman. He watched labor strikes fearfully. He listened to furious talk by anarchists. Some anarchists claimed themselves ready to kill each and every member of the middle class. The great appeal of *Looking Backward* was not that people believed it possible, but that it offered peaceful solutions.

The book remains a statement of the Ideal Society as contained in socialist theory. (Bellamy despised communism.) As a workable solution it does not have a snowball's chance in a blast furnace. As a statement of an ideal, though, it functioned to prepare people for change. In the next century elements of socialism would enter American life and business. In a world of conflicting opinions, and hatred between labor and industry, *Looking Backward* offered options. Frightened people were asked to think and talk about their problems.

## THE IRON HEEL

If Karl Marx had lived to read *The Iron Heel,* he would have begged for a second lifetime in order to refute Jack London. Marx spent his life in libraries. London spent his short life among working people, rich people, deadbeats, bums, literary people, and in libraries. London knew human beings, and how they behave.

*The Iron Heel*, published in 1907, purports to be a record written by Avis Everhard, later to change identity and become Felice Van Verdighan. She is killed. Someone picks up the record and publishes it, together with historical footnotes. The record, written by a woman, fits with socialist and communist ideologies. Everyone is equal. The female narrator is also a reflection of the women's movement at the turn of the century. The movement was, by then, a growing and vocal force.

The record tells how the trusts finally dispose of the middle class. What remains is the Oligarchy, a group of rich men. They know they are immoral, but they also know they are rich and powerful. They will lie, cheat, steal, manipulate, murder, buy governments, religions, armies, build their own armies, set up entire populations for destruction, and turn the working population of the world into slaves.

When in combat with the Oligarchy, the socialists are just as bad. Their difference comes because socialism, with them, amounts to religion. They work in behalf of their holy cause.

The Oligarchy overreaches itself. It causes such cruel conditions that socialists actually win seats in Congress. An agrarian movement called the Grangers also wins seats. The socialists and Grangers, in combination, constitute a majority. However, the Oligarchy refuses to seat the new Granger members. Since the Oligarchy owns the courts, nothing can be done.

The socialists fight back with extensive plotting and armed resistance. As years roll past, the working class is reduced to slavery. The working class becomes "People of the Abyss" (a term coined by H. G. Wells). They are dehumanized to the state of beasts.

The revolution arrives. It is beaten down. More years pass, and a second attempt is beaten down. Marx' theories are confounded. A new feudal society rises. The world has gone from shirtsleeves to shirtsleeves in three revolutions.

*The Iron Heel* is a forerunner of other predictive books about society and politics; the best known of them *Brave New World* and *1984*. It served the American people in a number of ways, not the least of which is a warning about the fruits of technology. In 1907, few, except Jack London, had the least notion of flying an airplane over a city and dropping bombs or parachutes. Airplanes were still power-driven kites.[2] In *The Iron Heel*, bombs are dropped from balloons.

---

[2]The Wright brothers made their first flight in 1903.

By 1907 news had recently arrived from the Russo-Japanese War (1904–5), and only Jack London understood that news because he had been a war correspondent. The news said: "Machine guns are more than simple artillery, and they can kill lots more people than anyone ever dreamed." London got the message and put it in his book. As will be later shown, hundreds of British, French, Russian, Austrian, and German generals did not get the message.

*The Iron Heel* asked Americans to think about alternatives, rather than buy panaceas. Although the book does show its author as an expert on socialist theory, its difference stems from the fact that the author understands that socialism, as a religion, is only another form of oppression.

In hindsight, the most important message of the book (because it is a book of messages, and not of characters) warns that technology will soon make it possible to construct a new type of government. There's a difference between a dictatorship and a totalitarian government. The world would soon learn this, to our universal sorrow.

## NATIVE SON

From *Looking Backward* (1878) to the publication of *Native Son* (1940) is a sixty-three-year jump. Since Richard Wright was not even born until 1908, it's a good question that asks how his book ties to the early socialist/communist movements. The answer has to do with Wright's being from Mississippi and growing up during a time when Mississippi was fervent on keeping the forms and content of slavery intact. Wright came from a place fifty or more years behind the rest of the nation. He came from a racial situation that offered the same degradation that immigrants knew during the nineteenth century.

In Wright's case, degradation carried the special ugliness of those Southern racial customs so well shown in the works of William Faulkner. Wright's move from Mississippi to Chicago was wise, because any black man who stayed in Mississippi had one of two choices: complete servility—or death. Wright would soon see how racial discrimination in the South was exchanged for racial hatred in the North.

*Native Son* is Richard Wright's best book, although his autobiography, *Black Boy* (1945), is widely read. *Native Son* tells of Bigger Thomas, a young Negro man in Chicago. It examines the social and cultural trap enclosing him. He is not only branded by the color of his skin, but by the industrial, economic, and political assumptions that control the world. Wright would explain Bigger in an address, "How Bigger Was Born," in which this paragraph appears:

> I made the discovery that Bigger Thomas was not black all the time; he was white, too, and there were literally millions of him, everywhere. The extension of my sense of the personality of Bigger was the pivot of my life; it altered the complexion of my existence. I became conscious, at first dimly, and then later on with increasing clarity and conviction, of a vast, muddied pool of human life in America. It was as though I had put on a pair of spectacles whose power was that of an x-ray enabling me to see deeper into the lives of men. Whenever I picked up a newspaper, I'd no longer feel that I was reading of the doings of whites alone (Negroes are rarely mentioned in the press unless they've committed some crime!), but of a complex struggle for life going on in my country, a struggle in which I was involved. I sensed, too, that the Southern scheme of oppression was but an appendage of a vast and in many respects more ruthless and impersonal commodity-profit machine.

Seeking understanding of these insights, Wright joined the Communist party in 1934. He lasted for ten years, but broke with the party because it could not handle original ways of thinking. After World War II he lived in Europe, largely because the political climate in America was such that he could not come home. Possessing less imagination than your average parsnip, the FBI wanted to try him for sedition, a charge it couldn't make stick. Middle- and upper-class blacks hated his guts, but not because of his politics. They didn't like him because he wrote honestly. Communists despised him as a traitor to their cause. The people who loved him then, and love him now, were, and are, his fellow writers.

In *Native Son*, Bigger kills two people, is defended by a Communist lawyer, and is sentenced to death. The book, which might have been nothing but a sermon about communism, is, instead, a great American novel. It is great because it takes a fully developed character, in an oppressive situation, and follows him to see what will happen. If he runs into social/political theory during the story, the theory does not get ahead of the story. The story is about Bigger Thomas, not communism.

Middle- and upper-class Negroes hated Wright because, as a superior intellect, and as a superior writer, he was not afraid to examine issues the upper and middle classes do not wish examined. The general reaction may be summed up by: "Why can't you tell stories about successful Negroes who own real estate and belong to the Episcopal church?"

Middle- and upper-class Caucasians hated Wright because he was a communist, turned socialist. By the time Wright broke with the Communist party, the word "communist" was a buzzword in America. People equated it with totalitarianism, not theory. To many people, "communist" was what "Satan" was to the people of Salem in 1692; and, as with Satan, "communism" also caused talk about "conspiracy."[3]

The two people Bigger kills are women: one Negro, one Caucasian. The women are also trapped in illusions. They are controlled by social and economic systems they do not understand. The communists, expressing an ideal of equality, prove fallible. In no other book I know is the combination of race, gender, and socialism so apparent.

As Wright discovered, communism was not particularly bad as a theory—only particularly silly. It assumed that economics formed minds, hearts, actions, insecurities, assumptions about power; and it assumed people are logical, which we are not; and that equality is something every human desires. In other words, communism wanted to do for the human race what the human race said it wanted, but didn't.[4]

*Native Son's* value lay in influencing thinkers and writers who, in turn, would begin to exert influences on racial and economic situations after World War II. It connects back to earlier socialist writing through a sort of innocence and hope, because at first, Wright, like earlier so-

---

[3]The obvious answer to such unhappy folk is "Yes, there is a Communist conspiracy. There is also a peanut growers' conspiracy. There are conspiracies among twelve-year-old boys who inhabit tree houses. There are conspiracies among people who manufacture paper dolls. But unless you can show it as a large and dangerous conspiracy, you're only blowing smoke."

[4]This reminds me of Twain's story *Extract from Captain Stormfield's Visit to Heaven.* A steamboat captain goes to heaven. He is issued a harp, but can't play a harp. He gets to join the heavenly chorus, but the "ignorant" chip in and spoil the music. He doesn't get to meet Moses or King David or the Apostles, because high mucky-mucks do not deal with riffraff. The story is a spoof on a heaven where nobody does anything he valued on earth; no sex, no drinking, no cigars, no cussing, no nothing, except flapping around on wings that do not work too well, and playing a harp, badly. Communism was like that.

cialists, did not have enough experience with communism or socialism to become disenchanted.

The power of ideas about the worker, and of myths about the worker, spread widely through the first half of the twentieth century. That, however, is getting well ahead of the story. Let us first turn to transitions from the nineteenth century to the twentieth, when the plucked chicken of Victorianism headed for the stew pot, and our contemporary world began to fledge.

# FUNNY BUSINESS

THREE FORMS OF storytelling brought America into the twentieth century: humor, satire, and poetry. We'll look at storytelling poets in the next chapter, but for now let's look at humor and satire.

## VARIETIES OF HUMOR

Humor is one form of search essential during times of corruption. Humor was thus an essential part of American writing as our nation entered the twentieth century. In addition, when you think of our overly serious religious origins, it's easy to see how America developed the need for humor. Since we've always been a nation stocked with plenty of working people, humor of satiric and sometimes raunchy proportions had to happen.

Our most famous humorist (also a satirist) was Mark Twain, who got his start using the tall tale. This is from "Baker's Blue-jay Yarn": "You think a cat can swear. Well, a cat can; but you give a blue-jay a subject that calls for his reserve powers, and where is your cat? Don't talk to *me*—I know too much about this thing."

## The Tall Tale

The blue-jay yarn is a tall tale, and it arrived late on the scene. Twain wrote most of his work after the Civil War, but a long time before the war, and to the present, the tall tale was—and is—a staple of American life. It is most often encountered among working people, or in the military, or in bars, where it runs under the name of b.s. From old Alaskan stories of weather so cold the flames on candles froze, to contemporary tall tales (currently termed "urban legends" by radio and television people who get taken in), the tall tale chuckles happily. It circulates in ways critical of society, or technology, or even business and religion.

Here is a social example: the story of the baby-sitter who gave the kid a bath, then dried it off in the microwave. It doesn't come up to Twain, and it's more than a little sick, but it shows how the tall tale knocks at the doors of conventional wisdom.

This sort of rap goes back to America's earliest origins, back to whenever a tyrant or god proved worthy of scoffing. In the example above, the god is technology, the tyrant is either children or the need for sitters.

Political example: A loyal constituent tries to give a U.S. senator a baby elephant, but the senator refuses because "I'd just hate to watch it grow up, grow old, and die." Whether against an eternity of politicians, or the tyranny of society, the tall tale is an element of political and/or social revolution.

From the eighteenth century on, America produced tall-tale spinners who also wrote mixtures of satire and straight humor. A lot of their work is no longer funny because they wrote about local matters that are now unimportant, but all of their work tells a great deal about the times in which they lived. It's almost impossible to find some of their work today, in part because much of it appeared in newspapers. Still, any American writer will probably want to be familiar with their names.

A roll of eighteenth- and nineteenth-century tall-tale spinners, and satirists, certainly includes Lucretia Peabody Hale, who wrote *The Peterkin Papers*, from which came a once-famous expression, "Ask the lady from Philadelphia," Thomas Bangs Thorpe ("The Big Bear of Arkansas"), Augustus Baldwin Longstreet (psuedonym, Timothy Crabshaw), Mortimer Neal Thompson (Q. F. K. Philander Doesticks, P.B.), Henry Wheeler Shaw (Josh Billings), George Horatio Derby (John Phoenix), David Ross Locke (Petroleum V. Nasby), Benjamin Penhallow Shillaber (Mrs. Partington—the forerunner of Twain's Aunt Polly), Charles Henry Webb (John Paul), Mercy Otis Warren (*The Adulateur: A tragedy*, and *The Group*, satirical plays), Charles Henry Smith (Bill Arp), Bret Harte,

Seba Smith (Major Jack Downing, our first political satirist), Frank Stockton (*The Casting Away of Mrs. Lecks and Mrs. Aleshine* and many others; though he is remembered today for his short story "The Lady and the Tiger"), Robert Henry Newell (Orpheus C. Kerr, *The Walking Doll: or, The Asters and Disasters of Society*), Edgar Wilson Nye (Bill Nye), Charles Farrar Browne (Artemus Ward), George Ade, who wrote such things as:

> Once upon a Time there was a slim Girl with a Forehead which was Shiny and Protuberant, like a Bartlett Pear. When asked to put Something in an Autograph Album she invariably wrote the Following, in a tall, dislocated Back-Hand: "Life is Earnest, And the Grave is not its Goal.' That's the kind of a Girl she was.

The championship poet who told stories in satirical verse was James Russell Lowell, as in *The Biglow Papers*: "Thet air flag's a leetle rotten, / Hope it aint your Sunday's best; / Fact! it takes a sight o' cotton / To stuff out a soger's chest:. . . ." This particular verse was about an Army recruiting officer who was drumming up cannon fodder for the Mexican War.

## Sophistication

Humor brought American writing into the twentieth century. After the Civil War, most of the tall tales came from the West, and most humor was slapstick. As humor entered the new century, it did not discard slapstick, but did pick up some pretty sophisticated drollery. While the world went through enormous change, humorists worked their hearts out knocking down conventional wisdom, such as:

> . . . Down in the turf where the daisies grew
> They planted John and his sister Sue
> And their little souls to the angels flew—
> Boo hoo.
>
> And what of that peach of emerald hue
> Warmed by the sun and wet by the dew?

Ah well, its mission on earth was through.
Adieu . . .

These verses are by Eugene Field on the problems attending the eating of green peaches, and possibly on the problems that rise from attending church services.[1]

Bill Nye, a contemporary of Twain, came from Boston. When he wrote about John Adams and John Quincy Adams, he said: "Neither of the Adamses were born in a larger house than I was, and for general tone and eclat of front yard and cook-room on behind, I am led to believe that I have the advantage."

Nye anticipated some awfully smooth humorists of the early twentieth century. The best would be Robert Benchley, who explained: "All of my friends call me Sweet Old Bob, or sometimes only the initials." He also wrote:

> The very words "fur-bearing trout" are offensive to me. So today I read that a man has reported to the Anglers' Club that he has discovered a fur-bearing trout. That's the way my whole life has been.
>
> At first I thought that I wouldn't read about it. "This is a free country," I said to myself, smiling sadly. "You don't have to read anything you don't want to read. Skip it, and go on to the next page. Keeping abreast of current events is one thing— masochism is another.
>
> . . .
>
> But that old New England streak in me, that atavistic yearning for a bad time if a bad time is possible, turned my eyes down into the column which was headed:
>
> FUR-BEARING TROUT AMAZES ANGLERS
> Its Pelt Is Called Sure Goitre Cure. . . .

During the twentieth century, humor would help haul the American people through world wars, the Great Depression, the Cold War, and immeasurable social change. In the library or bookstore, look for Og-

---

[1] In Laura Benét, *Famous American Humorists* (Dodd Mead, 1959).

den Nash, James Thurber, E. B. White, Ring Lardner, Damon Runyon, Clarence Day, Will Rogers, Don Marquis, Edward Streeter, Will Cuppy, Thorne Smith, H. Allen Smith, Max Shulman, and Dorothy Parker. These are not all of our humorists by a long stretch, but they are the ones you'll most likely find in print, or sometimes still available in used bookstores.

## SATIRE

Satire took firm hold as Victorianism hit a slippery slope that would dump it into the twentieth century. Satire from the past is one of the best ways of viewing the past. Satire takes what is real and cranks it up to the point where readers actually feel the weight of social or political conditions, rather than simply hear reports of them.

# Mark Twain

The best-known satirist is Mark Twain, who cut through Victorian pretensions about family in order to preserve the family. He did it largely through sarcasm and contrast. He denounced failure in families because he so loved his own wife and daughters. He was a family man who simply couldn't abide people who harmed their own families.

Twain was the most savagely honest writer since Melville. He never hid pain or anger or revulsion, although he sometimes downplayed his opinions about religion in order to sell books. He could use realism and naturalism, but was a whiz with the fantastic. He could satirize an entire civilization, as he did in *A Connecticut Yankee at King Arthur's Court*, by having a representative of American civilization do business with another corrupted civilization. The court of Ghengis Khan would have served him as well as did King Arthur's. It was all one to Twain. He showed that corruption destroys, and when corruption meets corruption, the result is the apocalypse.

Twain made a living both as writer and speaker. This was a time when speech making ("the platform," as it was known) served as a main source of entertainment. We cannot, today, imagine sitting and listening to speeches through the better part of an afternoon while loving every minute. In Twain's day, though, huge audiences would travel many miles to attend that sort of festivity.[2]

In both writing and speaking Twain went after conventional wisdom that claimed Progress as a god. He went after the falsity of Victorian style. In fact, there wasn't a whale of a lot he did not attack. As he grew older, and went through the personal hells of losing wife and a daughter through death, he began to drop issues and concentrate on the human race in general. His comments were not kind. Said he, "Heaven goes by favor. If it went by merit, you would stay out and your dog would go in."

## Booth Tarkington and Sinclair Lewis

Two other great satirists who operated during the early years of this century were Booth Tarkington and Sinclair Lewis. Both were popular, but for completely opposite reasons. Tarkington wrote to a broad and traditional audience, while Lewis attracted a new and indignant audience. Tarkington could be an overtly funny man when he wished.[3] Lewis exaggerates and lampoons, just enough to show characters and situations holding a spiritual content of Zero.

### THE SITUATION

To fully appreciate these satirists, we need to see a bit of what they saw:

They saw America turning into an industrial nation, and they watched the rapid growth of cities. They saw an emerging middle class of small businessmen, known as boosters.

The booster believed in "boosting" his own town, county, state. The opening of a fertilizer factory, for example, was cause for boosters to brag that "Midville" or "Pigeon Creek" was the grandest and greatest supplier of fertilizer in both the civilized and uncivilized worlds; and the boosters didn't see a blamed thing funny in the statement.

Our satirists also faced terrible urban situations. At the turn of the

---

[2]Attention spans were longer then. Language, and the way language can flower, was important. Lots of golden throats spoke from the platforms, Bob Ingersoll and Bill Nye among others.

[3]Anyone with the least interest in the business of art will surely wish to read Tarkington's *Rumbin Galleries* (1937). You'll laugh for a month.

century, the newcomer to a growing American city would find industrial desolation that we, in days of industrial pollution and auto pollution, would still have a hard time imagining.

Fires of industry, and fires for heating homes, were stoked with soft
coal. Together with soot, and mud mixed with soot, fell droppings from
horses. In the late-nineteenth century, and early twentieth, the country
went "horse-crazy." Fancy equipage, carriages, surreys, phaetons, snazzy
harness, matched teams; all of these combined with working delivery
wagons to crowd streets. In both farm and city, people kept stables. A
great many people owned far more horses than were, strictly speaking,
necessary. Street cleaners might work day and night (and street cleaners
did), but it was impossible to keep streets clean. In addition, at the turn
of the century, hardly any roads were paved, nor were streets. Filth
mucked together. Cities became breeding grounds for disease and, although disease found victims among every age group, the most vulnerable group was children.

Families were huge because of Victorian notions, fundamentalist religion, a rural ethic, and—for the majority—only rudimentary methods
and information concerning birth control. A family might have seven
or eight children, or many more. Only the lucky family would raise all
its children to adulthood. Children died frequently, sometimes two or
three in a single family, as disease swept across cities and spilled into
the countryside. Preachers explained the deaths as "The will of God,
Who never gives a burden you can't bear—and besides, little Georgie
or little Gracie is with the angels."

This, of course, was enough to drive writers crazy. I here declare
that a vast amount of fury rising in American writing during the early
part of this century came, directly or indirectly, from the deaths of
children.

For the purpose of the satirist, the changing social order, the filth in
the streets, and the grotesque celebration of business "boosterism" were
goads asking to be goaded.

## BOOTH TARKINGTON

One of the best descriptions of foul conditions comes from Booth
Tarkington's novel *The Magnificent Ambersons* (1918), which won the
Pulitzer Prize. He writes about industry, business boosters, growth, and
about Lucy, one of his characters:

What they [the business boosters] meant by Prosperity was credit at the bank; but in exchange for this credit they got nothing that was not dirty, and, therefore, to a sane mind, valueless; since whatever was cleaned was dirty again before the cleaning was half done. For, as the town grew, it grew dirty with an incredible completeness. The idealists put up magnificent business buildings and boasted of them, but the buildings were begrimed before they were finished. They boasted of their libraries, of their monuments and statues; and poured soot on them. They boasted of their schools, but the schools were dirty, like the children within them. This was not the fault of the children or their mothers. It was the fault of the idealists, who said: "The more dirt, the more prosperity." They drew patriotic, optimistic breaths of the flying powdered filth of the streets, and took the foul and heavy smoke with gusto into the profundities of their lungs. "Boost! Don't knock!" they said. And every year or so they boomed a great Clean-Up week, when everybody was supposed to get rid of the tin cans in his back yard. . . .

"Prosperity" meant good credit at the bank, black lungs, and housewives' Purgatory. The women fought the dirt all they could; but if they let the air into their houses they let in the dirt. It shortened their lives, and kept them from the happiness of ever seeing anything white. And thus, as the city grew, the time came when Lucy, after a hard struggle, had to give up her blue-and-white curtains and her white walls. Indoors, she put everything into dull gray and brown, and outside had the little house painted the dark green nearest to black. Then she knew, of course, that everything was as dirty as ever, but was a little less distressed because it no longer looked so dirty as it was. . . .

In Tarkington's work, one century dies and another is born. An entire way of life changes, as does society. *The Magnificent Ambersons* was followed by his novel *Alice Adams,* which also won the Pulitzer Prize. Its heroine is a young woman sucked into, and then rejecting, the illusions of higher society. These two books tell more about what went on in our country during those days than can be found in any other book.

This is true, at least, when Tarkington receives credit for trying to save what was good from the past while needling the bad.

## SINCLAIR LEWIS

Other writers saw little worth saving. Sinclair Lewis reached adulthood during this time. He did not begin publishing until 1920, but when he did publish he had the transition from the nineteenth to the twentieth century nailed. Three of his novels would do much to form ideas in American culture from 1920 until at least the 1960s. The first, *Main Street* (1920), did an even better job on the American small town than had E. W. Howe in the before-mentioned *The Story of a Country Town*. Here is the opening to Lewis' *Main Street*, and if it sounds like bitter fruit, recall that bitter fruit was part of the produce of our rural history:

> This is America—a town of a few thousand, in a region of wheat and corn and dairies and little groves.
>
> The town is, in our tale, called "Gopher Prairie, Minnesota." But its Main Street is the continuation of Main Streets everywhere. The story would be the same in Ohio or Montana, in Kansas or Kentucky or Illinois, and not very differently would it be told Up York State or in the Carolina hills.
>
> Main Street is the climax of civilization. That this Ford car might stand in front of the Bon Ton Store, Hannibal invaded Rome and Erasmus wrote in Oxford cloisters. What Ole Jenson the grocer says to Ezra Stowbody the banker is the new law for London, Prague, and the unprofitable isles of the sea; whatsoever Ezra does not know and sanction, that thing is heresy, worthless for knowing and wicked to consider.
>
> Our railway station is the final aspiration of architecture. Sam Clark's annual hardware turnover is the envy of the four counties which constitute God's Country. In the sensitive art of the Rosebud Movie Palace there is a Message, and humor strictly moral.
>
> Such is our comfortable tradition and sure faith. Would he not betray himself an alien cynic who should otherwise portray Main Street, or distress the citizens by speculating whether there may not be other faiths?

Volcanoes of wrath spouted when *Main Street* appeared. Lots and lots of people spotted the truth, and lots more were offended. The reaction taught Lewis that a writer could research something, show its flaws and foibles while puncturing comfortable myths, and serve literature while making a living.

At the same time that Lewis tore smug wrappers from small towns, he aligned himself with Willa Cather in his genuine appreciation of the farms built by immigrants to Minnesota. Knowing humans as he did, Lewis would expect considerable narrowness of view on the farms. He would not expect to find a lack of humor or generosity.

His next novel, *Babbitt,* appeared in 1922. George Babbitt is a businessman of the 1920s variety—i.e., not a captain of industry, or a J. P. Morgan type of pirate. He is a booster, a small businessman, destined so to be, and thus destined to cheer long and loudly over matters trite and dull.

Those volcanoes of readers' wrath cut loose again. The businessman of the 1920s was thought to stand with God at his right hand. *Babbitt* represented heresy to a great number of people, some of whom had even liked Lewis' work up to that point.

His toughest novel came five years later. *Elmer Gantry* takes on evangelical religionists. Its dark hero, Elmer Gantry, is as grim a character as can be found in American fiction. If we were to try to compare him with an American historical figure, he would be most like Richard Nixon, another man who began with ideals and ran purposefully down to gloom, then unto utter darkness.

In the work of both Tarkington and Lewis lies light more abiding than anything the nation's political and spiritual leaders handed out.

Tarkington begins with people trapped in illusions. Once the trap is sprung, people show their moral fiber. George Amberson, a spoiled brat, raised rich and completely despicable, is left destitute. He faces the family responsibility of caring for an aged aunt he doesn't even like. Instead of running, or making alibis, he takes a high-paid but dangerous job handling explosives. Honor is alive in him, as is the sense of duty.

Alice Adams is fooled into social climbing by one of the nastiest mothers to appear in fiction. Alice finally understands the shallowness of the world she attempts to enter. With her brother a fled criminal, her father ill and dying, and her mother abusing her father, she enters a business school. She has a tough road ahead, but at least a road without illusions. Tarkington's characters win out in the end, because while they are in situations that demand losers, they are not losers.

Lewis' characters get trapped into Main-Street-romance by empty situations and assumptions. Even at their lowest, they wish not to be low. They are still able to yearn for an ideal, even though they violate the ideal. Even Elmer Gantry, at the depth of foulness, knows he did not mean to become what he has become. The Ideal is always asserted in Sinclair Lewis' books. He is not a howler and wailer proclaiming: "All is lost."

It will pay the young writer in search of a voice and a vision to read these three satirists. The literature of which you are to become a part is one of the world's greatest. These satirists are foundation stones in the twentieth-century portion of that literature.

# SINGING THROUGH THE DARK

YOU CAN FEEL our writers searching as you read through their now-nearly-hundred-year-old pages. They stood at the beginning of the bloodiest century in history, and some already felt the movement of darkness. At the opening of the century, they could not predict World War I, or American involvement. Europe was a long way off. Steamships still carried auxiliary sail.

They could not know of World War II, or of monsters named Hitler, Stalin, Beria, Mussolini. They had intuition about such matters, because plenty of ghosts and specters appear long before World War I arrived and confirmed such things in the neighborhood.

In the middle of vast change, some of our writers must have felt they were the last moral force alive. They must have looked everywhere, tested every new sight and sound, trying to make sense of events. They did not quite understand that another crack-up was in progress.

The crack-up came because Victorian morality had altered, to become servile to Victorian style. When style became queen, and morality its handmaiden, morals no longer supported ethics.

## FAILURE OF RELIGION

Signal fires of change blazed high, heralding more trouble for religion and its possible contributions than all the writings of Charles Darwin and Sigmund Freud combined. Religion failed as a moral and ethical structure because it lost entertainment value.

The most dangerous hazard for religion came with the rise of communications. This rise brought new forms of entertainment that dealt a dreadful blow to the evangelicals. This is how the job was done:

Earlier we saw how the First Amendment to the Constitution separates church and state. Equally important, it guarantees freedom of religion. In America, this automatically meant churches were in competition with each other. America owned no "state church" as in England (Church of England), Norway (Lutheran), Italy (Catholic). Religions had to compete for customers.

In the past, American religions depended on doctrine, community (congregation), the social structure, and, importantly, entertainment. From 1620 onward, church on Sunday would serve as a main form of "getting together," and even enjoyment, for the majority.

With rise of communications, and ability to travel by rail, and then by automobile, entertainment became available to great numbers who might otherwise have settled for church. As cities grew, and as cars became common, people could attend plays, musical performances, or join lodges. Player pianos, phonographs, and, finally, radios, served as sources of entertainment. While religion still concerned itself with good and bad behavior, and with hellfire sermons against "demon rum" and other iniquities, it gradually lost its entertainment value. Little wonder that preachers of the period did such a tremendous amount of yelling. They tried—and you may be sure many of them were good men and true, if of small sensibility—to outshout the Devil.

## THE SINGERS

Balances shifted. While satirists tried to save what was good as they skewered what was bad, poets picked up where religion left off. Poets were among the major storytellers. Since poetry deals in image and emotion, it is perfectly suited to appeal to unanswered religious impulses, as well as supplying entertainment.

The poem-as-story was fairly new in our literature, although not new in our Western tradition.[1] Before the American Revolution, poetry was

---

[1]Storytelling, as we saw earlier, rises from the ancient past and was originally done in rhyme, as in *The Song of Roland*.

generally constrained, often religious and formal. Either that, or it was out-and-out doggerel, suitable to the aims of revolution. It might make good propaganda, but was to poetry what "Yankee Doodle" is to music, which is to say, just barely.[2]

After the Revolution, and until the Civil War, poetry in America ranged widely. The most popular poet was Henry Wadsworth Longfellow. Many other poets told stories. Some of the best known were Edgar Allan Poe, James Russell Lowell, and John Greenleaf Whittier.

## Henry Wadsworth Longfellow

Longfellow stands at the firm base of American storytelling in poetry. He was enormously popular. He could run language around the block, chase it up a tree, get it to climb across rooftops, then jump down to a dock and take passage on the good ship *Hesperus*. A lot of his stuff was romantic to the point of sentimentality. Nonetheless, more than any other poet he made poetry not only popular in the American home, but a necessity. His greatest popularity came before the Civil War. He bequeathed a legacy of storytelling to poets who came after the Civil War.

Longfellow set the stage for a major rash of great poets in the late-nineteenth and early-twentieth centuries. There is not enough space here to examine them all, but six storytellers among them are representative: Edwin Arlington Robinson, Edgar Lee Masters, Robert Frost, Carl Sandburg, Edna St. Vincent Millay, and Sidney Lanier, who died in 1881, but who belongs with this crowd. With Lanier, we may pause on behalf of an important point.

As we've seen, storytelling is a form of history. When you pick up a book, you pick up a piece of history even if the story was written only last year. In the role of historian, the storyteller has to mull facts, feel their weights, find their shape in relation to the story. Thus, the story published in 1888 may have been shaping for the writer's entire life, which in Lanier's case began in 1842. When we look at historical periods, it pays to remember that stories told during the period were shaped after considerable experience on the part of the storytellers. For

---

[2]An interesting sidelight: "Yankee Doodle" was originally a British song making fun of the awkward American colonists. The colonists, in a sassy mood, swiped it.

this reason, the "literary periods" we speak of are really only conveniences. Thus, separating writers by period rather than content is generally a mistake.

## Sidney Lanier

Lanier, who died young, lived before most of the twentieth-century poets who accompany him. If Longfellow set the stage for twentieth-century poets, Lanier set a foundation that would be best expressed in a period to which he is not supposed to belong. He asked poetry to extend beyond regions and across the nation. While Walt Whitman, the great generalist, sounded his "barbaric yawp across the world," Lanier, heavily romantic, talked about something more specific. Poetry might be about a certain town, or region, but its expression had to be one that included human experience within the entire nation.

Lanier was a concert musician who tried to combine music with poetry. Originally from Georgia, and a member of the Confederate Army, he died of tuberculosis contracted in a Union prison camp. In the poem "The Stirrup-Cup," Lanier knows he's dying. He uses a regional metaphor to examine the experience of all who face death. The stirrup-cup is a cup, almost always of sterling silver, used to drink toasts after a foxhunt.

### "The Stirrup-Cup"

Death, thou'rt a cordial old and rare:
Look how compounded, with what care!
Time got his wrinkles reaping thee
Sweet herbs from all antiquity.

David to thy distillage went,
Keats, and Gotama excellent,
Omar Khayyam, and Chaucer bright,
And Shakspere for a kind-dellight.

Then, Time, let not a drop be spilt:
Hand me the cup whene'er thou wilt;
'Tis thy rich stirrup-cup to me;
I'll drink it down right smilingly.

Lanier's legacy is displayed by Robinson and Frost of New England, and by Masters and Sandburg, who would both begin in or around Galesburg, Illinois. Millay, who also displays the legacy, originated not so much from place as from the pure breath of poetry applied to great human experiences. Her poem "Spring" is reprinted here, not because it is a story (although one can infer a story), but because it so perfectly captures the tone and style of much that was going on:

> To what purpose, April, do you return again?
> Beauty is not enough.
> You can no longer quiet me with the redness
> Of little leaves opening stickily.
> I know what I know.
> The sun is hot on my neck as I observe
> The spikes of the crocus.
> The smell of earth is good.
> It is apparent that there is no death.
> But what does that signify?
> Not only under ground are the brains of men
> Eaten by maggots.
> Life in itself
> Is nothing,
> An empty cup, a flight of uncarpeted stairs.
> It is not enough that yearly, down this hill,
> April,
> Comes like an idiot, babbling and strewing flowers.

If one is a great poet, that is the sort of poem one writes after a day that has been real bad, and also very good. It is a poem written when one suspects that chaos, and eternal night, hover just over the horizon. Darkness and hope characterize the period. Here is the same play, second act, in the theater run by Edwin Arlington Robinson:

### "Credo"

> I cannot find my way: there is no star
> In all the shrouded heavens anywhere;
> And there is not a whisper in the air
> Of any living voice but one so far

That I can hear it only as a bar
Of lost, imperial music, played when far
And angel fingers wove, and unaware,
Dead leaves to garlands where no roses are.

No, there is not a glimmer, nor a call,
For one that welcomes, welcomes when he fears,
The black and awful chaos of the night,
For through it all—above, beyond it all—
I know the far-sent message of the years,
I feel the coming glory of the light.

It is impossible to write iambic pentameter more smoothly than this. Meanwhile, a later poem, but same play, third act, in the theater of Robert Frost:

## "Come In"

As I came to the edge of the woods,
Thrush music—hark!
Now if it was dusk outside,
Inside it was dark.

Too dark in the woods for a bird
By sleight of wing
To better its perch for the night,
Though it still could sing.

The last of the light of the sun
That had died in the west
Still lived for one song more
In a thrush's breast.

Far in the pillared dark
Thrush music went—
Almost like a call to come in
To the dark and lament.

But no, I was out for stars:
I would not come in.
I meant not even if asked,
And I hadn't been.

If a writer wishes to get in touch with the depth and quality of human emotion, Millay and Robinson and Frost are good places to begin.

Millay's stories, like those of many poets, are often inferential. Frost, Sandburg, Robinson, and Masters just plain-out told stories. If their poetry was inferential, the inferences came on top of the story, not before.[3]

## LINKS TO THE PURITAN PAST

Our poets were firm echoes from the beginnings of American thought. Frost and Robinson are Puritans, but modern Puritans, looking for the writer's place in the new world forming. They show darkness of the American night, and they hold Puritan adherence to the idea that sensibleness can be found in form. They use meter and rhyme. They are unafraid of sonnets, and while anyone can tinker up a sonnet, only the bravest and best can write good ones.

They keep pointing out darkness and light. They write about the push and pull of good and evil as the century opens. Their world changes, and they say, "Yes, this is darkness. I suggest that everyone gets off his bucket and makes sure things do not get darker." And, they say, "Yes, this is light, and the human race has a real hard time keeping it lit; but if some of you folks want to apply yourselves by turning up the lamp, we will certainly not interfere." These storytelling poets are not preachers talking about what people should do. They tell stories showing how we all make choices.

If choices dump their characters into destruction, that is sad, but also true. If choices bring their characters to some spiritual understanding, or even to a noble heart, then that is also true, and doubtless preferred.

John Calvin would have been angered by this, since it suggests that predestination is nothing but old, cold soup. Martin Luther would probably claim this is what he talked about all along; i.e., individual responsibility. Robinson and Frost are as old, in some ways, as the Reformation. They were, however, dressed in modern clothing, speak-

---

[3]Another poet, most fascinating, was Amy Lowell, who could and did tell stories. She sometimes ran off the rails and wasted time in literary wars, her chief opponent an odd sort of fellow named Ezra Pound. It was a mistake for both of them. It is always a mistake when writers gang up on each other.

ing to a world of confusion, a world already hungering for order even as Victorianism died.

## LINKS TO THE QUAKER PAST

Sandburg and Masters are as old as Original Possibility, as old as the Quakers. They call on small towns and big cities to be great small towns and great cities. They are realists enough, recognizing the hardness of lives. They also recognize the greatness of the human heart. Here is Edgar Lee Masters, giving a nearly perfect example of how they wrote in a selection from his *Spoon River Anthology*:

### "Lucinda Matlock"

I went to the dances at Chandlerville,
And played snap-out at Winchester.
One time we changed partners,
Driving home in the moonlight of middle June,
And then I found Davis.
We were married and lived together for seventy years,
Enjoying, working, raising the twelve children,
Eight of whom we lost
Ere I had reached the age of sixty.
I spun, I wove, I kept the house, I nursed the sick,
I made the garden, and for holiday
Rambled over the fields where sang the larks,
And by Spoon River gathering many a shell,
And many a flower and medicinal weed—
Shouting to the wooded hills, singing to the green valleys,
At ninety-six I had lived enough, that is all,
And passed to a sweet repose.
What is this I hear of sorrow and weariness,
Anger, discontent and drooping hopes?
Degenerate sons and daughters,
Life is too strong for you—
It takes life to love Life.

I am reminded of this poem each time I hear young writers complain that our art is so hard to learn. It is sometimes necessary to remind them that happiness is not a right. The only right is the right to pursue happiness. It may help young writers and artists to hear that, if your art is pursued courageously enough, you almost always catch happiness. And, in catching, discover you somehow also learned the art.

## Carl Sandburg

More than any other poet, even Allen Ginsberg, Sandburg combines the overarching voice of Whitman with the power of storytelling. It's possible to pick up his great epic, *The People, Yes*, and find echoes of Whitman, as well as images that remain constant in our language. Here is a small excerpt:

> The little girl saw her first troop parade and asked,
>   "What are those?"
> "Soldiers."
> "What are soldiers?"
> "They are for war. They fight and each tries to kill
>       as many of the other side as he can."
> The little girl held still and studied.
> "Do you know . . . I know something?"
> "Yes, what is it you know?"
> "Sometime they'll give a war and nobody will come."
>
>   One of the early Chicago poets,
> One of the slouching underslung Chicago poets,
> Having only the savvy God gave him,
> Lacking a gat, lacking brass knucks,
> Having one lead pencil to spare, wrote:
>       "I am credulous about the destiny of man,
>       and I believe more than I can ever prove
>       of the future of the human race
>       and the importance of illusions,
>       the value of great expectations.
>       I would like to be in the same moment
>       an earthworm (which I am) and
>       a rider to the moon (which I am). . . .

# THE MARCH TOWARD ANOTHER
# CRACK-UP AND WAR

THE FIRST SEVENTEEN years of this century, before America jumped, or was dumped, into World War I, were prelude to crack-up of Victorianism. Victorianism cracked from outside forces in addition to internal pressures from its own rigid style. Three major forces were

> Inventions produced a new technology.
> Nationalism rose because of technology.
> Two modes of thought, Evolution and Psychology, could no longer be ignored or suppressed.

## INVENTION

These early years of the century, and those decades just preceding them, are rightly thought of as times of invention. Young giants walked the American scene sowing innovations as the mythical Jason once sowed dragon's teeth. These were days of Thomas Edison, George Eastman, and Alexander Graham Bell. They were, in fact, days when the keel for the entire twentieth century was laid: communications, technology of war, transportation, and, even, measurement of the speed of light. If American writing bloomed after the Civil War, an equal blooming occurred in invention.

Invention is the egg that hatches the chicken that lays the egg that hatches the chicken that brings forth all sorts of squawking things:

some admirable, some utilitarian, and some disgusting. In your life it has become popular to blame the products of invention for ills ranging from stunted growth of catnip to global warming. Complainers then turn around and bemoan the fact that the automobile, for example, was ever invented. That is an easy answer.

Inventors are not responsible when matters turn disgusting. Inventors develop an idea, and are responsible for the development. The society then takes the result of that development for its own, but often can't handle the responsibility. Thus, while Bell invented the telephone, we cannot blame him for scams run from boiler rooms. Or, on a lighter note, while Edison invented the phonograph, we cannot blame him for Christmas vocals by Liberace, or instrumentals by rock guitarists.

Here are a few of the inventions between 1865 and World War I:

> *Communications:* Typewriter, rotary press to print both sides of a page, modern photography including roll film and artificial light, telephone, mimeograph, stenotype machine, telephone switchboard, linotype machine, phonograph, radio tube, fountain pen, color photography, adding machine, comptometer, punch-card processing, wireless telegraphy, cathode-ray tube, and wire recorder (forerunner of tape recorder).
> *Weapons:* Machine gun, replaceable parts for weapons, steel processing enabling manufacture of modern artillery, smokeless powder, and hard and soft extraction of spent casings from the smallest rifle to the largest cannon. Not all of this originated in America, but all of it was revised, improved, and would be used by America.
> *Transportation:* Roads. Automobiles. Bicycles.

These last three were not American inventions, either, but American inventors preempted them and set about making improvements.[1]

---

[1]Macadam invented by John Loudon McAdam, Scotland, 1815; bicycle, the "safety" bicycle, J. K. Starley, England, 1885; automobile, Karl Benz and Gottlieb Daimler, Germany, 1885. They worked independently. The first vehicle running under its own power dates to 1769, when a French officer of artillery, Nicolas Joseph Cugnot, built a steam-powered, three-wheeled carriage to tow cannon.

The story of transportation in the late-nineteenth and early-twentieth centuries concerns introduction of cars and building of roads. Our nation did not build roads until

Innovations promised an amazing world, although the American world was not accustomed to thinking about such matters. Mechanical innovation was both drastic and new. Through most of history, mechanics had changed very little. In the eighteenth century, for example, the plow that turned soil was substantially the same type in use for two thousand years. In the eighteenth century, a simple household utensil, the fork, was known only among the upper class, and even then forks were brought out only when company visited.[2] Many signers of the Declaration of Independence had never seen a pencil, and those who had did not use the things because, at the time, they were crumbly and almost worthless. The great bulk of Western history is made up of people going about life in exactly the way their grandparents and parents went about life.

Because of invention, it appeared that twentieth-century society would surely break down, or possibly up. (It did both.) Customs would change. Even the English language would alter. Doomsayers and bleak prophets hung around the scene. In other words, matters stood about the same in the 1890s as in the 1990s, where legislators holler that English must be made an official language, or that immigration will destroy the American character.

## TECHNOLOGY

By the turn of the century, invention had produced a unified creature called "technology." Technology is more than the sum of its machinery and inventions. Technology is a force, and it produces ways of thinking. For example: Before widespread availability of electric light through the countryside (starting in 1937), it never occurred to people that some work could be done after dark, for the very good reason that it could not. When people planned work, they automatically thought in terms of seasonal light.

Technology heralded conceptual changes that went far beyond the

---

the advent of the modern bicycle because no one understood the notion of a day's trip for anything except business. When the modern bike was imported from England, the nation went more than a little crazy over the things. Roads began running everywhere. A splendid history is John B. Rae, *The American Automobile* (University of Chicago Press, 1965).

[2] A delightful rhyme from early America goes: I eat my peas with honey/I've done it all my life/It makes the peas taste funny/But it keeps them on my knife.

varities of work. Technology produced new forms of entertainment. It gave new perspectives to global business. Finally, it affected the way people perceived their lives. The effect came because technological changes demanded a whole new metaphor for civilization. No one understood this better than Henry Adams.

## Henry Adams

Adams was a storyteller, but first of all was an historian. In *The Education of Henry Adams* and in *Mont-Saint-Michel and Chartres,* Adams sums the story of the Western world, or at least of that world's beliefs. *The Education* is a story told to friends. *Mont-Saint-Michel* is a story told to a favorite niece.

Adams understood that changes in technology heralded changes of faith. In a famous passage from *The Education,* he examines the spiritual power of the Virgin Mary, as opposed to the mere force of the modern dynamo (symbol of technology). The Virgin Mary was spirit, thus power. The dynamo was only energy.

In *Mont-Saint-Michel and Chartres* Adams shows how Saint Michael, guardian and champion of the eleventh century, gave way to adoration of the Virgin Mary in the twelfth and thirteenth. The Virgin conquered Europe. The spiritual power of religious adoration set the tone for thought through all centuries from the twelfth to the nineteenth.

The combination of the two books gave this sum: The world abandons spiritual power on behalf of mechanical energy.

I will leave the accuracy of Adams' ideas to your reasoned judgment. My own judgment holds that Adams would help preserve America, not by denunciation, but by reminder that not all faith is founded in falsity, and that the human spirit transcends the machine.

### NATIONALISM

In the early part of this century, technology produced feelings of enormous strength among Americans. Machines allowed them to produce all sorts of other machines. Communications equipment allowed them to exchange information at incredible rates (when compared to the past). At the same time, Americans were dreadfully uneasy because of change. Sad to say, those feelings of strength combined with uncertainty and caused the rise of nationalism.

Nationalism is patriotism taken to narrow extremes. It is a form of prejudice and can be summed up in the following statement: "My country is precious and true. Everything else stinks."

Nationalism is not peculiar to America. All nations go through occasional fits of nationalism, and in all nations nationalism looks about the same. Strength (or the illusion of strength) combines with uncertainty. Uncertain people tend to yell a lot, and yelling raises tension.

The psychology of what happens next is simple: An excited person looks into someone else's face, sees his own excitement reflected in the other person's face, and becomes more excited. The other person, seeing rising excitement, then reflects more excitement. People bounce excitement back and forth, and tension builds.[3]

Nationally, tension propels social and political forces into action, and sometimes those forces head for war. In the early part of this century, nationalism set America up for World War I, as we'll shortly see; a war that became our third-largest bloodbath.[4]

## EVOLUTION AND PSYCHOLOGY

The other important reason for the coming crack-up of Victorianism was reaction to evolution and psychology. Evolutionary theory had been around for forty years, but the American people pretty much told

---

[3]This is the way mobs form. This is how lynchings begin, and how race riots take shape.

[4]I must give these unhappy figures sooner or later, so might as well give them now and be done with it. These are estimated American deaths in service for all of our wars:

American Revolution, 4,000
War of 1812, 2,000
Indian Wars, 1,000
Mexican War, 13,000
Civil War
    Union, 364,000
    Confederate 133,821
Spanish-American War, 11,000
World War I, 116,000
World War II, 406,000
Korean War, 55,000
Vietnam War, 109,000
Persian Gulf War, 3,115

Source: Department of Veterans' Affairs

themselves to let the preachers think about it. Psychology in America derived, in large part, from the work of the brilliant psychologist and philosopher William James. His work stemmed from evolutionary theory.[5]

Also as the new century opened, the European psychologists Bleuler, Jung, Adler, and Freud stood in the wings. Freudian psychology would soon become a fad. Evolution and psychology would come to be regarded as entities, not ideas.

## THE PROBLEM

Great numbers of people thought of these ideas as real creatures, as real as the Devil among the old Puritans of Salem. To other people they were vehicles on which a person might ride to wealth or freedom or sexual satisfaction. The popular mind did not think of them as concepts. For that reason it is probably well for us to think of them as influences. As influences, they were as disruptive to American peace of mind as was socialism. It worked this way:

Some folks avoided abstractions. They pictured their god as an eye in the sky, or an old man sitting on a cloud. They reduced evolution to the simple statement "Men came from apes." Psychology was "head-shrinking."[6]

Lacking abstraction, it's easy to take a complicated idea and reduce it to the level—if not the content—of prejudice. When such thinking ran rampant in years preceding World War I, it combined with nationalism. The reaction was fevered restlessness, insistence on the most conservative values, and the bombast it takes to lead a nation into war.

---

[5]James published *The Principles of Psychology* (1890), *The Will to Believe* (1897), *The Varieties of Religious Experience* (1902), and *Pragmatism* (1907). Pragmatism is an intricate philosophy holding that we operate on "truth" as we perceive it through the conjoining of facts ("conjunctive relations") from our experience. In general, we choose our "truth" based on what is expedient in light of our experience. It was a philosophy embraced by people who saw it as an easy answer for justifying all behavior, good or bad. William James, of course, would be appalled by such simple adaptations of a complex set of ideas.

[6]One task of the modern storyteller is to display abstract concepts in some, or, if lucky, all their mysteriousness. This task lies at the root of the fantastic. The modern storyteller does this because electronic forms either cannot, or will not. Television is about as abstract as a boot, movies somewhat better, but rarely, and theater is generally best when it goes for realism.

Refusing to think about the issues it truly feared, America took its anxiety about change and threw it against the German kaiser; the hated Hun.

It could have been a lot worse. America was a latecomer to World War I, not arriving until 1917.

## WORLD WAR I

In 1914 the Western world self-destructed. Historians still argue over the origins, but the classic account, *World War I,* by British historian S. L. A. Marshall, is doubtless correct. Europe had been arming since the end of the Franco-Prussian War in January 1871. The most dangerous part of armament was the machine gun. Almost no one understood it, especially the French.[7]

War came because, although no one—with the exception of Count Leopold von Berchtold of Austria—wanted war, everyone thought *others* wanted war. Lack of communication, a few well-pointed lies by Berchtold, and temporary absence of leaders from the seats of power combined to produce the world's first major war with modern weapons.

Casualties were incredible. No one could imagine the results of poor strategy and tactics combined with barbed wire and machine guns. In less than six months, what with the battles of Verdun and Jutland, France would lose 550,000 men, and England 400,000. Total military deaths for the war, all nations: 8,538,315. Total wounded: 21,219,452. Total missing or taken prisoner: 7,750,919. Total military casualties: 37,494,186.[8]

I find no reliable figure on civilian casualties, although I expect 50 million, military and civilian (the majority of civilians, Russian), would not be out of line.

This does not include victims of the influenza epidemic of 1918, which probably originated in Russia, and which was carried to America by our returning soldiers. Total deaths worldwide were 22 million, of which 10 million died in Europe and 6 million in India.

If we include victims of epidemic as war losses, 548,000 Americans

---

[7]A record of the nineteenth-century arms race that produced enormous cannon, and the machine gun, is contained in William Manchester, *The Arms of Krupp* (Little, Brown & Company, 1964).

[8]Source: U.S. War Department estimate.

died of the disease, bringing our total to 664,000. It's a rare war that does not kill more people from disease than gunfire.

There's no need to rehash that war, but it's worthwhile knowing the mood of our people. Writers would have to deal with that mood, and do their share in fashioning new shapes for a nation as it embarked on one of the most chaotic centuries in history.

## AMERICA RESPONDS TO WAR

As war opened in Europe, the noise level in America was already rising. As we've seen, automobiles were more numerous. Construction of roads, and improvements of streets, boomed, even in small towns. Preachers declared holy war against evolution. Evolutionists, not one whit brighter, vowed to wipe religion from the face of the earth. Socialists and communists yammered, while unions held strikes, some bloody. Strikers died. Anarchists killed people. The women's movement became electric, demanding suffrage. More people were leaving farms for the cities. Hubbub filled our streets.

Some people turned to war with anticipation, or even with relief, because war serves a goodly number. If it did not, we would quit having wars. War brings excitement during dull times. War also allows a lot of people to make a lot of money. When times are chaotic, war simplifies matters. While many Americans wanted no involvement at the beginning of World War I, plenty of loudmouths wanted to "plant Old Glory on the worn-out turf of every European country, and let America rule the world."

President Woodrow Wilson tried to avoid war. He actually won a second term on the slogan "He kept us out of war." Then Germany forced his hand. Many Americans backed Germany, at least in the beginning. If Germany had played smartly, it might have kept the United States from entering the war, because America at first had not chosen sides.

Germany did stupid things and England did smart things. Briefly: Germany denied journalists access to the front. It treated journalists poorly. England, on the other hand, treated journalists like kings. They were sent to the front in cars and were given staff officers to explain events. Naturally, reports from the British and French sides glowed. Reports from Germany did not.

H. G. Wells coined the phrase "The War to end all Wars." Many people bought the idea, a goodly number of them Americans.

England, with the agreement of Wilson (who finally accepted inevitable American involvement), opened a propaganda campaign in America. It spent $5 million, quite a lot in days when $20 a week was a good wage. People called "Four-Minute Men" crossed the country giving little speeches about German atrocities. They whipped up war sentiment, and newspapers did the same.[9]

Germany seemed almost suicidal. It declared a war zone around Britain and promised to destroy any shipping that transported war material. Wilson objected. Germany sank the tanker *Gulflight*. Wilson objected. Germany sank the liner *Lusitania*. Wilson objected. All of this happened in 1915, while America sat unprepared for war. The country divided between "preparedness" people, and people who still wanted to stay out.

By then, two hundred American lives had been lost because of the ship sinkings. Germany announced unrestricted warfare on all shipping. The fat hit the fire. After the election in 1916, America began to prepare. Even now, I think of what happened with deepest sorrow.

As I write this, a picture from World War I hangs on the wall behind my computer. It is a picture that was probably sold in dime stores. It shows ignorant innocence, and ignorant idealism. The picture is of a young doughboy in full uniform. He carries his rifle. He stands beside a white gate. Trees and a white house stand in the background. He is closing the gate. Inside the gate stands a beautiful hunting dog. The caption beneath the picture reads: "Not this trip, old pal."

For a while, it seemed the American people, whipped into a frenzy of patriotism, were each-and-every-one as innocent as that picture. That is not true, but seems so. Still, the majority of our people were like kids lining up to see a Frankenstein movie. They expected to go inside, sit in the dark, be deliciously thrilled for an hour or two, then step back into sunlight.

It didn't work that way. The movie ground on and on. Trench warfare gave way to something new, called a tank. Ordnance echoed

---

[9]A full account is contained in Phillip Knightly, *The First Casualty* (Harcourt Brace Jovanovich, 1975). Knightly is an English journalist. His book is a history of the war correspondent.

around the world.[10] Europe was bled white, its young men dead, an entire generation consumed in one great arterial flow of blood. America began to bleed. The movie ground on and on, then stopped; and there was no victory.

The best words to describe the ending of World War I come from a story written before the Civil War. This is the ending of Poe's "The Masque of the Red Death":

"And the life of the ebony clock went out with that of the last of the gay. And the flames of the tripods expired. And Darkness and Decay and the Red Death held illimitable dominion over all."

I've already given the casualty figures.

---

[10]To this day farmers in Belgium and France are still sometimes killed when their plows hit an unexploded World War I shell.

# THE 1920S; THE PIVOTAL
# DECADE

ILLUSIONS ABOUT THE War to End all Wars faded among power plays that produced the Treaty of Versailles in 1919. The treaty-writers, especially France and England, wanted revenge on Germany. The American president wanted a League of Nations, and equitable settlement.[1] A great deal of wrangling ensued. The treaty that resulted was not awful, but it was pretty bad. The League of Nations came into being, but Congress kept America from joining.

As American soldiers came home, and as President Wilson faltered with illness (and what appears in hindsight to have been monomania about the League of Nations), America turned to other matters. Some of those matters were reactions to war. The American people, and American writers and artists of all kinds, were left to sort out the aftermath. A great flowering of art was about to begin. It would help protect the nation from national leaders who contributed more confusion than leadership.

One of the worst was a copper-plated, double-dyed son-of-marriage between a klaxon horn and a billy club, one A. Mitchell Palmer, attorney general, a weird sort of Quaker who started a witch-hunt. He went after "Reds" because the baddest "bad people" of the world were communists. Palmer argued sweetly that what happened in Russia would happen in America if he and his minions did not save the coun-

---

[1]The League of Nations was a forerunner of the United Nations.

try. In 1920 he ordered people arrested and held without charges. Habeas corpus meant nothing.[2] At one point, Palmer had five hundred people picked up, held without charges, and not one thing was ever proven against any of them. This sort of red-baiting would continue, off and on, through most of the century. Palmer, who was the sort of man who makes you want to believe in Hell, would pass to his reward in 1936.

Another reaction to war's aftermath was expansion of the Ku Klux Klan. Its membership grew far greater in the North than South. It rose as a result of hate-mongering in which Henry Ford, among others, participated.

Ford targeted Jews, and once more pulled out the old flapdoodle that claimed Jews were in conspiracy to blow up civilization and own the world. A second scoundrel stood in the wings waiting for a way to broadcast his message of hate. We'll see Father Coughlin, priest of Royal Oak, carry his saccharine hatred against Jews, but we'll have to wait until radio gets established.

A third reaction was despair. Something called "The Lost Generation" appeared, and it would cause joy among literary critics of the next several decades. Literary critics are best left to their own devices since, these days, too many are only critical of each other. This business of "generations," though, is worth a short digression.

## GENERATIONS

The idea of a "Lost Generation" or a "Beat Generation" or a "love generation" or a "generation X" has little to do with people in a particular generation. In addition, the idea of "generations" as distinct entities cannot bear close scrutiny. People do not reproduce by gener-

---

[2]Habeas corpus (a "right" to the body) substantially means that the government must have an arrest warrant in order to pick you off the street or out of your house—unless police see you actually engaged in crime. It means that you cannot be held in jail unless you are charged with a crime. It is part of the constitutional guarantee against unjust imprisonment, and it stems from English common law as early as the fifteenth century.

Habeas corpus meant little during World War I. People were arrested for being pacifists, for saying the Allies were in for hard sledding, for saying Germany was efficient; in other words, any statement not amounting to mindless support of Allied causes justified arrest. The United States, while holding another witch-hunt, somewhat resembled totalitarian powers it would war against in the 1940s.

ations. They reproduce by intent, or by accident. Occasionally, social conditions are such that more time and motivation are available, and can be put toward intents and accidents. When that happens, a bulge appears in the census figures.

The terms "lost," or "60s," or "X" are convenient handles we use to describe a trend in society, and not an actual mass of people. Only a few people—usually around 5 percent—actively represent the trend. In the 1960s, for example, the so-called revolutionary movement was mostly confined to college campuses, and not all of them. The majority of students concentrated on their educations. During demonstrations, those students might attend and watch. Although only a very small percentage of students were actively engaged in demonstration, something important was happening. A large social trend occurred, and brought change, and we sum up by designating it a "generation." End of digression.

## THE "LOST GENERATION"

The Lost Generation was a mythical group of young people who felt betrayed. They were not quite sure what gave them a sense of betrayal. They blamed it on war. They blamed it on the shallowness of American society and culture. (They were old enough to know something of society, not old enough to comprehend the reach of the culture.) They blamed their parents, of course, because it seems one must when one is young. They greatly undervalued the entire history of the Occident, but the "mysterious East" was too much trouble to understand. In consequence, a few turned to art and letters. Most shrugged, dressed casually, and joined in revolt against Victorianism. In short, they started to have a party with singing and dancing, jazz and booze; about which more in a moment.

Young writers and painters did what young artists must. They struggled to gain control of their craft. In the 1920s, many of them hung out with a group of expatriate Americans in Paris. The action centered around a salon run by Gertrude Stein. She was not a storyteller. She was, however, a lover of art and language. She had definite ideas about language, and the power of language when used in ways beyond the swing-and-sway-of-everyday. You may wish to read her *What Are Masterpieces, and Why Are There So Few of Them?*. If you are twenty years old when you read it, I can almost certify that you will be cussing before finishing the first page. It's okay. By the time you are thirty, it will begin to make sense. By the time you become an aged person, you'll understand it, and be thankful.

As a group, it is difficult to take lost writers of the period very seriously because they weren't lost. We take them seriously because they did a good job. The idea of being lost in some special way, while being a writer or painter, doesn't work. If you're an artist, you feel lost in the first place and are fighting your way out. Nothing unusual about it. In addition, there is so much work that, although you may feel lost, you don't have time to be lost. We leave such matters to those bohemian elements who chug red wine, eat raw onions, burn candles at only one end, and talk interminably about Dada and Nietzsche.

## THE DECADE

Members of the Paris group would gain their voices in the late 1920s and through the 1930s, days when those voices were badly needed. We'll see them after we look at the decade, and a main influence that rose from the decade. After all, it would be a shame to brush past the most important decade of the twentieth century, and a near crime to pass up the seed of destruction that appeared with radio. Let us first look at radio, which is a symbol of the 1920s, and of the entire twentieth century.

## RADIO AND ITS LEGACY

The first commercial radio station was KDKA in Pittsburgh (1920), owned by a tiny outfit named Radio Corporation of America (RCA). That fact, and what came of it, explains at least half of American antics during the rest of the century.

Those antics would center around mass entertainment, and the vast American entertainment/amusement industry. They are best symbolized by two of the century's premier figures, Donald and Daffy Duck; not radio figures, but with web feet paddling in the pond of entertainment; a pond that began with the advent of commercial radio. At first the pond filled slowly. An older way of life still prevailed.

Use your artist's imagination. Imagine a world in which exists no electronic sound, and in most places no sound of engines. In 1920, people still heard the clop of horses, the rolling of carriage and wagon wheels, the murmur of voices. No one heard electric sirens, or the click of a stoplight changing red to green.[3] Music might arrive because someone in a neighborhood played a piano, or a church choir practiced. Sounds of civilization might include newsboys yelling headlines, or striking workers yelling at cops, or cops pushing people around—but nothing electronic.

This means that whatever happened, happened locally. A big world might lie out there, but people did not hear its voice. People did not feel connected except through newspapers.

Then—and suddenly—they could sit in small-town Maine or Kansas and hear live music played from Los Angeles. Connection to the greater world seemed on the order of a miracle.

Great power came with radio. Almost everyone listened. Some immediately learned "broadcasting." Others tied into ham radio. In the 1920s, the country went sincerely crazy over radio. The difference between then and now is that communication in the 1920s largely went from broadcaster to listener, a one-way street.[4] In the 1920s, the remarkable stride "forward," as represented by radio, came because of possibilities for entertainment.

Great optimism came as part of the package. Before radio, the average worker did not have money to afford first-class entertainment, although plenty of second-class entertainment abounded. Gramophones had been available but reproduction was poor.

Symphonies, operas, and theater were luxuries. Radio promised to amend the situation. Anyone who could afford a radio could now afford Culture. For a short while, radio actually did spread such culture—at least, with music.

Two problems rose. First: not enough culture was available. An inexhaustible supply of great music does not exist. Neither exists an inexhaustible supply of great literature. Second, even when supplies are bountiful, audiences divide, because of taste or lack of it. For example,

---

[3]The first stoplights in New York City appeared in 1928. They were ornamented with the bronze figure of a baseball player.

[4]Radio is limited because it goes in only one direction, broadcaster to listener, unless, of course, one can credit "talk radio," which is generally infantile, and heavily programmed. Computers, on the other hand, can communicate on the Internet in both directions, but are more or less limited to transmission of information; at least, that seems their best present use. Unlike radio, the Internet is not a very good carrier of emotional, humorous, or intuitive content.

I am not a big fan of Shakespearean comedy, although I'm a great fan of Shakespeare. I enjoy *The Tempest,* but if *Much Ado* is playing, my tasteless self would rather hear baseball.

Even that would be okay, except radio is a commercial proposition. The greatest number of listeners produce the greatest amount of revenue, and one thing predictable in our world is that bad taste resides with us always. As stations multiplied with the enthusiasm of goats, the fight for listeners turned nasty. Radio learned the code governing electronic entertainment:

1. Broadcast nothing of merit. Go for the groin.
2. Having gone for the groin, use sensationalism.
3. If sensationalism doesn't work, go for giggles.
4. It is impossible to overestimate the drawing power of babies, puppies, and breasts.
5. It is impossible to underestimate the intelligence of the average listener/viewer.[5]

As radio spread clatter and chatter across the nation, legitimate theater held its own, and even prospered. The movie industry blossomed in 1927 with the first talking picture, *The Jazz Singer.* Music became radiant with Gershwin, Ellington, and a parade of some of the best musicians the world has ever heard. Poetry, fiction, essays, and even some aspects of journalism contributed steadiness to the culture.[6] Architecture, and art nouveau, threw out Victorian roses, then produced graceful and well-stated lines. Meanwhile, radio puzzled, figuring out its code.

As the century rolled toward economic depression, then war, then television, the code would become rigid. A large segment of the American people would sink into the great jelly roll that is the American amusement industry. Demand for amusement would begin to outrank all other demands. As the century rolled toward old age, if not wisdom,

---

[5]I once listened to a television writer address a group of writers. He said exactly this: "When you write for television you must think like a baboon, because you are writing for baboons." He made the further point that nothing can be allowed on television that cannot be understood by the average twelve-year-old.

[6]One of our most brilliant journalists, Walter Lippmann, published *A Preface to Morals.* It didn't please the hidebound, but it has pleased and informed thoughtful people since 1929.

valid entertainment pandered its way down to the bottom levels of the popular mind, and thus became only amusement. Institutions began to change. Teachers, preachers, politicians, and, even, army generals were expected to perform with all the flair of stand-up comedians.[7]

"But," (you may say) "surely he makes too much of this. I confess that I am fond of Daffy Duck."

And why not? After all, daffiness is a part of the human condition, and the duck is only a cartoon. The problem is not the duck, but the debilitating force of amusement in the society. It was debilitating in the 1920s, and today has become even more so because of what it does to creative people.

American amusement, which must be pitched to the understanding of the average adolescent, is, by definition, mediocre. Adolescents are not mediocre, but forty-year-old members of the audience, who are fond only of amusements that please adolescents, have volunteered for mediocrity. Still, it's supposed to be a free country, and to each his own.

The problem comes because it takes a lot of creativity to produce a constant stream of mediocrity. Our nation sees legions of its most creative people engaged in trying to find ways to put new spins on mediocrity; and may the spirit of David Sarnoff, the original brains and heart of RCA, be with them. What a god-awful waste.

## 1920s SOCIETY

Other forces operated in the 1920s. They were

The Model T Ford, and other automobiles
Prohibition
Freudian psychology
Evolution
Jazz

A lot has been written about the automobile, booze, and jazz; and how they broke down order in the Victorian world. There is much to be said for those arguments.

---

[7]The best discussion of this is contained in Neil Postman, *Amusing Ourselves to Death* (Viking, 1985).

In 1920, a young lady in Victorian context expected to meet her future husband while sitting in a parlor, and in the presence of a chaperon. Young men would call. When things got serious, you can bet the young man would show up with a copy of Omar Khayyám's *Rubáiyát* bound in limp leather; a book that in those days was considered pretty "fast." When he got to the lines ". . . Here with a Loaf of Bread beneath the bough / A flask of wine, a book of verse—and Thou. . . ." things had gotten as serious as things could possibly get. A date was announced. They lived ever after, etc.

Nine years later, in 1929, a young woman expected to meet her future husband pretty much anywhere; but odds were good she would meet him at a party, with odds almost as good that the party would be at a roadhouse awash in Prohibition booze. A car would sit outside.

While they were important tools, booze and jazz and automobiles were really only vehicles on which the decade rode. The revolution lay in reaction to ideas of evolution and psychology, but even more in reaction to war and a rigid social order. At base, the 1920s became glitzy, then slimy, because a social system went tinhorn. To paraphrase George Ade, "It had all of its goods in the front window." Empty space filled the rest of the store.

A new god, one destined to rule the twentieth century, had been waiting in the wings since before the Civil War. Now it began its walk to center stage. Its name was Science—not Mary Baker Eddy's Christian Science, but *Science*. It would, people believed, surely cure the ills of society as well as human physical ills. It would create new machines, new medicines, and new social structures. "Science" became a term describing hopes of confused people as they viewed a dying social system.

To be boldly brief: Most of the boozing, sex, partying, boosterism, and vulgarity of the 1920s were a reflection of the American people's search for a new god and a set of beliefs that worked. Science was one big answer.

Psychology promised enough substance, and displayed enough superficial resemblance to science, to seriously bruise traditional functions of literature, art, and religion.[8] Psychology offered "adjustment," thus

---

[8]During previous times people turned to religious experience, or to art, or to books for understanding of the power of emotions. Those forms validated emotions as true

suggesting to Americans that they were subject to forces beyond them-selves. It suggested that Americans could no longer take charge and change situations. They could only adapt. In other words, psychology denied Original Possibility. It preached a religion as old as Puritanism. Metaphorically, psychology's covert message said that we were all sin-ners in the hands of an angry god. In spite of possible usefulness, psychology's message proved insidious.

Darwinism prospered, and the eternal human question of our origins seemed, on its face, answered. Humans evolved. Evolution suggested that people were far less important than their religions believed. With evolutionary theory, no godly fireworks took place during the Creation. No super-zap-father-figure snapped his fingers and undertook that Cre-ation in a six-day magic show.

The sum of psychology and Darwinism suggested to the subcon-scious: "You cannot change your world, and you ain't important, any-way." This amounted to more—if not better—Puritanism; and it was proposed to a nation that had its roots in Puritanism. John Calvin would have loved the message while hating its source.

The American people, bless their hearts, answered back with a certain amount of debauchery. It wasn't thoughtful, but at least it amounted to thumbing their collective nose at the universe.

It's difficult to symbolize a set of partially formed beliefs. In the 1920s the symbol may have been the Duesenberg automobile (it's a doozy), or it may have been naked swimming parties, or it may have been stately dinner parties with a gorilla as guest of honor, "Because, my dear, he is, after all, a distant relative."

Or, it may have been the Empire State Building, a symbol of science that was the culmination of the decade, being erected in 1930–31. Whatever the symbol, you may be certain it was a symbol in search of a belief. The decade resonates with unhappiness. Desperation lies in back of the dance styles, the "fast life," and sexual prowess. The popular mind felt that evolution denied religion, and the popular mind thought psychological repression was a desperate disease; and most repression was sexual. The way to cure repression was to behave as if one were not repressed.

The 1920s are important years because they set the stage for the rest

and worthy of understanding. Psychology, of course, largely viewed emotions as "trou-bled."

of the century. For example, our nation would see the same behavior, and much the same problems, in the 1980s. The 1980s so resembled the 1920s that we can call them twins. In the 1980s, a war had produced a disillusioned generation. A god—this one named Science—began to die. An older culture passed away as people sought quick financial success while hungering for a set of beliefs that worked.

In their search for beliefs, the people of the 1980s would blame social disarray on others. They would spout liberal rhetoric, but vote their pocketbooks. As in the 1920s, they would demand an education pointed toward making money and not pointed toward understanding of their conditions, or the human condition. A popular saying was "The one who dies with the most toys, wins."

They would discover, as did our people in the 1920s, that expensive cars do not bring much happiness. Money does not make you younger, or prettier, or nicer. Money will not keep you from dying. If anything, it separates people, and keeps them lonely.

# FIVE WRITERS OF THE 1920S:
# TWO RACES, ONE ATTITUDE

IN THE 1920S, issues of race, feminism, and economics began to knit together so tightly it is fairly impossible to separate them. The society, however, did not (and even today does not) see it that way. For that reason, writers of today share a task shared by writers of the 1920s. It is well to define that task, which is easily clouded by popular opinions.

American storytellers and artists have always gone to work in behalf of our people; in our case, the American people. The American people are highly diverse. It is easy for the popular mind to believe that writers and artists produce work intended only for special groups within the nation. Nothing could be farther from truth.

The writer writes what he or she knows, and so stories rise from points of view—racial, religious, sexual—all of the different ways we are raised, and the different communities we come from. Because of this, it is easy to slip into mistaken assumptions. People see a writer or artist working with his/her experience, and immediately reach for a category. Thus, these days it is customary to speak of "Women's Literature" or "African-American Literature" or "Native-American Literature" or "Gay-sexual Literature," ad infinitum. The American writer or artist need not pay much attention to this beyond simple courtesy. We pursue more-important business.

If a piece of work rises to the condition of literature or art, it doesn't make much difference who created it. If it does not rise to that condition, then it *sure* doesn't make any difference. The work of Richard

Wright, Toni Morrison, Harriette Arnow, and Pat Conroy does not qualify as literature because of race or gender. It is literature because the writer has approached the material with complete respect, told the tale with complete honesty, and has allowed the reader to enter a world the reader might otherwise never know. This is the art of the story. On this level of storytelling it is wrong, even insulting, to separate those writers into a special group, unless that special group is named "humanity."

For the good reason that experience teaches, writers may belong to special-interest groups, take up causes, complain bitterly, or celebrate with abandon. All of that will work just fine, until the moment they sit before a blank sheet of paper. At that point, it's time to become apolitical, aracial, and nonjudgmental.

Characters in the story may be political, or motivated by racial experience; and American literature is filled with judgmental characters from Ahab onward. The writer, however, stays out of it, because writing with a message can blow up in society's face. We already saw this in the case of Helen Hunt Jackson's *Ramona*, which was only a mild blowup. It's worth looking at a more serious blowup in behalf of the point that we need be nonjudgmental.

Here is an example of a story gone way, way wrong:

Back in 1906, an impassioned writer named Upton Sinclair wrote an exposé novel titled *The Jungle*, about excesses of the meat packing industry. Those excesses included the packing of spoiled meat, the boiling down of rats, spit, human body parts, feces, waste, floor sweepings, and everything else that fell into vats from which issued canned meat. The book is worth reading in order to get some idea of how our economic system once worked.

*The Jungle* is also a socialist tract. It documents criminal abuse of laborers who were treated no better than the animals they slaughtered. Cattle died pretty quickly. It might take as much as a couple of years for the system to completely kill a worker. Upton Sinclair wanted to introduce socialism, and thereby cure the plight of workers.

His story didn't play. The popular mind did not give two shakes about the workers. The popular mind yawned or protested about socialism. It did, however, raise raging whimpers because sausage being sold might actually be Polish (rumor had it that men fell into the meat vats and were rendered) in truth as well as recipe. The furor caused the installation of the Food and Drug Administration. It did nothing for socialism, or for immigrant workers. It caused trouble and some deaths because it raised the noise level over socialism. It escalated violence in the union movement.

Young writers of the 1920s, as now, had to learn the dangers of following a cause. They learned lessons about art, literature, groups, and the great beauty of humankind. It is one of the glories of the period that so much humane work came from a place where traps of secularism were abundant.

## HARLEM, NEW YORK, U.S.A.

Langston Hughes, Jean Toomer, and Zora Neale Hurston represent what is remembered as the Harlem Renaissance. The best-known is Langston Hughes, who is mostly celebrated these days for his poetry, and who had to do the most learning.

## Langston Hughes

As a beginning writer, Hughes's characters were not people, but lives lived on one side of the color line; including values, idiom, religion, and oppression of those who were then known as the American Negro. Hughes leaned toward portrayal, or picturing, rather than extended philosophy—at least, that is true of his poetry. He functioned as the classic storyteller supplying identity for his people, and his characterizations got better as he grew older. He shows characters *formed* by situations, more than *in* situations; for example, his story "On the Road."

He also functioned as essayist to explain "his people" to the rest of the American public. He had a big sense of humor, a tremendous sense of irony, and he loved being Negro. Depending on how he felt on a given day, he could be artist or politician. If one looks at Hughes and compares him to Twain, it's possible to see similarities. True, Hughes most often put the knock on white society, while Twain, being comprehensive, put the knock on everybody; but a comparison is apt.

Hughes began work during the Harlem Renaissance, which might also be called the second American Transcendental period. Harlem, in 1920s New York City, was a lot more flashy than Concord, Massachusetts, in the nineteenth century. Although plenty of Harlem's writing and music would show roots in Puritanism, the New Yorkers proved foot-free and fancy compared to stodgy old Massachusetts.

Hughes shows every characteristic we usually associate with young writers. He calls for an exclusiveness in art—i.e., "Negro art," and he jumps all over Negroes who value "white" art. He complains bitterly about publishers allowing Jean Toomer's novel, *Cane,* to go out of print, not realizing that if sales slowed, or publishers had to pay 10 percent royalty to God, the Bible would go out of print.[1] The young energy and young genius of Hughes could not have been better placed, and it will pay to take a look at his world.

Harlem, in those days, was not infested with corporate business. Business was locally owned. Later, as business boomed, corporations would move in and mess up the neighborhoods, something corporations have a way of doing. The best account of this is in Rosa Guy's novel *A Measure of Time.*

Harlem became a center of culture. At a time when the Ku Klux Klan stood at the height of its popularity through the Middle West, and when Jim Crow laws infested the South like vermin; when racial prejudice walked through streets and factories of the North, "Sophisticated America" discovered "the Negro." A certain amount of romanticism went on, about the same kind Victorians once accorded the American Indian.

This romance, though, rode high and wide accompanied by horns. Jazz reigned. King Oliver had begun his holy work in New Orleans, 1908, joined by Louis Armstrong in Chicago, 1922. Both did singles in New York in 1924, then returned to Chicago. Their musical reputations preceded them, no matter whether they moved east or west. Cabarets boomed, the horns talked, and poets spoke. White crowds gathered for the music. As Hughes and others complained, it got so a Negro man could not find a quiet spot to have a drink that was not infested by white people.

Hughes called on the future to produce the Great Negro American Writer and the Great Negro American Musician. He did not know that one of our soon-to-be-greatest American writers, Richard Wright, had just gotten the hell out of Mississippi. He may not have known that one of our greatest masters of music, Duke Ellington, was even then right down the street and in residence at the Kentucky Club (the former Hollywood Club).

---

[1] By this time Toomer had already announced that he was an American writer, not a Negro American writer.

As Hughes grew older, he fought harder and smarter, because energy ebbs as one grows old. He also got better. His level of sarcasm never quite got up to Twain when Twain was rolling, but it became awfully good. His storytelling became more complete.

Yet, it's for his poetry that Hughes is best remembered. It is also in his poetry that we see the clear transition from a writer with a limited cause to a writer with the greatest cause of all: humanity. Here is a sample of his young poetry, and it will break your heart. In 1925, he wrote "I, Too":

> I, too, sing America.
>
> I am the darker brother.
> They send me to eat in the kitchen
> When company comes,
> But I laugh,
> And eat well,
> And grow strong.
>
> Tomorrow,
> I'll be at the table
> When company comes.
> Nobody'll dare
> Say to me,
> "Eat in the kitchen,"
> Then.
>
> Besides,
> They'll see how beautiful I am
> And be ashamed—
>
> I, too, am America.

In 1947, after World War II, Hughes published "Freedom Train," a poem that heralded the vast change over racial attitudes that even then swept the nation. He pulled up images of discrimination where "colored" were kept off the Freedom Train, and images of men who died storming the beaches at Anzio during World War II. The poem ends:

> Then maybe from their graves in Anzio
> The G.I.'s who fought will say, *We wanted it so!*

Black men and white will say, *Ain't it fine?*
*At home they got a train that's yours and mine!*

Then I'll shout, *Glory for the*
  *Freedom Train!*
I'll holler, *Blow your whistle,*
  *Freedom Train!*
*Thank God-A-Mighty! Here's the*
  *Freedom Train*
*Get on board our Freedom Train*

Hughes had called for a great American Negro Writer. He gave it a shot, but ended up being a great American writer, instead.

## Jean Toomer

The other successor to Whitman, in addition to Masters and Sandburg, is Jean Toomer. Had Whitman been alive in 1923, and had he been handed a copy of *Cane,* he would have caught his breath. Whitman had written to poets of the future, and here was the future. The poetry in *Cane* is poetry, and the prose in *Cane* is poetry, and the people in *Cane* are people who would have had Walt Whitman chanting. The book is not exactly a novel, although it mostly looks like prose and tells stories, and it's not a play, although part of it is a play, and it is knitted together with poems.

*Cane* is also as Puritan as original sin. One chapter, titled "Becky," is another take on *The Scarlet Letter.* Toomer walked the road Hawthorne walked, and discovered what Hawthorne knew.

"And this," Whitman would insist, "shows you just how far you can go with poetry."

Whitman would be correct. *Cane* uses some of Whitman's technique. It piles on image after image after image. It also anticipates a lot of experimental work that would happen in the 1930s and 1940s. It sets the stage for John Dos Passos' experiments in *U.S.A.*, and for Steinbeck's three-act plays in the form of stories, the best loved of which is *Of Mice and Men.* And, like Dos Passos, and Steinbeck, there's passion and intensity reaching deeply into the subject. In the case of *Cane,* the subject is the Negro experience in the United States, historically, and North, and South.

## Zora Neale Hurston

As with Toomer, Zora Neale Hurston would announce that she was a writer, not a "black writer." In many ways, Hurston is sister to Meridel Le Sueur, another writer we'll meet soon. Both concerned themselves with the situations of a particular group, and within that group, women; and both went about their lives without taking advice from nobody, nohow. The steadfastness and courage displayed in their work elevates it to a level beyond concerns of economics and gender.

Hurston's writing anticipates the works of Toni Morrison and Alice Walker, in that she gives her audience a complete look at characters living in what was then called "Negro culture."[2] As with the best of our writers, she simply remained true to her material; showed her characters as they were; and, because she did it so well, allowed for understanding that could not come from history books, sociology texts, or editorials. As with Robert Nathan, who would come later, she could write a love story that will break your heart; and it isn't *True Romances,* and it isn't schmaltz. Read "The Gilded Six Bits."

These Harlem writers met the awfulness that rose in the wake of Reconstruction and the decline of Victorianism. They met it with poetry and stories and anger and hope. They interrupted the tranquil beliefs of the majority of Americans when it came to Americans with some African roots. These voices were among the most lasting of the several voices that worked hard in those days to validate all Americans as Americans, and worthy; and not simply worthy under the law.

## TWINS OF THE TWENTIES: F. SCOTT FITZGERALD AND CLAUDE McKAY

## F. Scott Fitzgerald

F. Scott Fitzgerald told the story of the 1920s by writing of his own life. As storytellers, we all portray ourselves to a greater or lesser extent, but Fitzgerald (and, a little later, Thomas Wolfe) did it most. Fitzger-

---

[2]We have Alice Walker to thank for rediscovering Hurston. One of the best spinoffs from movements such as civil rights, or feminism, is that they give us an opportunity to reappraise our literature.

ald's best book is *The Great Gatsby*. It has much in common with Dreiser's *An American Tragedy*. In each book, an ambitious young man buys
popular values, tries to make something of himself, and, in doing so,
self-destructs. This pretty much characterizes Fitzgerald, both as man
and writer. We need have no particular interest in his personal life,
beyond acknowledging struggles with booze and success and craziness.
His marriage was not made in heaven, but was a creature of the wild
side of 1920s society. In spite of pressures, Fitzgerald put together a
respectable body of work. He had a problem in writing, and that problem offers a lesson. The problem also gives a main justification for this
book:

Pick up any novel by Fitzgerald, and you will find a sharply focused
beginning. You will sense urgency, but especially anger. He will be
writing about a situation or a subject, and his characters will be fairly
objective projections. In other words, he's thinking of a situation or
subject first, and waiting on his characters.

Then his characters begin to form. They take over, as characters
should. As the characters come to life, Fitzgerald begins to understand
them so well he forgives them; by which I mean the opening pressures
of situation and subject disappear. Anger and focus drizzle away because the character becomes important, the situation secondary. This
would be just fine if the characters had enough experience and internal
fire to say to the author, "Tough noogies to the book you were gonna
write. This is the book we are gonna write."

It doesn't generally happen. The characters float. They do not know
where they came from, and cannot visualize a book of their own. They
are trapped without history. In this sense they truly are "lost," and the
idea of a "lost generation" carries some validity.

Here is an example of how both writer and characters seem to float,
unsatisfied with the reality of their lives, but occasionally happy with
transitory illusion; an illusion rising from the surreal. It comes from
*Tender Is the Night*. A group of people ride home from a party through
the streets of Paris:

> "Don't let Rosemary go home alone," Nicole called to Mary
> as they left. "We feel responsible to her mother."
> —Later Rosemary and the Norths and a manufacturer of
> dolls' voices from Newark and ubiquitous Collis and a big
> splendidly dressed oil Indian named George T. Horseprotection

were riding along on top of thousands of carrots in a market wagon. The earth in the carrot beards was fragrant and sweet in the darkness, and Rosemary was so high up in the load that she could hardly see the others in the long shadow between infrequent street lamps. Their voices came from far off, as if they were having experiences different from hers, different and far away, for she was with Dick in her heart, sorry she had come with the Norths, wishing she was at the hotel and him asleep across the hall, or that he was here beside her with the warm darkness streaming down.

"Don't come up," she called to Collis, "the carrots will all roll." She threw one at Abe who was sitting beside the driver, stiffly like an old man. . . .

Later she was homeward bound at last in broad daylight, with the pigeons already breaking over Saint-Sulpice. All of them began to laugh spontaneously because they knew it was still last night while the people in the streets had the delusion that it was bright hot morning.

"At last I've been on a wild party," thought Rosemary, "but it's no fun when Dick isn't there."

She felt a little betrayed and sad, but presently a moving object came into sight. It was a huge horse-chestnut tree in full bloom bound for the Champs Élysées, strapped now into a long truck and simply shaking with laughter—like a lovely person in an undignified position yet confident none the less of being lovely. Looking at it with fascination Rosemary identified herself with it, and laughed cheerfully with it, and everything all at once seemed gorgeous.

I'm not knocking a brilliant writer by citing this example, only trying to learn from him. After all, I'm the one who claims portrayal of character in situation is all-important. I am saying that Fitzgerald trapped himself because he was such a superior writer. He knows his characters, then sort of gets betrayed by them.

Fitzgerald teaches that writers need be firmly grounded in past and place. They need strong beliefs and strong disbeliefs; plus an open mind ready to change when it encounters new information. Fitzgerald was not firmly grounded because he sat smack, squat in the 1920s.

In addition, we learn from him that writing about situations while in the middle of them is the job of the journalist not the storyteller. Fitzgerald tried to capture the excesses of a groundless time while engaging in those excesses. He does such a good job on characters because, I think, he's working at a time when society was afloat. Characters were all he had. His books tend to wind down because his characters are trapped in the assumptions of their present, and are unknowing or uncaring beyond their present.

Fitzgerald apparently did not trust what he knew about the past. Ethical, moral, and especially artistic decisions were needed; and the information to make them was either not present, or rejected. The writer was himself trapped in situation.

Fitzgerald, and Claude McKay, who wrote in Harlem during the same years, are gemstones of the 1920s; intense, of momentous value beyond the size of their works. Between them, they catch the fierceness of the decade. Fitzgerald shows the glitz of the greater society, while McKay shows the glitter of Harlem; and both show disillusionment, anger, bitterness, and distrust. In each writer, though, sounds a call of hope, and a belief that happiness will be achieved by someone, somewhere, at some time. Even as the American mind went through the crashing of an old order, and the legacy of war, these writers offered assurance. Fitzgerald, like the earlier Melville—racked with pain and genius—would have taken up the world's pain to relieve that pain. The fight he made against the awful pressures of his life, and the 1920s, joins him with Hughes as one of the great voices of that time.

## Claude McKay

McKay's work is a perfect example of what can happen to fine books when we start dividing writers into "women" or "African-American" or "Native-American." Such categories may be suited to other needs of society, but have absolutely nothing to do with literature.

McKay is known as a black writer, a member of the Harlem Renaissance, and, as a novelist, has proven an embarrassment to professional "black folk" and professional "white folk" and folk who cannot read and understand clearly written English.

McKay, mostly remembered these days for his poetry, wrote three novels. One of them, *Home to Harlem* (1927), fits right in with the searching done by American writers in the 1920s. While Fitzgerald was raised in Minnesota, McKay came from Jamaica as a young man. The color of his skin prejudices professional readers, and so they read him as a black man instead of as an American writer.

When prejudiced African-American types read him, the general reaction is "Don't uncover dirty linen," or "Uncle Tom is playing to the prejudices of whitey." When neurotic Euro-Americans—or whatever we're calling the paler majority these days—read him, the reaction is "We'd better not talk too much about this guy. The African-Americans will think the Euro-Americans are getting their jollies."[3]

If Fitzgerald wrote about jazz and booze and plenty of sex, he was said to capture the spirit of the decade. If McKay wrote about jazz and booze and plenty of sex, he was said to tell bad things about Negroes. If Fitzgerald wrote about the excesses of greed, the wasting of human potential, and the waste of national wealth from high living, his work would be viewed as prelude to the Great Depression. If McKay wrote about excesses of greed, and wasting of human potential, and waste of wealth from high living, his work was viewed as a natural expression of an oppressed black man who would inexorably gravitate to communism. If his characters, in dialogue, blame the white man for their troubles half the time, and each other the other half, the easy answer says that McKay expresses his opinion—an answer that is, of course, not brilliant. McKay's characters express their own opinions.

Or, when expressing opinions: If Fitzgerald, in narrative, is critical of high society, he's called a social critic. If McKay, in narrative, is critical of Harlem society, he's called a traitor to the race. Here is an excerpt:

They went to the Negro Picture Theater and held each other's hand, gazing in raptures at the crude pictures. It was odd that all these cinematic pictures about the blacks were a broad burlesque of their home and love life. These colored screen actors were all dressed up in expensive evening clothes, with automobiles, and menials, to imitate white society people. They laughed at themselves in such rôles and the laughter was good

---

[3]I considered toning down this paragraph, then said, "Nope. If a man doesn't believe in the efficacy of race, I see no reason for him to put up with the soiled opinions of those who do."

Then I asked myself, "Why are you so angry?" The answer? "Because prejudice is a filthy thing, and prejudice from both sides of the color line has obscured the work of a splendid writer."

on the screen. They pranced and grinned like good-nigger servants, who know that "mas'r" and "missus," intent on being amused, are watching their antics from an upper window. It was quite a little funny and the audience enjoyed it. Maybe that was the stuff the Black Belt wanted.

Here is McKay being sardonic:

They bought tickets for the nigger heaven of a theater, whence they watched high-class people make luxurious love on the screen. They enjoyed the exhibition. There is no better angle from which one can look down on a motion picture than that of the nigger heaven.

And here he is, as confessional as any storyteller ever gets:

Ray had always dreamed of writing words some day. Weaving words to make romance, ah! There were the great books that dominated the bright dreaming and dark brooding days when he was a boy. *Les Misérables, Nana, Uncle Tom's Cabin, David Copperfield, Nicholas Nickleby, Oliver Twist.*

From then, by way of free-thought pamphlets, it was only a stride to the great scintillating satirists of the age—Bernard Shaw, Ibsen, Anatole France, and the popular problemist, H. G. Wells. He had lived on that brilliant manna that fell like a flame-fall from those burning stars. Then came the great mass carnage in Europe [World War I] and the great mass revolution in Russia.

Ray was not prophetic-minded enough to define the total evil that the one had wrought nor the ultimate splendor of the other. But, in spite of the general tumults and threats, the perfectly-organized national rages, the ineffectual patching of broken, and hectic rebuilding of shattered, things, he had perception enough to realize that he had lived over the end of an era.

And also realized that his spiritual masters had not crossed with him into the new. He felt alone, hurt, neglected, cheated, almost naked. But he was a savage, even though he was a sensitive one, and did not mind nakedness. What had happened?

Had they refused to come or had he left them behind? Something had happened. But it was not desertion nor young insurgency. It was death. Even as the last scion of a famous line prances out his day and dies and is set aside with his ancestors in their cold whited sepulcher, so had his masters marched with flags and banners flying all their wonderful, trenchant, critical, satirical, mind-sharpening, pity-evoking, constructive ideas of ultimate social righteousness, into the vast international cemetery of this century.

My dear friends: in the above paragraphs, Claude McKay, an American writer, just summed up, wrapped up, and gifted you with the position of the American writer in the 1920s.

# U.S.A.

THE GREAT BOOK about the 1920s (although not published until the 1930s), and one of the great books of the century, is *U.S.A.*, by John Dos Passos. Lots of people have read it once, some twice, and plenty treasure pieces and parts; shoving them beneath noses of friends while saying, "Here, here, that's what I mean. . . ." At which point our friends generally forgive us but often change the subject because few people, these days, wish to tangle with 1,450 pages, in either one or three volumes.

Dos Passos wanted to completely display the U.S.A. and its people. Not a chance. We're a big nation of immigrants. Even the American Indian was an immigrant in the far shadows of the past. We're also a nation of the descendants of immigrants, so crossbred that every blessed one of us is mongrel; a glorious nation of mongrel ideas founded in revolutionary principles and championing the rights of in-dividuals; while sometimes stomping on both rights and individuals. We're a nation of a hundred languages, or more; a hundred religions, or more; hundreds of just about everything—or more.

Dos Passos never had a chance of capturing the U.S.A., but he whaled away at it, and ended up sitting on heaps of what he went after. He certainly caught American society during World War I. He also caught the aftermath. He caught them, as Mark Twain used to say, "with all their things on."

Through his pages walk, run, stagger, or drift a collection of Americans going to war, or making a buck off the war, or using the war as an excuse to get laid. Union and industry beat each other bloody. Evangelicals rant. Nice girls read the works of Marx, Frank Norris, and Upton Sinclair; then attend strikes and get kicked around by cops. "Show up here again, sister, and we'll pick you up for prostitution."

Nice boys go to war. Some die, some get parts blown off, and some make a good bit of money. The Age of Advertising dawns from the honey-voiced land of the character J. Ward Moorehouse, who once was a nice boy, hisself.

And through it all runs poetry. Three great lyricists wrote during the 1920s. One was Dos Passos. The others were Jean Toomer, whom we've met, and Thomas Wolfe, writing in the 1920s and publishing in the 1930s, whom we'll look at directly.

Poetry in *U.S.A.* arrives during intercalary breaks. They are called "The Camera Eye." From an artistic point of view, they have uses. They break up the long narrative flow required for backgrounding so many lives. They serve as pop-off valves for the passions of the writer, much as the whale chapters in *Moby Dick* once served to release terrible emotional pressures on Melville. Most importantly, they give depth of feeling in a book so packed with information that human emotions might otherwise be lost. Here is a sample from *1919*, which is the middle book (*U.S.A.* is divided into three books). A soldier returns home from France:[1]

> throat tightens when the redstacked steamer churning
> the faintlyheaving slatecolored swell swerves shaking in a
> long greenmarbled curve past the red lightship
> spine stiffens with the remembered chill of the
> offshore Atlantic
> and the jag of framehouses in the west above the invisible
> land and spiderweb rollercoasters and the chewinggum towers of
> Coney and the freighters with their stacks way aft and the blur
> beyond Sandy Hook
> and the smell of saltmarshes warmclammysweet remembered
> bays silvery inlets barred with trestles
> the put put before day of a gasolineboat way up the creek
> raked masts of bugeyes against straight tall pines on the

---

[1] The uncle referred to is Uncle Sam.

shellwhite beach
the limeycold reek of an oysterboat in winter

and creak of rockers on the porch of the scrollsaw cottage
and uncles' voices pokerface stories told sideways out of
the big mouth (from Missouri who took no rubber nickels) the
redskin in the buffalorobe selling snakeroot in the flare of
oratorical redfire the sulpury choke and the hookandladder
clanging down the redbrick street while the clinging firemen
with uncles' faces pull on their rubbercoats

and the crunch of whitecorn muffins and coffee with
cream gulped in a hurry before traintime and apartmenthouse
mornings stifling with newspapers and the smooth powdery
feel of new greenbacks and the whack of a cop's billy
cracking a citizen's skull and the faces blurred
with newsprint of men in jail
the whine and shriek of the buzzsaw and the tipsy smell
of raw lumber and straggling through slagheaps through
fireweed through wasted woodlands the shantytowns the
shantytowns
what good burying those years in the old graveyard by
the brokendown brick church that morning in the spring when
the sandy lanes were streaked with blue puddles and the air
was violets and pineneedles
what good burying those hated years in the
latrinestench at Brocourt under the starshells
if today the crookedfaced custominspector with the soft
tough talk the burring speech the funnypaper antics of thick
hands jerking thumb
(So you brought home French books didjer?)
is my uncle

American poetry in this form and with this overreaching passion for
all things begins with Walt Whitman, progresses to Jean Toomer, is
expanded by Dos Passos, and will eventually show up in the 1950s with
Allen Ginsberg.

Dos Passos uses two other methods young writers should know and
understand. You may never need to use them, and it's certain you will

use them but rarely. You'll also have to invent your own spin on the methods. The way to praise Dos Passos is to do what he does, but in your own way, and do it as well as he did. Or better. The methods he used are powerful if they are not overused.

The first shows the reader what is happening on the periphery of the story. Dos Passos does it by inserting sections titled "Newsreel." Headlines and lyrics comment on the action. Sometimes they comment in a sardonic manner by being totally irrelevant. Here is "Newsreel VI" from the first book, *The 42nd Parallel*:

Newsreel VI
Paris shocked At Last
HARRIMAN SHOWN AS RAIL COLOSSUS
NOTED SWINDLER RUN TO EARTH
TEDDY WIELDS BIG STICK
straphangers demand relief.

*We were sailing along*
*On moonlight bay*
*You can hear the voices ringing*
*They seem to say*
*You have stolen my heart, now don't go away*
*Just as we sang*

*love's*
*old*
*sweet*
*songs*
*On moonlight bay*

MOB LYNCHES AFTER PRAYER

when the metal poured out of the furnace I saw the men running to a place of safety. To the right of the furnace I saw a party of ten men all of them running wildly and their clothes a mass of flames. Apparently some of them had been injured when the explosion occurred and several of them tripped and fell. The hot metal ran over the poor men in a moment.

## PRAISE MONOPOLY AS BOON TO ALL

industrial foes work for peace at Mrs. Potter Palmer's

*love's*

*old*

*sweet*

*song*

*We were sailing along*
*on moonlight bay*

The second method shows characters not directly involved in the action, but characters who have affected the world in which the action takes place. He writes of J. P. Morgan, Henry Ford, Thorstein Veblen, who wrote *The Theory of the Leisure Class,* Isadora Duncan, who was a dancer remarkably crazed and wonderful, plus a bunch of others. Here is the Unknown Soldier[2]:

## THE BODY OF AN AMERICAN

*Whereasthe Congressoftheunitedstates byaconcurrentres-*
*olutionadoptedon the4thdayofmarch lastauthorizedthe*
*Secretary-*

*ofwar to cause to be brought to the unitedstatesthe body of an*
*Americanwhowasamemberoftheamericanexpeditionaryforcein-*
*europe wholosthislifeduringtheworldwarandwhoseidentityhas-*
*notbeenestablished for burial inthememorialamphitheatreofthe*
*nationalcemeteryatarlingtonvirginia*

In the tarpaper morgue at Chalons-sur-Marne in the reek of chloride of lime and the dead, they picked out the pine box that held all that was left of

enie menie minie moe plenty other pine boxes stacked up there containing what they'd scraped up of Richard Roe and other person or persons unknown. Only one can go. How did they pick John Doe?

---

[2]You will shortly encounter the word "poppies." Poppies are a symbol of World War I. They scattered across the blasted Belgium and French landscapes, blooming among rot and rats, blood, decay, terror, mustard gas, and artillery.

Make sure he aint a dinge, boys,
make sure he aint a guinea or a kike,

how can you tell a guy's a hunredpercent when all you've got's a gunnysack full of bones, bronze buttons stamped with the screaming eagle and a pair of roll puttees?

... and the gagging chloride and the puky dirtstench of the year-old dead ...


*The day withal was too meaningful and tragic for applause. Silence, tears, songs and prayer, muffled drums and soft music were the instrumentalities today of national approbation.*


John Doe was born (thudding din of blood in love into the shuddering soar of a man and a woman alone indeed together lurching into

and ninemonths sick drowse waking into scared agony and the pain and blood and mess of birth). John Doe was born

and raised in Brooklyn, in Memphis, near the lakefront in Cleveland, Ohio, in the stench of the stockyards in Chi, on Beacon Hill, in an old brick house in Alexandria Virginia, on Telegraph Hill, in a halftimbered Tudor cottage in Portland the city of roses

in the Lying-In Hospital old Morgan endowed on Stuyvesant Square,

across the railroad tracks, out near the country club, in a shack cabin tenement apartmenthouse exclusive residential suburb;

scion of one of the best families in the social register, won first prize in the baby parade at Coronado Beach, was marbles champion of the Little Rock grammarschools, crack basketballplayer at the Booneville High, quarterback at the State Reformatory, having saved the sheriff's kid from drowning in the Little Missouri River was invited to Washington to be photographed shaking hands with the President on the White House steps;—


*though this was a time of mourning, such an assemblage necessarily has about it a touch of color. In the boxes are seen the court uniforms of foreign diplomats, the gold braid*

*of our own and foreign fleets and armies, the black of the*
*conventional morning dress of American statesmen, the*
*varicolored furs and outdoor wrapping garments of mothers*
*and sisters come to mourn, the drab and blue of soldiers and*
*sailors, the glitter of musical instruments and the white*
*and black of a vested choir*

—busboy harveststiff hogcaller boyscout champeen cornshucker
of Western Kansas bellhop at the United States Hotel at Saratoga
Springs office boy callboy fruiter telephone lineman longshoreman
lumberjack plumber's helper, worked for an exterminating company in Union City, filled pipes in an opium joint in Trenton, N.J.
Y.M.C.A. secretary, express agent, truckdriver, fordmechanic,
sold books in Denver Colorado; Madam would you be willing to
help a young man work his way through college?

President Harding, with a reverence seemingly more significant
because of his high temporal station, concluded his speech:

*We are met today to pay the impersonal tribute;*
*the name of him whose body lies before us took flight*
*with his imperi shable soul . . .*
*as a typical soldier of this representative democracy*
*he*
*fought and died believing in the indisputable justice of his*
*country's cause . . .*

by raising his right hand and asking the thousands
within
the sound of his voice to join in the prayer

*Our Father which are in heaven hallowed be thy*
*name . . . ;*

Naked he went into the army;
they weighed you, measured you, looked for flat feet,
squeezed your penis to see if you had clap, looked up your
anus to see if you had piles, counted your teeth, made you
cough, listened to your heart and lungs, made you read the
letters on the card, charted your urine and your intelligence,
gave you a service record (imperishable soul)

and an identification tag stamped with your serial number to hang around your neck, issued O D regulation equipment, a condiment can and a copy of the articles of war.

Atten'SHUN suck in your gut you c_____r wipe that smile off your face eyes right wattja tink dis is a choirch-social? For-war-D'ARCH.

John Doe
and Richard Roe and other person or persons unknown drilled hiked, manual of arms, ate slum, learned to salute, to soldier, to loaf in the latrines, forbidden to smoke on deck, overseas guard duty, forty men and eight horses, shortarm in-spection and the ping of shrapnel and the shrill bullets combing the air and the sorehead woodpeckers the machineguns mud cooties gasmasks and the itch

*Say feller tell me how I can get back to my outfit.*

John Doe had a head
for twentyodd years intensely the nerves of the eyes the ears the palate the tongue the fingers the toes the armpits, the nerves warmfeeling under the skin charged the coiled brain with hurt sweet warm cold mine must dont sayings print head-lines;

Thou shalt not the multiplication table long division, Now is the time for all good men knocks but once at a young man's door, It's a great life if Ish gebibbel, The first five years'll be the Safety First, Suppose a hun tried to rape your my coun-try right or wrong, Catch 'em young, What he dont know wont treat 'em rough, Tell 'em nothing, He got what was coming to him he got his, This is a white man's country, Kick the bucket, Gone west, If you dont like it you can croaked him

*Say buddy cant you tell me how I can get back to my outfit?*

Cant help jumpin when them things go off, give me the trots them things do. I lost my identification tag swimmin in the Marne, roughhousin with a guy while we was waitin to be de-loused, in bed with a girl named Jeanne (Love moving picture we French postcard dream began with saltpeter in the coffee and ended at the propho station);

*Say soldier for chrissake cant you tell me how I can get back to my outfit?*

John Doe's

heart pumped blood:

alive thudding silence of blood in your ears

down in the clearing in the Oregon forest where the punkins were punkincolor pouring into the blood through the eyes and the fallcolored trees and the bronze hoopers were hopping through the dry grass where tiny striped snails hung on the underside of the blades and the flies hummed, wasps droned, bumblebees buzzed, and the woods smelt of wine and mushrooms and apples, homey smell of fall pouring into the blood

and I dropped the tin hat and the sweaty pack and lay flat with the dogday sun licking my throat and adamsapple and the tight skin over the breastbone

The shell had his number on it.

The blood ran into the ground.

The service record dropped out of the filing cabinet when the quartermaster sergeant got blotto that time they had to pack up and leave the billets in a hurry.

The identification tag was in the bottom of the Marne.

The blood ran into the ground, the brains oozed out of the cracked skull and were licked up by the trenchrats, the belly swelled and raised a generation of bluebottle flies,

and the incorruptible skeleton,

and the scraps of dried viscera and skin bundled in khaki

they took to Chalons-sur-Marne

and laid it out neat in a pine coffin

and took it home to God's Country on a battleship

and buried it in a sarcophagus in the Memorial

Amphitheatre in the Arlington National Cemetery

and draped the Old Glory over it

and the bugler played taps

and Mr. Harding prayed to God and the diplomats

and the generals and the admirals and the brasshats and

the politicians and the handsomely dressed ladies out

of the society column of the *Washington Post* stood up
solemn

and thought how beautiful sad Old Glory God's
Country it was to have the bugler play taps and the
three volleys made their ears ring.

Where his chest ought to have been they pinned
the Congressional Medal, the D.S.C., the Medaille Militaire,
the Belgian Croix de Guerre, the Italian gold medal, the Vitutea
Militara sent by Queen Marie of Rumania, the Czechoslovak
war cross, the Virtuti Militari of the Poles, a wreath sent by
Hamilton Fish, Jr., of New York, and a little wampum presented by a deputation of Arizona redskins in warpaint and
feathers. All the Washingtonians brought flowers.

Woodrow Wilson brought a bouquet of poppies.

*U.S.A.* served the American people from its publication in 1930–36
until the Gulf War, performed during the regency of a president whose
name is forgettable. *U.S.A.* continues to serve American writers.

It served our people because it gave voice and shape to nebulous
sorrows. It gave shape to doubt and regret. The book is Puritan in
execution, but filled with anger over offense given to Original Possibility. It is not a socialist tract, nor a reformist tract (of which it often
stands accused), but a song of America and what we might become if
we quit making dumb mistakes. The book also allows us to understand
one major mistake: nationalism.

After World War I, and through Vietnam, the American people would
be asked to go to war, or, as with World War II, *have* to go to war; but we
would no longer regard war as glorious. Even in World War II, when
preachers dusted off platitudes about a "holy war," or in Korea, when
senators (resembling blowfish suffering from gastritis) spoke of "destroying Godless communism," Americans did not bite. Our people
now understood that patriotism was different from nationalism.

*U.S.A.* still serves American writers. After its publication, no honest
writer could, ever again, write a book about war in which there was a
winner.[3]

---

[3]Another strong book was published at this time, and it carried the same message.

This was important. War is traditionally surrounded by romance and sentimentality. Noble men ride off on horseback or jeep to defend their families, and some of them fall; nobly, of course. Their families weep, build shrines, and hang portraits of departed warriors, and the lucky old world is safe until the next tyrant stumbles into power.

In this sentimental version of war, brave men are dishonored by being seen as clichés. In this version, nice women do not get raped, children do not starve in gutters or die beneath destroyed buildings, and wild hogs do not grow fat on corpses left after a battle. Even our Civil War was not sufficiently grotesque to cure the tradition of a winner. Stephen Crane would write *The Red Badge of Courage,* and he would do a capable job of showing war. Even that book, though, carries the message that it's an ill wind . . . a young man grows up and finds self-understanding all because of a war . . . uh-huh. Yep. Tell it to the Marines.

Dos Passos wrote from compassion and anger. *U.S.A.* begins with

---

Here is a short excerpt from *Action at Aquila* (1937), by Hervey Allen. An eighty-year-old colonel of cavalry from the Civil War watches men going off to the Spanish-American War:

After the troops came the politicians, big, heavy-jowled, gloomy fellows in high hats and frock coats, looking each other brazenly in the face from the opposite seats of double victorias. They followed the flag. A roar of welcome greeted them from the Union League. Veterans and citizens knew who was worth cheering—who supported pensions and high tariffs. The funeral procession of the Republic moved on. . . . then came a long procession of the delivery wagons of leading Philadelphia merchants, who thus delicately took the opportunity to testify to their patriotism and to tout their goods at the same time. These marched past, like Christian soldiers, "as to war." Indeed, some of the oldest names in the city thus pressed towards the front, but turned aside at Walnut Street. The wagons were followed by a band playing hymns and a large delegation of the W.C.T.U. [Women's Christian Temperance Union] marching robustly and inveterately. Opposition was their meat, and the crowd fed it to them raw. After them came their sons in the various boys' brigades and cadet corps from the Sunday-schools of the city. Some young lady Christian Endeavourers in American flags brought up the rear. The very last unit of the van consisted of an old open wagon with semi-oval wheels in which upon kitchen chairs sat six ladies in six pairs of spectacles and concave profiles. "Lady Readers of Emerson," proclaimed the home-made sign over their heads. One of them waved a Cuban flag, probably a form of compensation. . . .

World War I and ends as the Great Depression smothers the nation. It is an insider's view of the 1920s.

It achieves artistic balance, which history cannot. When we read and write history, facts always run out of balance. How much, for example, did women's suffrage in 1920 affect women's views of independence, how much their views of responsibility? We can't say because other facts clamor for equal time. The facts of the stock market, and ordination (in the public mind) of the businessman as the new Christ, confuse our original question about women. It is only when a great writer shows as much as he can about what he sees, that a period comes completely to life.

Our literature now contains great books about war. Hemingway's *For Whom the Bell Tolls* is often misunderstood because it is experimental. James Jones' *The Thin Red Line* is equally misunderstood by folks who have a hard time wrapping their minds around the idea of death as a comic hero. Joseph Heller's *Catch-22* is easily understood. Harriette Arnow's *The Dollmaker* is still in print after nearly fifty years. Like *U.S.A.*, it is about more than war. As we'll see later, it is about America, and war. Tim O'Brien wrote *Going After Cacciato* from the Vietnam War, which also produced some of the best journalism ever written in the form of *Dispatches* by Michael Herr. In one way or another, all of these great books hark back to *U.S.A.*, or at least to the fact now ingrained in our writers that war produces no winners.

*U.S.A.* fully displayed the 1920s, and now leads us into the Great Depression, when our writers, artists, performing artists, and musicians preserved the soul of the nation.

# THE BIG BUST

MUCH HAS BEEN written about "the good old days of the Great Depression, when everyone rowed the same boat." Such writing is sentimental. The days were not good. Most people, however, *were* in the same boat. They couldn't stay there, though. The boat sank.

To this day, there are people who believe the Great Depression was simply a cost of doing business in the American Way. They believe it an aberration, but it wasn't. An economic system failed, and there's no whitewashing the fact. It did not falter. It failed.

Failure came because the system ran into problems for which it had not prepared. Some were

1. *The assembly line,* perfected by many manufacturers after being first installed by Henry Ford, allowed massive overproduction. Manufacturers had not learned how to expand markets for their goods.

2. *Industrialists* had not yet learned that their workers were also their customers, if their workers were adequately paid. Henry Ford provided an opportunity for business to learn this. He installed the $5 day for workers in his Ford plant at a time when $3 was considered a fair wage. Because he

paid so well, he could have his pick of workers.[1] And his workers could afford to buy his car.[2]

3. *Consumers* had not learned how to handle credit. In former days, people made payments on mortgages, but no large credit structure existed to handle durable goods. When cars and radios became, not oddities, but necessities, in the minds of most Americans, lots of people got deeply in hock. They could no longer buy the latest thing because they were still paying off the superexpensive radio purchased "on time" the year before.

4. *Advertising* sucker-punched consumers. The 1920s were years in which advertising stopped telling about the product and began suggesting that the correct brand of baking powder would cause a person to become radiant and sexual. Cars, soap, radios, sewing machines would do the same. Purchase of unneeded goods caused the illusion of a stable market, but the market for such goods became saturated.

5. *Two economies* ran side by side. The first economy used the regular system of banks, checks, stock market, real estate. The second economy used cash and dealt with illegal booze. Enormous amounts of cash ran through the economy, or went outside the country. Today, we see the same cash economy with the drug trade.

6. *Uncontrolled* speculation on the stock market allowed people to buy stock on margin while putting up only 10 percent cash. As the stock price went up, investors could sell for a profit. As long as the stock rose, they enjoyed a practically free ride. Such was the joy of leverage. But when stock prices fell, and margins were called, the ride bottomed out like a roller coaster to the center of the earth.

*Speculation* was not confined to the stock market. Speculation in land caused prices to rise. The land would then

---

[1] He could also control his workers. He intruded into their lives, regulating everything from their morals to their dress. He had his own police force.

[2] Because of mass production, by 1925 the price of a new Ford had gotten down to $260.

be reassessed for taxes, which would rise. Meanwhile, prices for crops kept falling. By 1929, a lot of farmers could not make back seed money, let alone pay the high tax on their land. The stock market crash in October 1929 signaled the beginning of the Great Depression, but economic depression had been around for a lot of people all through the 1920s.

A *"bubble"* appeared in the stock market, and also in the land market. Bubbles are not new in economics. As early as 1637, in Holland, a bubble occurred over tulip bulbs, remembered in history as tulipmania. Speculation drove prices so high that a particular variety of tulip brought 2,600 guilders—as much as a house in Amsterdam—for a single bulb. When the bubble burst back in those olden days, thousands of people went bankrupt. In 1929, people lost everything in the American stock market and in land speculation. A bubble occurs when an object—be it tulip bulb, or blue-chip stock, or acreage—becomes overvalued because people have become crazed with the idea of profit.

In the final analysis, the economic system failed because no one had control of industry. America—and the world—saw the uncontrolled power of industry create economic depressions.

Warning signs had been around for at least thirty years. In America, industrial enthusiasm, coupled with speculation in land, and manipulation by trusts, caused bad economic downturns in 1873 and 1893. The country lived through them and returned to the semblance of prosperity. That is why depressions were regarded as normal cyclical events.

## THE WORLD OF THE 1930S

If we could jump back to 1930s America, you would believe you were visiting another nation. People would speak English, but just about everything else would look different. There were no four-lane roads or shopping centers. Suburbs were virtually unknown. In small towns, and often in large cities, there was no such thing as waiting in line at a store or a movie. Customers were few. Long-distance travel still moved largely by train.[3]

You would also see a nation without much in the way of government support programs. There were no social security, veterans' benefits, aid to dependent children, unemployment insurance, or any other subsidy. Education received funding from the local level. The federal government was relatively small, even minuscule compared to the U.S. government of today.

Most women did not work outside the home. They married and had children. Single women generally had such shabby jobs—or, at least, shabby pay—that marriage was their most hopeful option. During the 1920s, the American people rebelled against Victorianism, but basic Victorian attitudes about family hardly changed at all.

For at least half of the nation's population, the extended family still operated. Uncles, cousins, nephews, aunts, grandmothers, and grandfathers lived within a few miles of each other. During the Great Depression, extended families operated on very basic levels. Literally, the farm folk fed the town folk, because while no one had money, at least farms could grow food.

Much of what Americans knew as truth would be proved wrong during the Great Depression. One main truth was:

*American men were raised to believe that any good man could always find a job and support his family.*

Not true. Men would search day after weary day, month after weary month, trying to find work. Men would dress in their best clothes in the morning and carry shoes and socks in a paper bag. When they got to a store or factory to inquire about a job, they would put on their shoes and socks. After they inquired, and were told there was no work, off would come the shoes and socks. Because, when those shoes wore out, there would be no new shoes. Men would walk all day rather than spend the nickel it took to ride a bus. Because, when that nickel was spent, they did not know when they would see another nickel. This is how bad it was:

Unemployment reached 26.7 percent by 1934, roughly 34 million people who had not a cent of income. Relief agencies (and they were

---

[3]Airmail and commercial airlines started operating in 1927. The first capable airliner would be the Douglas DC-2, in 1932. It could carry twelve passengers at a speed of up to 150 mph.

few and far between) could not handle the need of so many people. Cities went broke because few people could pay taxes. Schools shut down. Worst of all, bad times would not quit. The Great Depression ground on and on and on.

When over 25 percent of the nation's population does not have a dime's worth of income, people starve. Seeing their hungry children, men are reduced to begging, and some to theft; although crime rates remained low.

During the Great Depression, most men did not blame business, or government, or the economic system, for their troubles. They blamed themselves, because they still believed that any good man could get a job and support his family. For that reason, a great deal of guilt ran through society in those days, together with a great deal of helplessness.

A second main truth concerned women. *Women were raised to believe in family as the one bastion that must never be breached.*

Such training was a remnant of Victorianism, and a sound remnant it was. All else might go—banks, political systems, even churches—but the family must stay intact. Men might concern themselves with whether the new president, elected in 1932, was a saint or a demon; but women didn't waste their time. When Franklin Roosevelt became president, the American woman knew she had an ally. Roosevelt promised much, and delivered much, but it took several years.

For the first few years, the Great Depression ground on, unending, month after month. As it progressed, an entire generation of young people felt continual frustration. People expected to use their twenties to get established, then married. They expected to work hard, raise kids, and expected their kids to work for the family. This belief arose from the Puritan tradition, and from practical forms of rural life.[4]

A nation of people who expected to work, wanted to work, and who derived much of their self-worth from work, had no work. Roosevelt's New Deal attacked the problem by setting up the Public Works Administration, hiring men to work on the nation's physical problems.

---

[4]When people moved to cities, children were expected to help in the family business. If the father was an employee, he most likely worked a six-day week. He was not expected to do chores that could be handled by the rest of the family. The five-day work week did not become standard until the late 1950s. I recall, in the late 1940s, thinking it very "neat" to have Saturday afternoons and Sundays off. We went from a six-day week to five-and-a-half, to five.

Men built or repaired bridges, roads, and dams. Young men worked in the Civilian Conservation Corps, building lodges and trails, or did reforestation in national parks. The nation hired its own citizens to restore the infrastructure. It was a good idea, and worked far better than expected.

There were some problems. People took great pride in being independent. They hated to receive charity. In a nation of workers, it somehow seemed wrong to be employed by government instead of business.

As the Depression progressed, patterns developed that are still fondly remembered by people who lived them. The patterns may be summed up by the phrase "people helping each other."

Help appeared in all sorts of ways. A woman might cook up a kettle of vegetable soup, then take it down the street to a neighbor's house. She would claim she had folks coming over, but they couldn't make it. Would the neighbors keep this from going to waste? A man would show up at a house where the husband might be gone looking for work. The man would have a truckload of saw-ends that could be used as firewood. "They give them away at the mill, missus, and since I was coming this direction . . ."

The crime rates were never high.[5] Thousands of men were on the road. Many looked for work. Others drifted, picking up a job here or there, never settling down. They were called "tramps" or "hoboes." Many and many a time I've seen a man in filthy clothes show up at my grandmother's door asking for a hand of work and a meal. Grandmother always found some chore, and always found some food to give him. She would not offer food without work because that would insult the man's pride. Hardly anyone was afraid of these men.

Families, whether extended or not, fought to survive through eleven years from 1930 until our entry into World War II. It may be gloriously recorded that most of them made it, although to this day I do not fully understand how. I remain in awe of their ability to endure and create, while sustaining the democratic ideals of America.

Some families did not make it. Two of the great novels of the century

---

[5]These days it is popularly believed that poverty causes crime. If that were true, the nation would have self-destructed during the 1930s. Crime is a product of "easy money," an emphasis on materialism, and lack of education in practical and ethical matters. Thus, we see about the same behavior among corporate officers as we see in ghettos.

are *The Grapes of Wrath* (1939), by John Steinbeck, and *The Dollmaker* (1954), by Harriette Arnow. Each traces the destruction of a family, the first through economic depression, the second through war. We'll look at *The Dollmaker* when we get to the 1950s, and will consider Steinbeck in the next chapter. For now, let us look at the president.


## FDR

Franklin Delano Roosevelt represented a clean break from traditional ways of thinking about government. Roosevelt saw the American people as a national resource, not simply as a labor pool. He saw the nation as belonging to Americans, not to industrialists.

Roosevelt's administration introduced elements of socialism. These elements had more to do with controls on business and the installation of social service programs than with nationalization of industries. To this day, you will hear businessmen curse the memory of Franklin Roosevelt, but the hard fact is: he—and the integrity of the American people—saved the capitalist system.

Capitalists couldn't do it because the profit motive got in the way. Unions couldn't do it because unions, like most organizations, become greedy or corrupt as their power increases. In the 1930s, government would be the one force that could save the economic system.

Social programs stemming from Roosevelt's New Deal did not contradict capitalism. In fact, they addressed one of capitalism's big problems: People who had money did not spend it during the Depression. They were afraid. Thus, money did not circulate. This caused the economic system to lie dormant.

If, however, a Social Security check arrived each month, it could be spent. This planned circulation of money through social programs is one tool built into our system to ensure that another Great Depression does not happen. It does not, of course, ward off an inflationary depression. Inflation causes cheap money. Cheap money causes cheaper money. "Value" and "wealth" become relative, or hidden. The economy spirals downward.

In addition to the social programs of the New Deal, Roosevelt enlisted the love and confidence of great numbers of Americans. He did it through plain speech over the radio in addresses called "fireside chats." He discussed the problems of the nation: unemployment, the concentration of too many people in industrial centers, the greed of speculators, and the excesses of the banking system. He addressed the American people in a manner politicians almost never use: straightforward, honest, and with confidence that the American public can understand complex situations and complex answers. For the majority, faith in Roosevelt was only slightly less than faith in God, which is why he was elected to an unprecedented four terms.[6]

Faith in God was also a factor; or, rather, forms surrounding religion were factors that played a big part in American life during the Depression. The main force may not have been belief in God, but reliance on local church congregations that served as extended families. As a thoughtful resource, religion did not distinguish itself during the Depression.[7]

## ENTERTAINMENT

One of the strongest sustaining forces came from the entertainment industry. Movies and music supplied sparkle in the midst of darkness. These were days of the big bands, and among those bands one could find something to suit any taste; from sentimental ballads to swing, and all from the bells of glorious horns. Even rock and roll has roots in the period. A form then known as "race music" held the essential beat of rock and roll.

Movies were among the great entertainment bargains, and by the 1930s the movie industry had worked through most of its glitches. These were days when fantasies about good times held sway. In those movies, ladies in gorgeous gowns descended spiral staircases of polished marble while orchestras supplied background. There were other kinds of movies as well, but people needed fantasy. The world outside the

---

[6]Roosevelt was either loved or hated. There was no in-between. I can remember how much my grandmother adored him, and how my father despised him. As illustration, I can remember a newspaper report saying that the government was controlling disease by testing prostitutes who gathered around army camps. My grandmother's response: "That is not true because Mr. Roosevelt is a good man and he wouldn't let something like that [prostitution] go on." My father's comment on the day Roosevelt died: "The bastard finally did something right."

[7]As a child, I can remember a Lutheran preacher guilt-tripping a congregation by telling them the Depression was a visitation by God because of the excesses of the 1920s. Since this occurred in a Midwest town of five thousand, you may be sure the man's congregation had not been doing much "excessing." They took the rap, though.

movie house remained a gray world of unemployment; or, if a man had a job, constant fear of unemployment.

Double features were always shown, and, if it was cold outside, and a person had nowhere to go, it was possible to stay in a warm movie theater for hours. Lights did not go up after a single showing. Price of admission ranged from 10 cents for kids on Saturday, up to as much as 30 cents for adults; perhaps more in cities. One night a week, the movie houses gave away free dishes.

Historical novels found wide readership. Most were romantic, many poorly researched, but all of them served to satisfy hunger for romance. The two biggest novels of the period are *Anthony Adverse* (1933), by Hervey Allen, and *Gone with the Wind* (1936), by Margaret Mitchell. Mitchell's book would become the ideal of the form and won the Pulitzer Prize, but Allen's is much the finer book. It is perfectly re-searched and beautifully written. It takes place in eighteenth-century Italy, Spain, Africa, England, and America. Since it is twelve hundred pages long, few people, except writers, read it these days. Mitchell's book is about the Civil War.

People wanted novels about America—the earlier in our history, the better. They wanted an America successful, brilliant, and peopled by humans only slightly less interesting than angels. A Revolutionary War, or a Civil War, might be going on in the novel, but the event was only background for characters who were smashingly beautiful and brave. Many such novels resembled soap operas; but, in their way, they served. This demand lasted until after World War II. As late as the early 1950s, drugstores still rented popular novels just as grocery chains now rent videos.

The 1930s were also the heyday of radio, which was as shabby during daytime as is present-day television. In the evenings, though, music and theater and comedy carried the nation. Radio might have done more, but the admen took their toll. Electronic entertainment seems destined to be the creature of snake-oil salesmen; a pity for the possibilities.

If Americans during the 1930s needed romance, they also needed realism. To fully understand the importance of the major writers—Thomas Wolfe, Meridel Le Sueur, Sinclair Lewis, Ernest Hemingway, and John Steinbeck—it's well to note that they wrote not simply to answer their own confusions, but the confusions of the time. A nation that knew itself on the way to greatness had suddenly stumbled. No one could explain the stumble. The American people still seemed the same. American institutions looked sound, but proved a bit rotten. Days of easy money turned into days of no money at all.

Writers are at their best when they express what other people feel, but cannot express. When people are trapped in an undefined situation, they feel helpless. Great writers can define situations. Once the American people understand a situation, they generally act with character and purpose.

# OUR WRITERS AT THEIR BEST

THE 1930S WERE so filled with confusion and change it would take a full book to show everything our writers did. One of my heroes, Katherine Anne Porter, picked up the short story and wrote it with fullness that even Hemingway could not achieve. Eudora Welty did amazing things with both the short story and the American South, as would Carson McCullers (although she did not publish until 1940). Stephen Vincent Benét, and his sister Laura Benét, took American history for their own, both in poetry and prose. Sherwood Anderson puzzled the inflictions by commerce upon life, and the infliction by small towns upon thought. It was a golden age of theater, lit up by dramas by Eugene O'Neill and Clifford Odets among others. In order to offer an overview of the American writer engaged with the American world, many fine writers will be skipped. For this I grieve.

Let us look at a few who handled main issues among Americans during the Great Depression:

## THOMAS WOLFE

Into the confusions of the 1930s stepped Thomas Wolfe. His novels are not read much these days, but young writers will wish to read *Look Homeward, Angel* and *You Can't Go Home Again*. More than any other writer, Wolfe serves as a transition from the 1920s to the 1930s.

Wolfe's voice romped through the 1930s with needed passion. While other writers would do different, and equally important, work, none would sound the bell of memory so well as Wolfe. In the midst of economic depression, he remembered the good times, the important times, and times when families were fixed in certain, if not happy or honest, orbits. He was a vicious social critic, but sensual, filled with energy. He didn't mind making a fool of himself on the page if, by being a fool, he got the job done.

Equally important, Wolfe validated confusion at a time when confusion caused shame among a great many people. He did it by being confessional. His work is intensely personal, autobiographical, and sometimes barely on the edge of artistic control. Wolfe died young, and there's no telling what he might have produced as he gained authority. What he did produce, however, was a hymn of faith in the goodness that resides in otherwise damaged things.

Wolfe loved family. He loved the South. He loved America. He knew all of his loves were flawed. Families were institutions in which love might exist, but which also held betrayal. The southland with its heat and manners and gentleness was, to Wolfe, womanly. At the same time, the South could be small and mean and cruel.

Wolfe understood that we are all raised in the company of certain truths. For example, we have traditionally been raised to believe a young man and a young woman meet, fall in love, get married, raise children, and ride into the sunset after having lived happily ever after. We've been given an ideal. Almost no one actually lives this way, and many marriages fail. When they fail, people generally feel defensive and guilty. It was not supposed to end like this. What went wrong?

What went wrong, of course, is we weren't told that in order to reach the ideal one must work awfully hard, and even then the ideal may be beyond reach. Just because something doesn't work, though, doesn't mean the basic idea is wrong. This was Thomas Wolfe's message to America. The best plan is to acknowledge the truth of the ideal, make changes, and try again. In marriages, the basic idea may work the second or third time around. With nations, it's equally complicated.

Americans knew our nation was sound, but something dreadful had gone wrong. Our people had a hard time believing in themselves. Wolfe wrote of basic goodness that can exist among humans. Here is a passage from *You Can't Go Home Again*:

The train had hurtled like a projectile through its tube beneath the Hudson River to emerge in the dazzling sunlight of a September afternoon, and now it was racing across the flat desolation of the Jersey meadows. George sat by the window and saw the smoldering dumps, the bogs, the blackened factories slide past, and felt that one of the most wonderful things in the world is the experience of being on a train. It is so different from watching a train go by. To anyone outside, a speeding train is a thunderbolt of driving rods, a hot hiss of steam, a blurred flash of coaches, a wall of movement and of noise, a shriek, a wail, and then just emptiness and absence, with a feeling of "There goes everybody!" without knowing who anybody is. And all of a sudden the watcher feels the vastness and loneliness of America, and the nothingness of all those little lives hurled past upon the immensity of the continent. But if one is *inside* the train, everything is different. The train itself is a miracle of man's handiwork, and everything about it is eloquent of human purpose and direction. One feels the brakes go on when the train is coming to a river, and one knows that the old gloved hand of cunning is at the throttle. One's own sense of manhood and of mastery is heightened by being on a train. And all the other people, how real they are! One sees the fat black porter with his ivory teeth and the great swollen gland on the back of his neck, and one warms with friendship with him. One looks at all the pretty girls with a sharpened eye and an awakened pulse. One observes all the other passengers with lively interest, and feels that he has known them forever. In the morning most of them will be gone out of his life; some will drop out silently at night through the dark, drugged snoring of the sleepers; but now all are caught upon the wing and held for a moment in the peculiar intimacy of this Pullman car which has become their common home for a night.

Two traveling salesmen have struck up a chance acquaintance in the smoking room, entering immediately the vast confraternity of their trade, and in a moment they are laying out the continent as familiarly as if it were their own backyard. They tell about running into So-and-So in St. Paul last July, and—

"Who do you suppose I met coming out of Brown's Hotel in Denver just a week ago?"

"You don't mean it! I haven't seen old Joe in years!"

"And Jim Withers—they've transferred him to the Atlanta office!"

"Going to New Orleans?"

"No, I'll not make it this trip. I was there in May."

With such talk as this one grows instantly familiar. One enters naturally into the lives of all these people, caught here for just a night and hurtled down together across the continent at sixty miles an hour, and one becomes a member of the whole huge family of the earth.

Perhaps this is our strange and haunting paradox here in America—that we are fixed and certain only when we are in movement. At any rate, that is how it seemed to young George Webber, who was never so assured of his purpose as when he was going somewhere on a train. And he never had the sense of home so much as when he felt that he was going there. It was only when he got there that his homelessness began.[1]

## MERIDEL LE SUEUR

During the Great Depression, our writers sorted through confusion to give shape and form to a society in trouble. One trouble came because communism made a heavy pitch for the minds of the American people. The pitch didn't work, but it threatened. America did not go communist during the 1930s for a number of reasons. The strongest reason was that our people still believed in our country and the democratic system. Writers reinforced that belief.

A second reason came because the ideals of the labor movement remained in the society, even though the movement had precious little

---

[1]Here is Carl Sandburg on the same subject in his poem titled "Limited."

I am riding on a limited express, one of the crack trains of the nation
Hurtling across the prairie into blue haze and dark air go fifteen
    all-steel coaches holding a thousand people.
(All the coaches shall be scrap and rust and all the men and women
    laughing in the diners and sleepers shall pass to
    ashes.)
I ask a man in the smoker where he is going and he answers:
"Omaha."

clout during the Depression.² Meridel Le Sueur, a vigorous unionist, owned the same confusions and passions owned by multitudes of working people. Le Sueur addressed working America and, especially, American women. In *The Girl,* Le Sueur struggled with definitions of womanhood. She called the 1982 reprint of the book a "memorial to the great and heroic women of the depression." And so it is, and it is also more. Every word of the book is based in fact.

Le Sueur's writing has been treated as anarchist/socialist/communist/feminist; and she was none of these, because, while she would take up a cause (she was a lifelong member of the Communist Party), she was first of all a writer. Here are two passages. In the first, the Girl has discovered she is pregnant. She talks with five women, one old with a mind that wanders, and one who is a prostitute. As writers, you'll probably also enjoy seeing what happens in dialogue when no quotation marks are used:

I feel lonely, I said.

Oh stuff, she cried, why you aren't alone now, she laughed, he will dog your heels now all right, day in and day out. Try and be alone now! Ho! she cried laughing, she'll be kicking around like a sack full of kittens in no time. Ho, you are not alone now, whether you like it or not.

You had to laugh. She was so comical peering into my face, stroking my arms.

I know how it is, she said, you can't break people apart from each other and not have them get bitter in the belly. But lubchick, look! we are all here ...

Clara said, You should go on and have it now. And it will take care of you in your old age. You couldn't be any worse off, could you?

Belle said, Don't have it taken out.

Clara said, Don't do that. That's what's the matter with me, it gets you sooner or later.

---

²Marxists hated labor unions. According to Marx, the proletariat would become so oppressed it would revolt and seize the means of production. Labor unions worked for better wages and conditions. Marxists had to be against anything promising permanent benefits for the proletariat. Logically, if things got better for working people, there would be no need for revolution.

Amelia said, I don't know what it is, something used to come over me. Everytime one of mine was born, I'd say I was never going to have another, and then something would come over me, and all I would want was to be sitting on the back porch sewing on a blanket and thinking I was going to have a baby, and then I would get like that and I would feel good. No matter how hard it was for me I would feel good.

Clara said, O, a man can always be raising some dough for whiskey or ten bucks for those pills for an abortion, but no money to have it.

Belle said, And they're at you day and night. You can't lie down in the daytime the way it is.

We're dumb. We're fools, Clara cried bitterly, taking all their filth one way and another, getting poisoned with it.

Amelia said, It isn't the man. A man is a mighty fine thing, there is nothing better than a man. It's the way we have to live that makes us sink to the bottom and rot.

That's me, Clara said, I'm rotting.

Butch's mother licked up the stew. I have to go now, My husband has come to take me home. I see him out the window.

You are home, mother, Amelia said, sit still.

Oh no, I'm not home. We had red roses on the wall. I seen ropes and swivels this afternoon so this must be Uncle John's house, and we will have to hurry to be home by night . . .

And here is Le Sueur on the labor movement:

Amelia said: There is no use saying it is this and that, it is men, it is women, it is one thing and another. We all got to be alive, and not lay down, and *fight* for it. We got to be men and women again and want everything and dream everything and fight for it, so? I know how you feel. When my husband first was a union man I only favored it because he was my husband and he was in favor of it. But when I got the news that he was dead and his brother came in to tell me he was dead, I was different after that.

I listened to her closer now. I am different too, I thought. How did he die again

*We had six children then, she said, the biggest one was Ella she*

*was eight, going on nine. The youngest was inside me. When he went that morning in the strike, I told him there was going to be trouble, and he might get killed, and he said to me, I'll never forget it, he said, he'd better die fighting than be a scab or live like a mouse. I said if he died the raise wouldn't do him no good. He said it would do the others some good. He said it would do the other union men good, and he wasn't no man if he didn't stand up and fight with the others.*

It's beginning to snow, Mrs. Rose said, looking out the window. Big white flakes like faces looked in the window.

I didn't think scabs were he-men nohow, she went on, they don't hold up for their rights. I figure a man who don't hold up for his rights is no man nohow. Woman either. That goes double for women.

The fire burned hot. I put in another stick. We had seven sticks left. After that we would have to go to bed to be warm. People began to come in, doors slammed below. The snow was falling. Everybody talks about their lives this time of night.

And here is Le Sueur in a testament of faith that I cannot read without weeping. She tells how the book came together. She was with a worker's group of women who told their stories.

They looked upon me as a woman who wrote (like the old letter writers) and who strangely and wonderfully insisted that their lives were not defeated, trashed, defenseless but that we as women contained the real and only seed, and were the granary of the people. This should be the function of the so-called writer, to mirror back the beauty of the people, to urge and nourish their vital expression and their social vision. . . .

## REALISTS, FANTASISTS, FABULISTS

When the fires of the twentieth century are banked, the one writer who may continue to stride through history will be John Steinbeck. He was brilliant, emotional, fearless in his attempts, and consummately lucky. If Roosevelt proved the right politician at the right time, Steinbeck proved, equally, the right writer. He had a lot of help. A few fellow writers were Ernest Hemingway, Philip Wylie, James T. Farrell, Damon

Runyon, James M. Cain, William Sydney Porter (O. Henry), and Dashiell Hammett, and at least a hundred others. Some are regarded by the literary establishment as heavyweights, and others as lightweights.[3]

We can look at Steinbeck by thinking of two major issues he faced in the 1930s:

One major issue was grayness. Depressions are gray, whether individual and psychological, or economic and national. Vitality seeps away. Creativity flees. Life ceases to be life and becomes only motion as people can barely bring themselves to take one step after another.

A second problem was dehumanization of the American people. In the 1930s, dehumanization came from a failed system. It also came from forces that tried to eliminate the value of the individual by manipulating language: thus men and women would be spoken of as workers, or the masses, by communist and other political groups. Businessmen and politicians called anyone who did not love them "Reds."[4]

Further dehumanization came from hate campaigns using radio as a vehicle to spread their filth. In the 1930s, with plenty of hatemongers in attendance, a nasty little piece of flimsy who called himself Father Coughlin, priest of Royal Oak (Michigan), became a self-styled economist. He at first supported Roosevelt's New Deal, then turned against it. He used radio to attack the Jews, and railed against the "Jew Deal."

Another preacher who would be a disgrace in the eyes of all honest clergy was Gerald L. K. Smith. Smith served as mouthpiece for Huey Long, governor of and then senator from Louisiana, a Southern demagogue who had the good grace to get assassinated. (The man who killed Huey had, in Southern terms, a very satisfactory family reason. Huey "Kingfish" Long, it appears, fished after a lady who was married.)[5]

After the Kingfish went to his just reward, Smith formed a bond

---

[3]As writers, we may be glad for the literary establishment, so long as we understand that we need make our own judgments about important books. If we take our view from the literary bias currently in vogue, we miss a lot of good books, and will likely accept a distorted version of history.

[4]The same sort of buzz entered our language in the 1970s when people became "persons." Such usage can only be endorsed by the insecure or demented; people who have yet to explain why a chairperson is nicer than a chairman or a chairwoman. Before agreeing to dehumanize language it will be well to remember that when Stalin dehumanized people by changing them into workers, it became easier for him to kill 20 million.

[5]The masterful novel *All the King's Men* (1946), by Robert Penn Warren, is modeled on Huey Long.

with Coughlin, and the two founded a political party while vowing to lick Roosevelt. In the election of 1936, Roosevelt received 60.7 percent of the vote.

Of these two major problems of grayness and dehumanization, I think dehumanization was clearly worse. Dehumanization comes not only to the hated, but to the hater. It reduces everyone who gives it credence.

## JOHN STEINBECK

Steinbeck understood the perils of dehumanization as he addressed communism.

Great writers do not generally take sides. *In Dubious Battle* tells the story of Jim Nolan, who, for many good reasons, including the deaths of his father and mother, does field work for the Communist party. The organizer is Harry Nilson. The field men are Mack, Dick, and Joy. Burton is a doctor. There are other important characters, but the situation Steinbeck examines centers around these. The writer, exploring the truth of the material, discovers the callousness of communists. Mack will use anyone and anything to further his cause, a strike among fruit pickers in California. The book also shows idealism, faith in humanity, and self-sacrifice.

In addition, the situation spits forth viciousness of landowners whose political clout allows them to run the police and the newspapers. A few small landowners, and others sympathetic to the strike, must hold their tongues or suffer. One man's barn and crop are burned, and another man's lunch wagon burns. Strikers are beaten to death, or shotgunned. Doc Burton questions all of it, and we readers are left with an understanding of a situation in which everyone is partly wrong.

Not even Steinbeck's later *The Grapes of Wrath* would be so definitive when it came to showing opposing forces in the society. *In Dubious Battle* gave voice to national anger, despair, and voice to sorrow. It stood in opposition to two systems, communist and capitalist—both corrupt. It allowed the understanding that both systems could be rejected in behalf of a better way.

## JAMES T. FARRELL

These were days of turmoil in city streets, and of violence, gangs, and a failure to persuade young people of the values attending civilization. These problems are still with us, and in the 1930s, they were not new. They extend backward as far as the American Revolution. In the 1890s, Stephen Crane had written *Maggie: A Girl of the Streets*. In the 1930s, James T. Farrell would write the trilogy *Studs Lonigan*. The rapid recognition of these books brought other stories and novels that searched for faith in the middle of urban chaos. In this tradition, Nelson Algren would later write the story "A Bottle of Milk for Mother," and Harold Robbins would write *A Stone for Danny Fisher* (1952). The books and stories deal with children and grandchildren of immigrants. The Studs trilogy began after Farrell wrote the short story "Studs." The opening of that story gives a sense of what was being done by writers dealing with the streets:

IT IS RAINING outside; rain pouring like bullets from countless machine guns; rain spat-spattering on the wet earth and paving in endless silver crystals. Studs' grave out at Mount Olivet will be soaked and soppy, and fresh with the wet, clean odors of watered earth and flowers....

At Studs' wake last Monday evening everybody was mournful, sad that such a fine young fellow of twenty-six should go off so suddenly with double pneumonia; blown out of this world like a ripped leaf in a hurricane. They sighed and the women and girls cried, and everybody said that it was too bad. But they were consoled because he'd had the priest and had received Extreme Unction before he died, instead of going off like Sport Murphy who was killed in a saloon brawl. Poor Sport! He was a good fellow, and tough as hell. Poor Studs!...

For Studs will be miserable in Heaven, more miserable than he was on those Sunday nights when he would hang around the old poolroom at Fifty-eighth and the elevated station, waiting for something to happen. He will find the land of perpetual happiness and goodness dull and boresome, and he'll be resentful. There will be nothing to do in Heaven but to wait in timeless eternity. There will be no can houses, speakeasies, whores (unless they are reformed) and gambling joints; and neither will there be a shortage of plasterers. He will loaf up and down gold-paved streets where there is not even the suggestion of a poolroom, thinking of Paulie Haggerty, Sport Murphy, Arnold Sheehan and Hink Weber, who are possibly in Hell together because there was no priest around to play a dirty trick on them.

## HENRY ROTH

The great book about immigrants, and one that attacks grayness, comes from this period. Henry Roth's *Call It Sleep* (1934) tells about a Jewish child, David Schearl, growing up in New York. He has a gentle mother, a hardworking and cruel father who is a desperate man working harsh jobs. These are people in a dual battle. They fight against, or flee from, ancient angers of a European background. They also fight against the harshness of New York ghetto life.

I read *Call It Sleep* many years ago, and have just listened to it on tape. Since reading is an auditory experience, as well as visual, some books tape very well. Roth's book is one, and I hardly know whether it is better to read it first, or hear it first; but one would surely wish to do both. Few writers can get into the mind of a child so fully and with such empathy as Roth. I think no other writers love their characters more deeply than does Roth, and no other writer sounds a firmer note of hope.

## WILLIAM FAULKNER AND
## RICHARD WRIGHT

Two of our best and toughest novelists are William Faulkner and Richard Wright. (We've already seen Wright in the context of socialism/communism.) These two wrote in the generation after Chesnutt and Johnson. They never got so distracted by communism (Wright) or movie writing (Faulkner) to cease doing what was innate. They could be only writers, not worth a whole lot for anything else, for which we may all give thanks. Neither was especially nice, but being nice was not their job. They tried to tell the truth of characters in situations. Because of who they were, and what they dealt with, those situations were eternally surrounded by race.

In *Light in August,* Faulkner wrote of Joe Christmas, a man capable of "passing," but Christmas may or may not be Negro. He is murdered in a terrible fashion. As we've already seen, Wright tells of Bigger Thomas in *Native Son.*

Faulkner, from Mississippi, evoked brutality in a way most Northern writers handling similar situations could not, or at least did not. So did Wright, who, coming from Mississippi and Arkansas, and moving north, understood brutality in Chicago in a way matched only by James T. Farrell and Sinclair Lewis.

Faulkner and Wright are coupled in this book because they are so linked in my own past. They deeply influenced most of my writer friends and me during the late 1940s and early 1950s. In our discussions, we covered the entire range of subjects over which young writers fret. We figured Faulkner as a white guy writing about the deep ugliness, sin, and sorrow of Southern racial practices. We figured Wright as a black guy who wrote only about the truly terrible stuff faced by black guys. Our attitudes were reinforced because we lived in the border South, Kentucky, and, in my own case, had a background in small-town Indiana. Neither place was kindly in racial matters, but urban Kentucky pulsed with a little less cruelty than rural Indiana.[6]

We young writers were so overwhelmed by excesses we saw in American society we could see Faulkner and Wright only in terms of race. We had to live through some history before we understood that they wrote about people first, subjects second. Faulkner's work is awash in history. Wright's work is awash in social analysis. In addition, both wrote about characters dealing with other equally great matters, Americanism among them. These two, more than any other writers, set the stage for the civil-rights movement that would arise after World War II.

## ERNEST HEMINGWAY

A terrible feature of the Depression was an attack on the American people's sense of their own worth. We've already seen how Meridel Le Sueur worked to restore the faith of women in themselves.

---

[6]At the time—the witch-hunt 1950s—we did not understand that publishers tried to hide Wright's communism. We did not see Faulkner's deep and abiding concern with history, especially with historical forces arising from the Civil War and World War I.

During the Great Depression, American men were under attack. Men who could not find work felt guilty, ashamed, angry, and helpless; and, for the American male, there is probably nothing in the world worse than feeling helpless.

No one worked against this feeling of helplessness more than Ernest Hemingway, one of the badly used writers of the twentieth century. His work was extremely popular. His style is electric. Of late, his work has fallen on hard times. When the feminist movement gained momentum, it took on the character of all such movements; i.e., despite a great and admirable cause, and despite leadership from many, if not all, informed and intelligent people, a certain amount of mindless noise was generated. The same sort of shallow minds that would ban *Huckleberry Finn* from schools insisted that Hemingway's work was "sexist."

Total drool, of course. Great writers aren't sexist, because if they are, they're not great writers. The best-drawn character in *For Whom the Bell Tolls* is Pilar, a woman. Women in Hemingway's work may find themselves in tough situations, or they may find themselves dealing with jerks, but they are always their own selves. Hemingway's best book, *For Whom the Bell Tolls*, was written while the author thought in Spanish and wrote in English. In that sense it is a complete experiment, and if one reads it with a mind-set of English, some of it sounds a little silly. If, though, one reads it with a mind-set of Spanish, it's wonderful.

Hemingway wrote mostly about things concerning men. At a time when men were attacked at the very roots of their identities, he reinforced the value of male roles. When we set all literary and/or prejudiced chitchat aside, it's fair to say that Hemingway's work served men in the exact same manner that Le Sueur's served women.

## DASHIELL HAMMETT

Hemingway was not alone. Dashiell Hammett produced work so stark, yet so complex, that any attempt to dismiss him as a mystery writer would be a glaring error. In *Red Harvest* (1929), he deals with mob control and mob wars in a town called Personville, nicknamed Poisonville. The bad guys are bad, and the good guys are bad in a good way, and the whole book is a morality play. Forces of light and dark run through the actions of tough guys. The value of traditional male ideals is enhanced because even some awfully cynical people can still hold them.

## JAMES M. CAIN

The strongest writer in this tradition, after Hemingway, was James M. Cain, who, from 1934 through the 1940s, wrote *The Postman Always Rings Twice, Serenade,* and *Mildred Pierce,* among others. In *Serenade,* Cain created a bisexual hero and got away with it. (The topic was thought unspeakable long after World War II.) Cain also put the knock on the hypocrisy of society and custom. In dealing with sex, mindlessness, and misuse of power, he announced a sea change in American thinking.

During the Great Depression, Americans retreated into many of the forms of Victorianism. That made sense, because the Victorian period was remembered as a time when society had been stable and many people fairly well off. Cain knew that those attitudes could not last; his work became a goad against the rigidity of Victorian forms. His novels also serve as introduction to one of our most interesting writers.

## PHILIP WYLIE

Philip Wylie was tremendously prolific. He wrote from ideas rather than character, and his ideas were often snarly. By 1934, he had published seven novels before his first really successful novel, *Finnley Wren.* The title page pretty much describes Wylie's complete works:

FINNLEY
WREN

His *Notions* and
*Opinions* together
with *A HAPHAZARD
HISTORY* of HIS
*Career* and *Amours*
in these MOODY YEARS,
as well as SUNDRY RHYMES,
FABLES, DIATRIBES

AND LITERARY
MISDEMEANORS

A NOVEL IN A
NEW MANNER
by PHILIP WYLIE

Wylie can flip dialogue and insights, and keep flipping until the
reader sits sort of stunned. In the following passage, Finnley Wren,
aboard ship, is approached by a girl he's never met.

The girl was feminine and very sweet despite the short skirts,
bobbed hair and conscientious rakishness of the early American
flapper. She was a dark girl, not very tall, with a rapturous
mouth and oblique, private ways of presenting herself even to
strangers which were both charming and imaginative.

She sat down in front of Finnley, crossed her legs, and said,
"There was a porpoise yesterday, but I'm afraid it's gone"

He nodded. "I find them like that. Quite unreliable. It's part
of their fascination. But I can recommend the waves. We had
several fine ones an hour ago. It's a pity you missed them. The
color of tourmalines."

"Of course," the girl continued, edging a little closer to him,
"there are two kinds of tourmalines."

"I referred, naturally, to the South American variety."

The girl yawned. "I've been sleeping all afternoon."

"So I noticed. In your dress."

"Is it so badly mussed?"

"Just a little. On one side. And there are fingerprints on your
cheek."

"I usually take off my dress before I go to sleep," the girl
replied. "But I wasn't able to do it today. I wanted my state-
room door open and mother made me choose between that
and a dress. So I went to sleep in my dress." She leaned forward
and stared at him, her deep eyes wide open. "I trust I'm not
offending an habitual peeping Tom."

"No offense."

She shook her head several times. Her hair was as dark as

his own and faintly perfumed. "Shall we get married?" she said.

"Or shall we walk around the deck?"

"Or both?"

"Are you very hard to marry?" Finnley peered back at her anxiously and their faces almost touched.

"Dreadfully. There are the Sirens. And there is the Cyclops."

"Did you get A in Ancient History, too?"

"B plus."

"And how will I recognize these hazards?"

"The siren is my mother. Young men who see both of us fall in love with her. As if she were a plum pudding and I were a raisin."

"I see," Finnley replied with sudden comprehension. "And the Cyclops?"

"My father. Can you play golf? Did you ever collect postage stamps? Are you terrified by little men with bass voices? Do you get seasick? Do you believe that progress depends on national advertising?"

Wylie provoked readers all through a long life. His imagination would try anything. In *The Disappearance* he made all the women in the world vanish, in order to examine men's idiotic assumptions about women. In *Opus 21,* after World War II, Christ appeared in the cockpit of the *Enola Gay,* the plane that dropped the atom bomb on Japan. Wylie was a feminist long before 95 percent of living Americans were born, and the feminist movement has been unable to handle him; a mild way of saying that he is, officially, a writer whose very guts women are supposed to hate.

The whole flap arose from his book *Generation of Vipers.* That book holds a chapter about the American Mom, begirdled, bridge-playing, controlling; in fact, women exhibiting all of the more loathsome characteristics associated with Victorianism.

As he grew older, Wylie would ruefully say that he had spent a lifetime, plus millions of words, damning the actions and beliefs of men; and had written only twenty-one pages about the commoner sort of women. For that he was hated roundly and soundly. Since Wylie would come to have about the same opinion of the human race as that held by Mark Twain, I have no doubt he found the situation droll.

More than any other writer, Wylie gave the American people something to talk about, worry about, and swear at besides depression. He served the cause of ideas during a time when creativity might well have been buried beneath despair.

## O. HENRY

It's hard to say how much of American endurance came from the spirit of the people, and how much was a reflection of writing, fundamentalist religion, plus entertainment. Some of the most popular writers portrayed basic goodness and idiosyncracies of "regular folks." Sometimes they wrote humor. William Sydney Porter, who wrote under the name O. Henry, was about as well loved as any writer ever gets, and for more reasons than are readily clear.

He died in 1910, but although writers disappear, books have the half-life of radium. During the Great Depression his writing became a mainstay of middle and rural America.

He was the one and only master of the trick ending. He could conceal some element the reader should have been told on page one, and spring it in the last paragraph. In "The Last Leaf," for example, two young women live in a walk-up apartment in New York. Both are artists. Living downstairs is an awfully old and awfully failed artist named Behrman. An empty canvas, awaiting the masterpiece he always says he will paint, has been sitting for twenty-five years. One of the young women, Johnsy, catches pneumonia. She watches cold wind blow leaves from ivy that climbs a wall outside her window. She says when the last leaf falls, she will be gone as well. Sue, the other young woman, is desperate because Johnsy's doctor says there is only a one-in-ten chance, unless Johnsy can find some interest in life. The leaf does not fall. Johnsy decides she has been horrid for expecting to die. She recovers. The trick ending arrives when the two young women discover that Behrman has died of pneumonia, caught when he went outside to paint that last leaf (his masterpiece) on a wall behind the ivy.

Contrived. Sentimental. A little tacky, no doubt. Formula writing. And yet, O. Henry made it work. Over and over. In one guise or other, he must have told that same story six dozen times.

His work succeeded, I think, in the same manner Norman Rockwell paintings succeed. Only people who receive radio messages from Martians through fillings in their teeth can believe an O. Henry story or a Rockwell painting. At the same time, anyone with a sense of humor can believe the sentiment that lies behind the sentimentality. We respond to the affection in the work; for both writer and painter are warmhearted. O. Henry was one of the kindest men who ever lived, and behind his formulas lie genuine kindliness. The stories are always affectionate, and always somehow funny. Sometimes they were straightout humorous, as in "The Ransom of Red Chief." During the Depression, they performed like small dance routines that break up the seriousness of a dark and awful play.

## DAMON RUNYON

Damon Runyon told stories in which bad guys were really good guys, or at least carried mild streaks of goodness. His stories center around the social lowlifes of New York City. He uses slang and satiric language. In "Butch Minds the Baby," four guys plan to crack a safe, but one guy has a wife who makes him baby-sit. The safecrackers take the baby—and carriage—to the job. Butch gets away from a cop because no cop, anywhere, will figure that any safecracker, anywhere, is going to have a kid along.

Here is a sample. Three of the guys have just learned about a $20,000 payroll languishing in a safe:

Well, it seems that Harry the Horse and Little Isadore and Spanish John wish to get the money out of the safe, but none of them knows anything about opening safes, and while they are standing around over in Brooklyn talking over what is to be done in this emergency Harry suddenly remembers that Big Butch is once in the business of opening safes for a living.

In fact, I hear afterwards that Big Butch is considered the best safe opener east of the Mississippi River in his day, but the law finally takes to sending him to Sing Sing for opening these safes, and after he is in and out of Sing Sing three different times for opening safes Butch gets sick and tired of the place, especially as they pass what is called the Baumes Law in New York, which is a law that says if a guy is sent to Sing Sing four times hand running, he must stay there the rest of his life, without any argument about it.

So Big Butch gives up opening safes for a living, and goes

into business in a small way, such as running beer, and handling a little Scotch now and then, and becomes an honest citizen. Furthermore, he marries one of the neighbor's children over on the West Side by the name of Mary Murphy, and I judge the baby on the stoop comes of this marriage between Big Butch and Mary because I can see that it is a very homely baby, indeed. Still, I never see many babies that I consider rose geraniums for looks, anyway. . . .

Runyon taught us to laugh at ourselves, because life had gotten just a little too serious.

## DOXOLOGY

As we move from the Great Depression toward World War II, and to the close of a period in the history of the American writer, it's fair to ask how well writers succeeded in presenting new myths, and generating new ideas during a time of cant, confusion, and misdirection, a time stretching from 1865 to 1940.

Remembering those times, it also pays to remember that America has not always been a great nation. It had to be built. Successes had to be registered. Mistakes had to be made.

In addition to guilt attending the aftermath of the Civil War, the American people also responded to growth, Reconstruction, exploitation of national resources and of people. They dealt with new inventions, immigration, settlement of the west, nationalism, world war, and economic depression. Bells in church steeples rang out against evolution, psychology, and were finally muffled by radio. Admen emerged clattering like jackpots on slot machines. Labor unions rose. Corporations replaced captains of industry. And, behind it all, the assembly line smoothly spat forth automobiles, radios, and gadgets.

Our writers—both the ones we remember, and ones now forgotten—sought for form and shape and sense within formlessness. The nation was in search of itself. Given the circumstances, I think our writers did pretty well. When they were joined, in the 1920s, by great artists, architects, musicians, playwrights, and composers, they did very well indeed.

They validated the hard work of people on the land by introducing a combination of practicality, romance, and naturalism. The farm and countryside became a stiff-necked, but moral, resource for the nation, a resource built on both Puritanism and revolution. It was also founded in the self-confidence rising from the "can do" attitude of pioneers; the "can do" of Original Possibility. Neither Europe nor England could produce anything comparable, although they had other working myths.

Our writers were the main voices insisting on the value of our people. Writers took on the issues of race, feminism, and economics. When the nineteenth century departed and the twentieth began, our writers were chief among those who denied the paper-thin forms of Victorianism while insisting on those parts of Victorianism that held merit. Finally, when the nation lay strapped beneath depression, our writers were singers, social realists, performers, and, even, revolutionaries; maintaining a tradition going back to 1776.

And we could learn to laugh at ourselves only because some of our writers could laugh at themselves.

Our nation might have made it through those years without our writers, but a fair question asks: Would the nation have wanted to go through those years without its writers? The answer: Of course not.

Another, even better question asks: Without our writers, what kind of nation would have emerged?

The answer: Doubtless a nation without a firm identity, a nation without kindness, and one with only a small ethical base.

# PART III

# WORLD WAR II

A FEW OF our writers tried to handle the greatest bloodbath in history, but storytelling about World War II would have to wait until after the war for at least two reasons:

First: Telling about a situation while sitting right in the middle of the situation is the job of the journalist. Second: Our writers and artists were stunned. World War II lay so far beyond ordinary experience that even savvy participants, generals, journalists, and Hemingway, viewed it in fragments. The very best of them saw only pieces and parts.

The popular journalist Ernie Pyle had covered the European campaign. When that phase ended, he had no interest in the Pacific war. The military begged him to cover the Pacific theater, and he reluctantly agreed. He died from a sniper's bullet on the island Ie Shima. He had never been careful about wearing a helmet and was shot in the head. A nation, by then well accustomed to mourning, mourned.

If it seems odd that millions of people felt stricken by the death of a journalist, perhaps that very oddness is key to the difference between the America of the 1940s and the America of today; when, in the popular mind, journalists are nearly as detested as lawyers.[1] It is key to

---

[1] Part of Pyle's popularity stemmed from work done before the war. He traveled around the nation for five years writing of places and people; apple knockers, top fallers, cowboys, and presidents of companies. The best of those writings are in his book *Home Country*, which is a collage of prewar America.

the difference in public attitudes about World War II, as opposed to the attitudes about tacky and unexplainable wars from Korea to the end of the twentieth century, when brave men and, latterly, brave women, have been asked to step forward in defense of questionable assumptions.

We can begin to understand the mind of our people, and their sorrow over Pyle, by looking at what they saw: the biggest war in history.

World War II truly was a world war—or, rather, a series of wars happening all at once. Take a globe of the world and give it a spin. With your eyes closed, place a finger on it to stop the spin. Odds are 90 percent or better that your finger will hit a war.

War raged through Europe, the Middle East, Africa from the northern states to the southern rubber plantations; and war pounded Russia, China, and Australia. South America and Central America served as fueling stops, and as bunkers for Germans and their money. The South Pacific, all of Asia, North America from the Aleutian Islands south, struggled in the grim fist of war. No ocean in the world remained safe for shipping. Even the Arctic and Antarctic proved not remote enough and were touched by war.

I wish I could avoid writing about the horrors of that war, but do not wish to dodge definition. So much romantic, sometimes even humorous, claptrap has been written about World War II that young writers may get sidetracked by bad information.

And, as if cheap writing was not bad enough, television arrived after the war. The public was treated to sitcoms about prisoners of war; the sitcoms not mentioning starvation, lice, disease, brutality, and massive death among prisoners. You may trust me when I say that in World War II, there were no jolly German colonels running prison camps, or cartoon Japanese majors being fooled by rollicking GIs.

Given a mixture of honest and dishonest information, people of today have a hard time understanding American thought and action during World War II. Americans at war were less than idealistic. The nation felt that it had its back to the wall, and survival came before courtesy or law. Understanding of our people's behavior comes more easily when we look at war's two great victories. The first victory is

## DEATH

Death is not war's greatest victory, but death is an obvious victory. The generalist (and storytellers are, by necessity, generalists) will see that total deaths in a war include those killed during preparation, execution, and aftermath.

If we add the millions killed in Russia as Stalin prepared for war to the numbers Hitler killed within his country; and if we add in the purges throughout China, as well as workers killed worldwide by faulty manufacturing equipment—and—if to these we add natives of islands, the men and women killed on African plantations, and the deaths of refugees, I venture we'll have 50 or 60 million killed before a single combatant falls. Estimates for deaths during World War II vary, but a figure of 60 million is generally considered reasonable. I venture that 100 million is overly conservative, once we add in deaths occurring during the prelude and aftermath.

It isn't possible to conceptualize 100 million deaths. The storyteller doesn't even try. The storyteller comes to understand a single death, then further understands that the death happened over and over and over.[2]

Such is the power of *The Diary of a Young Girl*, a journal kept by Anne Frank, a young Dutch girl who was not a storyteller. We read the book and find the blooming of thought, of hope, of friends, and the first thoughts about friendships with boys. We read of parents and ambitions and things that are beautiful. Then the Nazis arrive, the journal ends, and Anne Frank is destroyed with less compunction than the destroyers would feel over putting down a dog. All dreams are gone. Our tears remain.

This was one death. It happened 100 million times. Seen in this manner, it is possible to get an inkling of the total catastrophe of World War II. The American people reacted to this amount of death in harsh ways, as we'll shortly see.

---

[2]"The death of one child is a tragedy; the death of 20 million is a statistic."
–Joseph Stalin.

## DEHUMANIZATION

The greatest victory of war is dehumanization. There is not a solitary thing one can do for the dead, or expect from the dead. They have entered other realms, including the realm of history. The living, though, keep living.[3] As war swirls, whirls, walks widely, civilized values depart. Let us take one symbolic example of dehumanization, see how it came about, and we can then understand war's greatest victory.

## HIROSHIMA

The use of the atom bomb at Hiroshima on August 6, 1945, is cited these days to illustrate any number of points about "right" or "wrong." It's a favorite subject among English and philosophy professors who use the event as stimulus to get a class thinking. What some professors understand, but do not tell their classes (because they hope the classes will discover it on their own), is that "right" and "wrong" do not exist in modern war. There is only Wrong.

Although individuals in war may exhibit courage and integrity, the nature of weapons certifies the wrongness of war. It isn't possible to use any sort of bomb without killing noncombatants. The same holds true for the overwhelming firepower of armies. These days, a single squad carries more firepower than a nineteenth-century battalion.

In order to understand Hiroshima, it is necessary to understand the accumulation of wrongs. We do this because writers cannot settle for superficial understanding. Let us view that accumulation one nation at a time.

## JAPAN

During World War II, Japan stood but a short distance removed from a feudal society. It owned a rigid system of belief in loyalty, duty, and

---

[3] I have never been in combat, but have seen enough death at sea to say that great heroism happens *after* a war ends. When combatant soldiers return, marry, raise families, and remain sane—or, at least, not dangerous—and continue to contribute to the society, those soldiers are heroes.

obedience to rules. Racial hatred was as much a part of its culture and armies as were weapons. Japan had ambitions against China, one of its traditional enemies. The Japanese thought of the Chinese as animals. The Chinese, not one whit brighter, thought the Japanese laughable. Both nations considered Koreans with loathing. Americans were held in the same low esteem.

Holding that other races and cultures were subhuman, the Japanese army operated with a degree of cruelty we generally find in barbarian cultures. In addition to the Bataan Death March and other atrocities, the Japanese literally raped the Philippines.[4]

The attack on Pearl Harbor on December 7, 1941, while spectacular, is understandable. It was done for military advantage. The great wrongness of Japanese warmaking came from actions that gained no military advantage.

## GERMANY

The German army was, without question, the best-trained and best-equipped army in the world. Had Hitler left military decisions to his generals, outcomes might have been more serious than they were.

In the early years of the war, the German army was unstoppable. That kind of power is seductive. In your own experience you've watched two sports teams go at each other when one team is clearly superior. At some point, the game in no longer in question. One team has won; the other has obviously lost. The winning team, with time still on the clock, begins pounding, running up the score, going into a sort of frenzy to see just how badly it can thump the other team. This kind of conquest marked the German army and the German soldier in the early years of the war. The difference, of course, is that score was kept in terms of lives destroyed and cities burned.

German aims for the annihilation of Jews carried far beyond death camps. It affected the minds and hearts of Germans who, at some other time or place, were people you might wish to know.

Historian Chris Browning has documented this in his book *Ordinary*

---

[4]In the mid-1990s Japan paid compensation to Filipino women who, during World War II, were forced into sexual service for the Japanese army. The Japanese called them "comfort women." Rape and murder were also common.

*Men.*[5] It is the record of a German police battalion. The battalion received orders to round up Jews and shoot them. The battalion consisted of average citizens, carpenters, grocers, shoemakers; not soldiers. The men were given a choice: to go into a city and kill, or stay behind and avoid killing. The reaction—and actions—of the large majority of the men, even though those actions happened more than fifty years ago, will terrify you.

German leadership dictated German cruelty. Cruelty became a synonym for German conquest. Hitler claimed, as doctrine, the superiority of the "Aryan race."[6] This doctrine went beyond the Nazi party. It infected a nation and a nation's soldiers.

## RUSSIA

When Russia fought back, it fought as Russia has always fought: It threw masses of humanity into the face of guns. Russia has always owned an abundance of soldiers it considered expendable. Russian losses in World War II were catastrophic. Exact figures are unknown and will probably remain unknown, but they are somewhere between 20 and 25 million. This figure is in addition to those millions already killed by Stalin as he prepared for war. When German arms finally failed in Russia, revenge fell on the retreating army. Of ninety-one thousand German troops taken prisoner after Germans lost the Battle of Stalingrad (1942–43), only five thousand would eventually get back to Germany.

## ENGLAND

In the early days of the war, when France fell with little more than a whimper, England faced the possibility of a Europe controlled by Germany.[7] England faced decimation. It had to strike hard and keep strik-

---

[5]Christopher R. Browning, *Ordinary Men: Reserve Police Battalion 101 and the Final Solution in Poland* (HarperCollins, 1992).

[6]Hitler borrowed heavily from Nordic and Scandinavian legends and from German myths that arose before the Crusades. It is a good deal easier to understand World War II, and Hitler's Germany, if one reads Norman Cohn's *The Pursuit of the Millennium*, subtitled *Revolutionary Messianism in Medieval and Reformation Europe and Its Bearing on Modern Totalitarian Movements* (Harper & Row Torchbook, 1961). It's a tough read for young people, but it's worth the work.

[7]Germany actually occupied the Channel Islands.

ing in order to survive. The combined force of England, Australia, Canada, the United States, and volunteer forces from at least thirty other countries would defeat Germany. In order to succeed, massive war crashed on the heads of German civilians. The Allies pretty much bombed around the clock, the Brits bombing during night raids and the Americans during days. Bombs were first directed against military targets, then against cities. The Allies believed they could break German morale by killing German civilians. It was not uncommon to bomb towns and cities that contributed little or nothing to Germany's war effort.

## AMERICA

In the beginning, American arms against Japan were directed at military targets. As war progressed, air attacks on cities were aimed at breaking the nation and the nation's spirit. Horrible as it was, the atomic bomb did not begin to kill as many people as did firestorms, caused by dropping tons of incendiary bombs on cities, so that fire became a self-feeding, self-sustaining destroyer.[8]

By the time the atomic bomb was dropped on Hiroshima, America had lost 400,000 military dead; this in a nation of 131 million. For three-and-a-half years, a propaganda machine had cranked out stories of German and Japanese atrocities. Radio, newspapers, platform speakers, politicians, preachers, and journalists all joined in to aid the war effort. In school classrooms, children were taught that Japanese were a lower form of life. I know this because I was one of those children. The entire nation lay covered with propaganda.

And 400,000 were dead. The American people did not know the extent of loss because that was a military secret, but I venture not a man, woman, or child in the nation did not experience loss. The dead soldier might not be a relative, but a kid who lived down the block or across the street. Everyone knew someone who had died.

Secretary of War Henry L. Stimson would later publish a justification for using the atomic bomb, written at the direction of President Harry Truman. Substantial rational reasons are given for the use. They include the argument that the bomb saved a million American lives, and countless Japanese lives; which may or may not actually be the case, de-

---

[8]A firestorm was also used to destroy the German city of Dresden.

pending on the unknown state of Japanese morale, which has been variously reported. An American invasion of Japan might well have been a bloodbath.[9]

But that is begging the point. At the time, most people in America were so sick of death and fear and loss that, had Japan sunk into the sea, the majority of people would not have turned a hair. The majority would have hollered hallelujah.

The Japanese, equally sick of death and fear and loss, would have done the same were the roles reversed.

The point is that war achieved its greatest victory. It literally *dehumanized* the entire world. Wrong was added to wrong, and two wrongs were added to two more, and the sum of wrong was multiplied by factors of a thousand, a hundred thousand, a million; and thus discussions of "right" or "wrong" in the dropping of the atomic bomb become academic exercises.

Had Ernie Pyle been alive when the bomb dropped, he would not have had a word to say, because Pyle remained one of the few voices of civilization sounding clear above the rabble. Pyle did not understand strategy, tactics, or politics. He understood soldiers, wrote about them, and told their individual stories. He wrote about their hometowns and their hopes for leading a clean life after the war. Pyle was one of the few voices in a war-torn world that claimed the human spirit, and human hopes, as still valid. And that is the reason why we mourned him.

---

[9]Some historians have proposed that the bomb was dropped in order to intimidate Stalin—not Japan, because Japan was already whipped.

A second reason may well have been that power is seductive. The problem with a dread new weapon is that its very existence asks for its use.

# THE SECOND AMERICAN
# REVOLUTION

AT THE CLOSE of World War II America gradually discovered itself on center stage. Our army and navy were victorious. The nation owned the most powerful weapon the world had then seen, the atomic bomb. No other nation had one. America stood in a position to dictate terms, command large stretches of empire, and, as a government, control vast portions of the globe. Instead of conquest by force, the nation turned to conquest by commerce.

Much of the world lay knocked flat, its industrial base knocked flat as well. American industry sat with healthy facilities, and a workforce wanting peaceful work. Europe and Japan needed rebuilding. In fact, most of the world became customers for American products. The nation embarked on a period of prosperity unparalleled in its history.

With prosperity came the growth of cities and further exodus of people from farms. The entire social structure began changing. Back in the 1920s, the nation had rebelled against Victorianism. Then, in the 1930s, Victorian values reasserted themselves because of the Great Depression. During World War II, those values once more began to crack because the pressures of war, and the great loss of life, made a lot of Victorian pretensions look purely silly. After the war, remaining Victorian values struggled with the values of a growing industrial nation.

For the American writer, a lot would happen quickly because the nation embarked on a revolution.

## THE SOCIAL REVOLUTION

The revolution was not political, but social and economic. It was marked by these features:

The movement from farm to town caused the breakdown of the extended family. Something called "the nuclear family" appeared. It was made up of father, mother, and children; no cousins, uncles, aunts, or grandparents. The extended family, a traditional means of emotional and economic support, broke down.

Reaction to economic depression and war caused the nation to embark on a frenzy of building and, literally, economic joy. Anyone who poured concrete was thought to be engaged in holy work, no matter what was being built.

Changes in the physical and social landscape caused marriage, divorce, birth, madness, suicide, education, and crime rates to race upward.

New ideas entered society, especially the idea of "social conscience," which we'll look at after a bit.

The good news is that most change during the second revolution had roots in the principles of the first American Revolution, in concepts of the Rights of Man, and ". . . with liberty and justice for all." Much of what happened after World War II also came directly from ideas of Original Possibility and Original Good. Original Sin was also represented because the nation embarked on self-criticism that would last through the rest of the twentieth century.[1] The nation changed rapidly on its surface, but our formative ideas remained. At the time, no one could say, with any precision, just what the blazes was happening.

With the advantage of hindsight, we can now get a pretty clear picture. These forces operated:

---

[1] No other nation in the world has so deeply examined, and reexamined, reasons for guilt as has this nation: guilt over slavery, the treatment of women, the environment, and other misdeeds. If, in the past fifty years, we had spent as much time correcting problems as we spent trying to make each other feel guilty (while also trying to rewrite history), our problems would be greatly lessened. I know of no better illustration than this "guilt-tripping" to show how founding ideas (in this case, Puritanism and Original Sin) stride across centuries to affect the present.

## Need for Normality

People who had rarely known normality except by hearsay hungered for "things to get normal." After all, if one has endured eleven years of catastrophic ecnomic depression, followed by four years of catastrophic world war, hunger for normality is reasonable.

"Normality" meant marriage, a house, an education, a job for the man, a car, a refrigerator instead of an icebox, a cookstove that didn't run on firewood, and kids who would eventually lead to grandkids. Those wants may seem obvious to us now, but to Americans after World War II, the wants seemed optimistic. Fifty years ago, for example, a refrigerator and an electric or gas range seemed luxuries to as many as half of our people.

As we've seen, many Americans, even most, came from the countryside or had parents and grandparents on farms. Much of what they knew were codes that worked for two centuries in rural America. The country boys and country girls came to town. They looked around, shook their heads, rushed toward marriage—and moved to the suburbs.

## Suburbs and Women

Suburbs held a built-in contradiction. During the war, many women had learned a measure of independence. Then, suburbs moved women away from economic and social action almost as effectively as had Victorianism. No one planned it. At the time, no one gave it two thoughts because everyone was busy striving for normality.

People moved to suburbs because they couldn't afford a house in town and they sure-as-the-world didn't want to run a farm. A new house in the suburbs was easy come by, thanks to mortgages under the G.I. Bill. A man named William Levitt applied mass-production methods to house building, which brought down the price of houses. Suburban houses were not expensive; they cost less than $10,000 as late as 1958; roughly 2½ years' salary.

The movement of women away from the center of action did not bring immediate distress. Distress over women's roles arrived a few years later, as understanding started catching up with change that had occurred during the war.

War changes came about because women worked beside older men in factories. (Men to age forty had been in the army or essential industries, or on farms.) As factory workers, women enjoyed excellent pay.[2] Overtime pay became standard. Women got used to having their own money instead of depending on a husband to earn the family living.

Wartime money had also offered a bit of freedom. Because of rationing and lack of consumer products, one could not buy much, but a lot of partying went on. For some women, love affairs came and went with passing troop trains. A measure of freedom thus attended most women's lives, although many did not exercise much freedom. They worried about husbands or brothers or boyfriends overseas, and stayed close to home. Whether drinking and dancing, or keeping a steady hand in matters at the church, pretty nearly everybody prayed; and, what with the number of killed and wounded in action, some of the prayers didn't seem to work. The sum amounted to women's roles under enormous pressure and in enormous change, although, at the time, even the most emancipated women could not estimate the far-reaching consequences.

## RACIAL ROLES

If roles for women changed, Americans still identified as niggers, china boys, chinks, the yellow peril, slant-eyes, as well as wops, spicks, yids, kikes, mackerel snappers, dagos, dinges, eight-balls, micks, squareheads, spooks, hunkies, polacks, and siwash changed as well. These words started to falter in vulgar usage as awfully nice things began happening.

## PRELUDE TO INTEGRATION

A nation had just emerged from literal hell, but a hell it went through united; not simply as states, but united as a people. Ideas of Original

---

[2]Labor-union demands boomed during the war, but industry didn't care. Industry charged the government for products on the basis of actual cost of production, plus 6 percent profit. Thus, if the cost of production got kicked up by high wages, the 6 percent profit grew. Labor unions, being institutions, turned into power-mongers, some as dirty as nineteenth-century industry had been. There would be a shake-out among unions, and a reduction in their power, starting with the Taft-Hartley Act (1947). There would be further reductions during the 1970s and 1980s.

Good emerged once more. Although hate-mongers still circled the action with vicious messages, those messages were mostly discounted. The American world did not lay covered with daffodils, but matters improved greatly.

That improvement had roots in presidential actions prior to World War II. Before President Franklin Roosevelt (and advocacy by Eleanor Roosevelt, who didn't let her husband get by with a whole lot when it came to ignoring domestic policy), the idea of racial equality shone remote as the farthest star in the most distant galaxy; and that statement is *not* an exaggeration.

Roosevelt integrated the U.S. Post Office. Then World War II took Americans of all backgrounds to war, even though discrimination continued to exist. Industry hired whoever could fill jobs, although discrimination also existed in factories.

In consequence, after the war, our nation stood ready to handle integration. The Supreme Court, which traditionally follows major trends in public opinion, ruled in *Brown versus The Board of Education of Topeka* (1954) that the doctrine of "separate but equal" was not valid. Schools must be integrated. By then, some Americans of types both dark and pale had already enjoyed the hospitality of local jails for pushing integration.

What followed was an exciting and hopeful time for great numbers of Americans. Integrationists rose all across the nation. While the large majority of activists were black, a solid minority were white. A camaraderie came into being that, for those who experienced it, remains warm in memory. In many ways, we, as a people, have not been so united since. I miss it.

Resistance rose in that part of the South that Southerners usually term "sorry."[3] Looking back on those days, it is difficult to identify who was the lowest of the low. If I had to choose, it would be Orval Faubus, governor of Arkansas, who became so low, he could walk under a snake's belly while wearing a top hat. He did not really care about

---

[3]We did not have the *Miranda* warning or other protections in those days, and police pretty much did what they wanted. As illustration: In Louisville, as late as 1956, I was working a job with two friends who were black. After work, I drove them home. One sat in the front seat, one in back. I dropped the first guy off, and the man in back didn't move to the front seat since it was only a two-block drive to his house. A cop worked both of us over pretty good. It offended the cop because it looked like a white guy was acting as chauffeur for a black guy.

integration one way or the other. He cared about winning the next election. He fomented a mob, and then ordered out the National Guard to protect the mob. The National Guard had the assignment of keeping Negro children out of Central High School.

Another piece of human waste was "Bull" Connor, head cop in Birmingham. Other people, certain mothers in New Orleans known as the Cheerleaders, displayed mouths like flushings of a toilet, and brains colder than those of a corpse. The Cheerleaders demonstrated outside schools. I always knew the Ku Klux Klan sported creatures both smelly and cowardly, but those New Orleans mamas gave new meaning to the word "stink." If you own a strong stomach, you may want to watch a bit of news footage from those days.

Nothing I've ever seen is uglier than a mob, and the 1950s saw the American South plagued by mob action so mindless that, in comparison, an attack by sharks looks like the height of gentle reason. If that had been all the South displayed, I would be saddened to have lived anywhere near the place.

Many Southerners favored integration, and for at least three reasons. It was the right thing to do. It was inevitable, so the South might as well get it over. It was too expensive to segregate kids, educate them, and have them bail out for the North the minute they got high-school diplomas.

These three elements were pointed out by many people, none more delightful than Harry Golden, who published a newspaper called *The Carolina Israelite*. Harry owned a droll sense of humor. He pointed out that whenever interreligious dialogue took place, it was always a meeting between Reformed Jews and Unitarians (a sort of funny statement because God, Himself, cannot tell the difference). On interracial meetings, Harry wrote, "A group of colored and colorless got together last night. . . ." He introduced "The Vertical Negro Plan for Integration," in which he argued that the races mingled beautifully in the South. Negroes fixed the food, swept the floors, cut the lawns, took care of the children. He concluded that white people and black people worked together just fine as long as black people didn't sit down. Therefore, he argued, integration was a cinch. Just take all the chairs out of the schools.

Martin Luther King, Jr., had some support across the broad range of Southerners of all colors. King also found opposition from elements of the black power structure. Many black businessmen, preachers, and social workers saw their power on the wane if integration became fact. Enlightened cynicism became the order of the day. Among many integrationists, the NAACP was known as the National Organization for the Advancement of Certain People. I know this statement does not accord with popular history, but popular history is wrong.

It was a new Civil War fought in the streets of North and South, and in behalf of understanding by Northern and Southern minds. An otherwise-united nation stood divided on the issue, but, through the 1950s and 1960s, would gradually come together. Backsliding began in the 1970s, but that is another story that must be told by someone else.

## THE NEW DEITY

We need think of another element facing writers in the 1950s. World War II had been won through courage, supply, and manufacture. Industry, which traditionally acted badly (as we have seen), proved its great worth. While only government could have gotten the country through the Great Depression, only industry could guarantee success in World War II. Germany and Japan were defeated by brave men, but also by American industry, which produced weapons, trucks, and ships faster than the enemy could destroy them.

During the 1950s, American production continued to boom at wartime rates, but products supplied peacetime markets. A way of thinking had lurked near the popular mind since at least the 1920s. Now the thought took shape:

## SCIENCE AS GOD

Industry strode the land as an expression of science. Science seemed omnipotent, promising a cure for any and every ill of individual and society. As the century rolled on, industry became taken for granted. Science stood as a separate creature, creating miracles.

The big news after World War II was not nuclear energy, but penicillin, followed by the Salk vaccine for polio. If both seem like routine miracles in these days of scientific wonders, it's time for another jog down memory lane.

Here are a few diseases that once laid waste this nation and the world, diseases that medical science would sweep away: smallpox, diphtheria, scarlet fever, typhus, polio, whooping cough, mumps, tuberculosis, syphilis, and cholera, one of the all-time favorites of world history.

Science became godlike, then revered, because it made huge promises—and kept them. The national attitude rapidly changed to belief in science.

An example of that rapid change can be seen in the ways Americans raised their children. As the 1950s opened, any kid who thought well of Buck Rogers, and who talked about going into space, found himself at the doctor. His parents feared him mentally disturbed, or a dreamer; both conditions considered deadly.[4] But, by the end of the 1950s, most everyone understood we would go into space. Thus were kids encouraged to do well in math. People began to admire science for its advances into what was considered the last frontier.[5]

Few Americans, if any, realized that after World War II science literally took over traditional powers owned by God. Our scientists split the atom. Biologists predicted understanding of the structure of life. Doctors performed organ transplants, healed the blind. A growing network of communications promised that soon we would see all and know all. Newsreels of the period hyped a future containing technological miracles: automobiles run by atomic power, superhighways on which would run vehicles following electronic beams.

If this seems sort of silly today, it was not silly then. Most Americans had grown up burning wood or coal for heat. They had no experience with air-conditioning, ballpoint pens,[6] automatic transmissions, turn

---

[4]The doc was not a specialist. America was about to discover "the identity crisis," but we weren't there yet. The 1950s were days when doctors were still trusted implicitly, as were ministers and schoolteachers. The doctor had little changed in form or ability from the men pictured in a powerful novel of the time, *Not as a Stranger,* by Morton Thompson.

[5]Many conservative people still made dire predictions about space and flight. These were the same types who once claimed one could not exceed speeds of 60 mph in a car without exploding. After a car surpassed 60 and didn't explode, their estimates went to 100 mph before the big smash. The same types, in the 1950s, claimed no one could ever get to the moon because it was like building a tower to heaven in order to view the face of God. And no one, it was claimed, could live if he flew past the speed of sound. Their voices got drowned out by sonic booms.

[6]The first ballpoint pens caused a sensation. They sold for $25 to $50 and were regarded as miraculous because they could write underwater. That was about all they

signals, power brakes and steering. Fluorescent light, plastics, aluminum building materials, dial telephones, four-lane highways; these, and hundreds of other innovations, were completely new to nearly everyone. In addition, a marvel of science (one that would prove the scourge of the twentieth century) appeared in 1947. We had gotten rid of cholera, but now the nation suffered a new plague: television. Cholera was cleaner.

## TELEVISION

Television enjoyed an untrained but willing audience that regarded television as a magnificent contribution from science.

At first, television did not understand its markets, but it learned fast. Advertisers proved eager to participate. Politicians took awhile to catch on, but by the end of the decade, even they understood that a medium, greater than any manure spreader ever known in the history of agriculture, lay composting at their feet. By the end of the decade, television stood ready and willing to spread for anyone with a buck.

"But," one might protest, "selling things is the American way."

Yep. I have no quarrel with free enterprise. I quarrel not with advertising, but with assumptions that accompany advertising; assumptions at least as old as publisher William Randolph Hearst in the early twentieth century. Yellow journalists assumed the way to sell newspapers was to go for the groin. As I've attested elsewhere, television took to this proposition like a cat to tuna. It cheapened society's view of the human experience.

Many other elements existed in the 1950s, but two proved interesting to writers:

## PRACTICALITY

Practicality became the watchword of the 1950s. It is easy to understand how people who experienced economic depression and world war were not likely to get real spiritual. They intended to get educations, make money, and give full rein to a nesting instinct too long denied. They

---

could do because the first inks would not feed smoothly. At the time, no one stopped to think that almost no one ever has much occasion to write underwater.

did not give two snips for anything that could not be used for building houses, or jobs leading to aught but bags and bags of groceries.

In consequence, they wanted their kids raised in the "real world." In the 1950s, perfectly sincere people not only wanted to "off" Santa Claus and the Easter Bunny, they wanted to get rid of "Snow White," "Rumpelstiltskin," all of *Grimm's Fairy Tales*. The most progressive wished to rewrite miracles of the Bible to conform with scientific explanations.

Any work of imagination became suspect. As writers, you can readily see exactly how our writers would react. American writing would soon embark on a golden age of imagination.

Another issue affecting writers came about because, together with integration, our nation discovered something it called "social conscience"; a grand concept arising from ideas of Original Possibility, though not always well used.

## SOCIAL CONSCIENCE

In the past, the word "conscience" applied to individuals. Back during the Great Depression, much of the economic and spiritual help people gave, or received, derived from personal conscience. Our churches and charities depended on individual contributions and actions. In the 1950s, the nation started to mull over the idea that a society could have a conscience, and society should accept responsibility for the well-being of all its members. This would have both good and ill effects.

Social conscience arose partly because structures of Roosevelt's New Deal remained in place, although Roosevelt died four months before the end of World War II. Part came from necessity. With the exodus from farm to city, and disappearance of the extended family, American society attempted to replace the extended family with social programs.

Psychologists, sociologists, and social workers stepped into the breach that economic depression, war, and urbanization had caused in society. A tug-of-war for the conscience of America began then, and continues today.

The value of social conscience can be seen in contemporary educational programs such as Project Head Start, and in civil-rights and equal-rights legislation. The danger of social conscience came from excursions into relativism. That danger became so great that it will get special consideration in a later chapter.

The 1950s are traditionally thought of as a time when the flavor of America turned plain vanilla. Nothing could be farther from truth. It was an exciting decade with unexciting leaders. The American people actually seem to have replaced the president and Congress when it came to leading the nation.

There was, however, a war going on in Korea. A nutcase named Joseph McCarthy engaged in a witch-hunt. Both the war and the witch-hunt derived directly from the world's fear over totalitarianism. In the 1950s, the Soviet Union lurked like the beast of the Apocalypse. To understand, we'll have to take a face-to-face look at that beast.

# WHEN THE WORLD WENT MAD

THE BACK HALF of the twentieth century (and especially the 1950s) saw a world suffering the trauma of shock. From the 1950s until the 1990s the threat of nuclear holocaust would never be far from public consciousness.

In the American mind, nuclear holocaust became linked with totalitarianism, and totalitarianism became linked with Soviet communism after World War II. The roots of witch-hunting in the 1950s lay in the fact of totalitarianism. Jack London had warned of its coming back in 1907 (see pp. 174–76). When totalitarianism arrived in the 1930s, and produced World War II in the 1940s, at least a few people understood London's warning.

Totalitarianism actually was a new creature crawling across the face of history. To fully understand the latter half of the American twentieth century, it is well to pause for a brief look at the creature:

The nightmare had begun back in 1931, in China, where like a butchering dream, totalitarian war spread across the world. The nightmare also dwelt in the Soviet Union, Germany, Japan, Spain, and Italy. A dark fledgling hatched onto the pages of history, squawking with a new voice, although the voice was old in spirit; a spirit even older than the Spanish Inquisition. Throughout the centuries, tyrants had been at one with that spirit, but Inquisitors and tyrants had always been frustrated as their best efforts turned to dust. They could never be totalitarians.

For example: even conquerors like Genghis Khan had not succeeded. He once pressed horsemen from Mongolian steppes to conquer half of the then-known world. His sons would conquer as far west as present-day France. Conquering a city, and before riding on (had he not burned it, leveled it, and killed everyone in sight, which was his usual practice), Ghengis Khan installed an administrator. That administrator, seeing the khan's horsemen riding away, felt alone and lost. He looked about, saw trouble on his personal horizon, and began cutting deals. The broken city that he administered would soon bury its dead and return to a daily round of building, procreating, trading goods, writing poems, and dreaming. The khan's dreaded horsemen rode elsewhere, killing strangers.[1]

Unhappy tyrant, the khan. He could conquer a world, but couldn't control it because he rode away. He could earn people's hate, but could not so oppress them they would learn to kiss, with adoration, the shadow of the hem of his robe. Not even the European Church, at the depth of its infamy, proved able to succeed. Neither tyrant nor church could be totalitarian.

This new fledgling, totalitarianism, hatched from a nest woven of technology and fabrication. It grew awkwardly, the first of its kind, and unclear about its power. It hatched from a world of purified steel using the Bessemer process (1856) and William Kelly process (1857): techniques that would produce modern cannon, machine guns, rifles, train rails, high-compression engines, trucks, tanks, tools for the making of tools. It fledged on assembly lines; learned to squawk and talk by radio, telegraph, loudspeaker, telephone. Its ships no longer carried auxiliary sail; some were even submarines. The creature grew flight feathers, to spread wings capable of hauling troops and bombs.

It soared above a confluence of forces. The world had never before seen totalitarianism because the world had never seen a combination of tools and ideas that make totalitarianism possible.

Never before could armies be moved with the speed of trucks and trains, or attack with the speed of planes. It had not been possible to direct logistics by radio. Generals could not make decisions based on reports from commanders in the field while action was taking place.

Now occupation forces no longer needed to be fixed, but could be

---

[1]An extremely good study is contained in Harold Lamb, *Genghis Khan, the Emperor of All Men* (Garden City Publishing, 1927).

moved like checkers. Technology allowed full surveillance of resident populations. Populations in occupied territories became atomized. People were made to fear each other. Old scores could be settled by accusations about disloyalty. Neighbor could not trust neighbor. Children were taught in school to denounce parents to the police. A great hush fell over occupied territory.

This new tyranny resembled older forms in some individual matters. Dictators, generals, admirals, bird colonels, bureaucrats (railway directors—police chiefs—holy Christian ministers proclaiming Aryan Truth) expressed power through contempt, ego, symbol—the sacred cross—jackboots goose-stepping—flags, red rags, hammers and sickles, swastikas.

And, because egos were involved, mistakes occurred as power coalesced. This new creature resembled a mighty engine, a machine expressing power beyond human experience, at first beyond human imagination. Let us view some mistakes:

In preparing for World War II, Stalin need not have killed 20 million of his own people through starvation; 10 million would surely have served. Stalin did not understand the power of transportation. He needed to bring food from country to city, and did not understand how quickly grain could be seized and moved. Such power need be learned.

When war arrived, the military mind of Japan, closer to Genghis Khan than to Hitler, misunderstood dangers in tools; of equipment needing oil, of assembly lines in other nations. It did not understand the engine's appetite for endless reserves of steel, fuel, and people. It needed not only an oil reserve, but a reliable way to transport oil; and American submarines stopped that transport.

Nor did Hitler understand, even as Nazi Order became the watchword, that the creature depends on certainty. Totalitarianism has one direction: forward. It may fan out in a march toward domination, but confusion rises with a change of mind, a pause, a lapse at the head of the column. Thus Dunkirk served a world because the massive British Expeditionary Force escaped certain destruction at Dunkirk (1940) while Hitler hesitated. The British army lived to fight another day. Dunkirk revealed the creature's flaw.

And, the creature of totalitarianism must extend into the countryside. "Be not content with the comfortable boundaries of cities." Such should be the inscription above the disgraced bones of Nationalist-

Chinese leader Chiang Kai-shek, who lost power to Mao Tse-tung because he did not extend his influence beyond cities.

And: "The creature is not jolly." Such, the inscription above the dangling corpse of Benito Mussolini, the Italian tyrant who would have liked totalitarianism; but, with bombastic self-importance, forgot to pay attention to forces at play right beneath his nose.

And: "The creature fails when men retain their pride," an epitaph for Francisco Franco, whose Spain forgot him one minute after he died.

Mistake. Error. Flaws.

In *The Origins of Totalitarianism* (1951), historian Hannah Arendt explains that the creature came off the nest with a gale of ideas beneath its wings. Nineteenth-century thought, exemplified by Charles Darwin and Marx, viewed the development of life and the development of society as constantly changing; improving (ideally), refining (perhaps), and raising new species and ideas, for future extinction or decay.

Because of Darwin and Marx, the idea of change thus became a theoretical constant, and that was something new in human thought. When change became a constant, it followed that war would inevitably become part of the equation.

What frightened Americans, who hold a mythology of individualism, was that totalitarianism deemed the individual meaningless. Totalitarianism claimed to operate in a world of inevitable forces. It said that meaning could only be found in great causes, in the dialectics of history; dialectics that drove economic necessity or racial theories.

When the value of the individual became theoretically meaningless, German leadership considered the German extermination camps merely expressions of historical necessity. They could not be cause for guilt. Murder became not murder, only an iron requirement from the dictates of history. The situation, though inevitable, was even perhaps sad.

In the aftermath of World War II, our American shudders changed to astounded horror. As the world learned of Belsen, Dachau, Buchenwald, and Auschwitz extermination camps, our hearts grew cold. Totalitarianism displayed things that should never be seen, acts unspeakable; the open mouths and rotting eyes of 6–8 million sprawling corpses.

Totalitarianism had produced murderers and monsters more fearful than any medieval pitchforking devils of Hell, because in medieval hells (it was once believed) devils rejoiced in torture, took pleasure from screams, grew fat on the bite and endless repetition of eternity.

These new monsters, though, gave off light both low and cold. They confessed no loyalty to joy, only loyalty to duty. In her book about the Nazi mass-murderer Adolf Eichmann, Hannah Arendt finds him nondescript; a boring man, unimaginative, puzzled by all the fuss: a tidy monster, more-or-less efficient.

After World War II, the victorious Allies held the Nuremberg Trials for Nazi war criminals like Eichmann. Those trials became defining moments for the twentieth century. The world bowed to expediency as the trials stretched international law to the breaking point. The trials were held under ex post facto law; i.e., laws written after the crimes were committed. These trials were justified in hearts, if not in minds, by clear evidence of acts beside which simple atrocity paled.

The trials did not change the totalitarian creature, but helped define its nature. The creature took shape in the minds and hearts of the world. We understood that totalitarianism arises when the popular mind is insecure, or starved for easy answers, or lies paralyzed with fear. In the 1950s, the world, comprehending the nature of the creature, turned wide eyes and frightened stare toward the Soviet Union. Stalin and his henchman Lavrenti Beria promised World War III, a worldwide totalitarian state, and the end of civilization.

Writers and artists, together with society, stepped into the second half of the century with the knowledge that—with weapons at the ready—the nations could, like fated houses, sink into a tarn. The earlier struggle between capital and labor lay only a little stale in memory. The word "Communist" now took new meaning in America, but the popular mind quavered, thinking the word had carried the same meaning all along. In America this fear was expressed by witch-hunts and denunciations through much of the last half of the twentieth century. The most powerful example occurred in the 1950s.

## WITCHERY

Joe McCarthy, junior senator from Wisconsin, was one of Congress' leading alcoholics; no small distinction in a community where some members use good red whiskey when they brush their teeth. McCarthy was also a leading paranoid schizophrenic, his madness an indulgence, since mental instability is a luxury congressmen rarely afford themselves.

McCarthy embarked on a crusade against communists in the early fifties and hit what he figured was a lucky streak. He literally stumbled into one of America's main fears. Russia was obviously a totalitarian government, and the world had just seen what totalitarianism could accomplish. The wreckage of war lay across the world.[2] Then Russia developed nuclear weapons.

McCarthy surrounded himself with a group of "investigators" whom he called "fine young men," but who, in retrospect, look like a bunch of hoods. He claimed he possessed evidence placing great numbers of communists in the U.S. State Department, in universities, and in the movie and music industries. As he gained confidence and grew more boozed if not more crazy, he even suggested that communists infested the U.S. Army.

He pulled back from that one just in time. In the early 1950s, it was hardly wise to bad-mouth any organization instrumental in winning World War II, and then fighting in Korea.

He did manage to spread loyalty oaths all through business and government and the military, although every military man and woman had already sworn an oath to protect the nation and the Constitution. McCarthy's oath read: "I am not now, or ever have been, a member of any organization dedicated to the overthrow of the U.S. Government." One brave chap, I recall, checked "Yes," and in an explanatory note added: "Member of the Democratic party."

Congress, and a spiceless president, together with leaders from a whole lot of universities, ran like bunnies. The U.S. Senate put up with McCarthy even as McCarthy destroyed careers with never an ounce of proof. President Eisenhower detested the man, but applied no pressure. McCarthy, without an iota of hard evidence, used only accusation and innuendo.

*Universities* fired professors and canceled classes in history, economics, and political science.

---

[2]As late as 1968, wreckage had not been completely cleared from West Berlin, leave alone East Berlin. In both places, bombed buildings had been bulldozed. Brick and rubble sat in huge stacks. The few remaining prewar brick buildings were pocked where they had been hit by bomb fragments.

*The movie industry* blacklisted actors accused by McCarthy; the blacklist was really a roll call of shame—but not shame on the actors. The heads of studios cowered before the senator.

*The music industry,* only a little worse than the movie industry, crawled on its knees.

*The publishing industry,* only a little less worse than the movie industry, whimpered its way into the sunset. It imposed censorship by removing anything mildly objectionable from its backlists and by deleting entire passages in new releases of classics. This, from an industry that during the war saw fit to make dollars by publishing Adolf Hitler's *Mein Kampf.*[3]

For a while, in the 1950s, hate-mongers who circled the action scarcely knew which way to turn. Minorities were acting uppity, and now, McCarthy claimed, many Americans were communists. Other Americans, including most writers, claimed Joe McCarthy issued a musty stink reaching all the way back to the Salem witch trials. What was a poor hate-monger to do?

In general, the haters put bumper stickers like "Love it or leave it" and American flags on their cars. The haters joined the John Birch Society, a dreary organization founded by a candy manufacturer, a fudge maker (honest-to-God, the guy made fudge as well as spreading it) named James Welch.[4]

McCarthy did not last long because he drank himself to death. And, I'm pleased to report, because in 1954, the U.S. Senate finally got fed up and condemned him for contempt. While McCarthy operated, though, he showed America how deep was its fear. The USSR was nobody's joke. After engaging in hot wars across the world, and a hot one in Korea, our nation entered one more war: the Cold War.

It's no wonder people were afraid and uncertain. In the presence of

---

[3]While most publishers subscribe to one or another ethical standard, there are elements in the publishing industry that would gladly print the Declaration of Independence on toilet paper if it would make a buck. Then, at the end of the year, those elements would get together, throw a big party with plenty of champagne, and give each other awards for public service.

[4]The John Birch Society was named after a dead soldier who would not have been pleased to have a group of paranoid kooks using his name. The John Birch Society would hold center stage in the affairs of the lunatic fringe until the advent of Jerry Falwell and his Moral Majority.

a totalitarian Russian state, and spooked by a man who should have taken up residence in a rubber room, society, politicians, and religion faltered. Large parts of society tried to regain the illusion of normality by trying to stuff all of us back into a bottle labeled "the good old days." As we'll see in the following chapters, it didn't work.

# . . . Comes a Shift in Wind and Tide

There's a saying among historians: "If it's fewer than fifty years old, it isn't history, it's gossip." Historians know it takes fifty years for dust to settle over actions of the past. While we can see past actions well enough, we can't see accurate relationships *between* actions. When events are too close in time, evidence is clouded.

Perhaps the premature writing of histories is the base for the popular belief "History is a lie we all agree to believe." That statement, so beloved by folks who live with their own manufactured facts, misses the point. History is the best truth we can discover from thoughtful evaluation of a body of evidence.

For that reason, a problem arises as we begin viewing the American writer from the 1950s onward. I lived through those days. I knew/know many of the writers, either personally or by correspondence. As a young writer, I loved some, stood in awe of others, and detested a few even as I admired their work. And, as a young writer, I went through drills young people seem obliged to follow; mistakes all over the place, while using dreams and hard work to cover confusions.

And, as it seems we all do, I went through my "Young Turk" period, where I yammered about my betters, talking and occasionally writing stuff that would make a cat blush.[1]

---

[1]I once actually put the knock on Saul Bellow for his characterizations, and you can imagine how deeply it must have affected the poor man. I'm certain my adolescent

Thus, what you read about the next decades will be skewed. There's a temptation to wander into stories about writers. For example, anyone who ever knew Stanley Elkin has a "Stanley" story.[2] There's temptation to gossip, or make judgments based on personality, and not on work. Also, it's impossible to accurately place the work of friends in a larger context because you know what your friends hope and how hard they pursue their dreams.

Another problem arises because, during this period, publishing changed. The publishing business has traditionally valued bestsellers and big bucks, but as the population grew, and as markets for novels and short stories changed, some superior writers were completely shoved aside. This indifference to talent had probably been going on through most of American publishing history, but in the past fifty years, it seems to have intensified. In the early part of this century, publishing had traditionally been a privately owned (and ofttimes catty) business that offered some interesting literary forms to maintain its reputation as a godfather to art. Immediately following World War II, for example, it was still possible to write a novel in the form of a long narrative poem and have it published by a major house.[3]

---

opinion forced him to publish *Mr. Sammler's Planet,* of which, more later, and I've been red-faced ever since.

[2]Stanley could find a person's weakest point within ten seconds of meeting. He was perfectly capable of sitting outside a public pool, accosting the first ten-year-old boy who came along, and saying: "Hey, kid, I saw you pee in that pool and I'm gonna tell your moth-a." He didn't do it out of malice. It was sport.

[3]*Beach Red,* by Peter Bowman (Random House, 1945). It begins:

> Oh, say, can you see by the dawn's early light
> the glimmering haze squatting on its moist gray haunches and
> guarding the waters with a battleship resting across its knees,
> searching in diminishing circles until it challenges its own eyes.

Another excerpt, talking about generals:

> And so they sit in rooms that are far away
> and point to charts on the wall and indicate little
> bits of tinted paper stuck in a sandbox, and say,
> "Take this island, envelop that position, break through right here."
> And nobody's legs give way under them, and nobody starts
> coughing and spitting blood, and nobody carries in a boy
> that's too old to cry and too young to swear
> and too lifeless for either. And nobody sticks him in
> the sand and says, "This is Joe," while all the

Then, over years, publishing became corporate. Publishers moved their offices into high-rent districts. They raised their overhead and tried to standardize content in order to sell millions of copies. Important books still get published, but it's a knock-down battle a good deal of the time.

Faced with my own bias, plus these other problems, I've altered this book's format for the years after World War II. Instead of going by decade I'll take the period 1945 to the 1970s, and write of a few trends that engaged me. So many writers worked during these years, it will be possible to mention only a small number. A lot of superior writing, even writing by some of my best friends, must be left out. That makes me feel as depraved as the lost and lamented John Calvin claimed for our souls' estate.

So much for the preamble.

American thought moved away from dogmatic proclamations of absolute "right" and absolute "wrong" on subjects ranging from religion to child raising to banking. Our nation turned to examine its identity. We, the nation, knew we were changed, but did not understand why. With the exception of the Jews, who owned good reason for religious questioning (as we'll see in the next chapter), the nation no longer asked most questions in religious contexts.

Most questions had to do with American society. In the spirit of the 1920s, Americans questioned remnants of forms left over from Victorianism. People questioned the useless remnants, as well as those with some value.

For example, ideas of Romance took a beating as the old pioneer spirit of the nation temporarily turned corporate. As the corporation man stepped forward wearing his gray flannel suit, he actually engaged in a sort of economic romance, or at least in economic illusions.[4] Ro-

---

traffic cops present nod their heads in agreement and murmur,
"Yes, General, yes indeed, General, how right you are, General."

Random House also published Vikram Seth's *The Golden Gate,* a novel in verse, in 1991.

[4]During the 1940s and 1950s, Americans set out to rebuild the world. Many corporation men of those days were idealists of a bold and rather wonderful sort. They had endured economic depression and world war. Now they set out with true belief that they could build a world in which no one, anywhere, would ever be hungry, ever again.

mance still lived, but only here and there. And just barely. Romance simply faded before practical points of view, although sentimentality always remained with us.

As American thought changed, there would be talk of something called "the new morality," as well as something named "situation ethics." In general, the new morality would deteriorate to "if it feels good, do it," and situation ethics are, by definition, not ethical; the point being one needs bring ethics to a situation, rather than allow the situation to dictate ethics. Still, morality and ethics once more became concerns of great numbers of Americans. It marked a beginning of genuine turmoil in American thought.

While Americans turned their attention to practical matters, they were glad to read books of theory: political, international relations, invention, social, and economic. Fiction still held large appeal to a nation relatively inexperienced with electronic media. Americans read all sorts of fiction, except science fiction. Even as they taught their kids about "the real world," and denied the fantastic, they created their own fantasy by reading the scientist Willy Ley, who wrote of rockets and space travel. They oohed and ahed over space illustrations by Chesley Bonestell. They pursued fantasy through books written from scientific points of view, and endorsed by scientists.[5] Meanwhile, their kids bootlegged science fiction, tons of it.

The result of all this was that the nation once more rose on its intellectual back legs, smarter by several rods, and sassy. Books, more than television, would remain a way of life into the early 1960s, and would then get a boost from the enormous college generation of those days. American writing flowered in the aftermath of war.

The late 1940s and early 1950s saw many of our writers explaining World War II. Some of the most important books were Harriette Arnow's *The Dollmaker*, James Jones' *From Here to Eternity, The Thin Red Line*, and *Some Came Running*. James Michener published *Tales of the South Pacific* and *Sayonara*, followed by *Hawaii*. Herman Wouk published *The Caine Mutiny*. Kenneth Dodson published *Away All Boats*.[6]

---

[5]A good example, and a personal favorite, is Kenneth Heuer, *Men of Other Planets* (Viking, 1955).

[6]During World War II, our writers had mostly published work about matters other than war for reasons already shown. One of my favorites from those war days is Jean

## HARRIETTE ARNOW

The most important book of the period, and in my estimate the greatest book of the century, is *The Dollmaker*. Published in 1954, it has never, to my knowledge, been out of print. Most people read *The Dollmaker* only once because it's a book that alters life. No one is ever likely to emerge from that book unchanged.

Gertie Nevels and her family move from the Kentucky hills to Detroit during the war so her husband Clovis can get a job. The family falters, begins to fade, and by the end of the war looks at final destruction. It is a book about war, but also a book about art, family, the basic call of religion that far exceeds the twaddle of fundamentalism; it is about the firmness of custom, and how custom, honor, and, finally, hope come near to extinction when moved from a mountain community to a big city. Art prevails at the end of the book because all that remains is the sacrifice of art. If that sounds contradictory, it will not be so after reading the book. *Moby Dick* is held as the great American novel of the nineteenth century. *The Dollmaker* is doubtless the great American novel of the twentieth. I feel this way because, more than any other novel I know, it stands for the twentieth-century American experience. We did not grow into an urban, industrial society without pain, hope, and art.

Arnow wrote several other books. The best, after *Dollmaker*, is *Hunter's Horn* (1949). She must have fallen in with a bad editor in *The Weedkiller's Daughter*, because the book is cut too heavily. She also wrote history. Her best is *Seedtime on the Cumberland*, about settlement of the Cumberland plateau.

---

Stafford's *Boston Adventure*. Pearl Buck published *Great Son*, about Seattle, and Steinbeck wrote *The Moon Is Down*, a little allegory about humans caught in war. He tried to remind us to remain human, but the book was largely ignored. He also wrote *Bombs Away*, a piece of propaganda about how jolly it is to fly across the world dropping bombs on people while getting your gizzard shot out. We all do, from time to time, odd things.

The most popular book, and the best, came from William Saroyan, who wrote *The Human Comedy* (1943). It's about a kid in a small town who delivers telegrams. Some of the telegrams "regret to inform" of soldiers killed in action.

## JAMES JONES

The biggest splash after World War II came with James Jones' *From Here to Eternity*. It tells of lead-up to the war, taking place in the professional army in Hawaii. The book shows more than the army. It tells a story of economic depression in America, of survival, and, like *The Dollmaker*, deals in the power of art on the artist; in this case, a bugler named Robert E. Lee Prewitt. The book ends in the aftermath of the attack on Pearl Harbor. It is not really a book about war, but about the spirit of people too proud and too tough to complain because life is hard.

Jones published *Some Came Running*, a novel written at a time when he worked under the influence of James Joyce.[7] In *Running*, Jones wrote of postwar America, and small-town life that had so taken Sinclair Lewis. Jones' novel is filled with characters drawn so powerfully that we know them, as Mark Twain used to say, "by the back."

While the nation tried to forget the war, our writers tried to record, explain, understand, and preserve the record. The strongest combat novel from World War II is Jones' *The Thin Red Line*. It is a novel about an infantry company on Guadalcanal, and Death is the comic hero.[8]

## JAMES MICHENER

Other important books were Michener's *Tales of the South Pacific* and *Sayonara*, novels in which racial prejudice raises its filthy head to destroy dreams and lives. In this case prejudice was directed at Japanese and Pacific Islanders. Michener became the first major writer after the war to throw the subject of race into the postwar turmoil. He would be followed by Ralph Ellison's *Invisible Man* and James Baldwin's *Go Tell It on the Mountain*.

---

[7]Joyce's *Ulysses* served as a challenge to lots of writers in those days. Joyce's work followed patterns laid out in William James' essay titled "Stream of Consciousness." Because of those patterns the reader can easily identify bursts of stream of consciousness in Joyce's work. Jones took stream of consciousness a step further by weaving it into narrative through skillful transitions. The writer sees him weaving in and out, but most readers do not even realize that anything marvelous is happening.

[8]The other great combat novel from that war is *Fires on the Plain*, by the Japanese writer Shohi Ooka.

James Michener holds an important place in the hearts of writers from those days. His novel *The Fires of Spring* is a testament of faith in the importance of young writers. It acknowledges their struggles, and it understands how the honest struggle in art leads to genuine happiness. If that were all he did, we would treasure him.

In the 1950s, though, Michener began writing his big books that take readers on excursions across the world. As with all writers, some of the books are more enjoyable than others, and a couple are flops; but all are instructive. Michener reinvented storytelling as done by those men of ancient times who went from camp to camp telling tales. His books instruct, entertain, and the best of them satisfy completely. My favorites are *Hawaii* and *The Source*, in which Michener becomes a modern Josephus.

And, if we were asked for cause to show that stories are needed by cultures, Michener would provide a perfect example. He did for four decades what our world presently attempts to rediscover through other forms of storytelling. A brief digression is wanted for purpose of illustration:

## DIGRESSION

These days, our nation seems information-crazy. A sound journalistic form, variously termed "literary journalism," or "creative nonfiction," now has a hard time getting published. Magazines currently print what they call "service pieces": little bites of information helpful to the reader, but served up with no creative sauce. In addition, rapid growth of the Internet rides on the back of the exchange of information.

I have no doubt that the quick rise of video rentals is in direct correlation to this flood of information now distributed by the snippet, because a video is a complete experience; be it good or bad. A video has an organizing principle. Information limited to the organizing principle of a snippet may well be interesting, but it isn't satisfying. Cultures want, and need, stories. End of digression, and return to James Michener.

During the 1950s, as Michener began publishing those big books, America came under an onslaught of information similar to what we see today. New ways of viewing the world, new insights into human behavior, and new notions of a society's obligation to its members flowed about our heads with no more clarity than most of us can find in the Book of Revelations. Ideas were sometimes mistaken for facts in the public mind—i.e., the question "Is there life on Mars?" was rapidly turned into the statement "Science has found life on Mars."

Michener gave information by using the organizing principle of the story, and the man could tell a story. His information was interesting; but, more importantly, it could be understood in context. Michener was not the only writer to do this with information, because any storyteller does, but Michener did it most obviously.

Times, they were a-changing. In our literature, realism would give way to social realism. That social realism would be in the spirit of earlier works; of Crane's *Maggie,* Dreiser's *Sister Carrie,* and Farrell's *Studs Lonigan.* After World War II, well into the 1970s, one strong force in American writing dealt with society and culture. Writers from Jewish backgrounds set the pace. Writers from gentile backgrounds chipped in and helped. American writers set out to re-create the American world, making it better than the original. Writers worked at a new mythology, one that asked for understanding our people by understanding their social context. Many writers still do the same, and they still make improvements. It's an honor for us to be part of it.

# SHALOM

IN THE 1950S, work by Jewish writers came to the fore, although plenty of Jewish writing lies in America's earlier literature. To those writers and books already mentioned should be added a moderately romantic *The Fire Eater* (1941), by Henry J. Berkowitz, and *Kasriel the Watchman* (1925), by the brilliant short story writer Rufus Learsi.

Others include Joseph Opatoshu, who wrote in Yiddish. Isaac Bashevis Singer spent his first thirty-one years in Poland, then came to America as a newspaperman for the *Jewish Daily Forward*. Dorothy Parker and Leo Rosten belong with the humorists and satirists.

## BUDD SCHULBERG

The big push to social realism after the war, and until the seventies, seems prompted by a novel published in 1941: *What Makes Sammy Run?*, by Budd Schulberg. The book caused a sensation, was widely read, and even unimaginative people understood that a new force entered American life. Schulberg was a marvelous storyteller. His subject was a Jew.

To properly understand the power of the book we need pause to remember that in 1941 the American world was saturated with hate-mongers stretching all the way back to the 1920s. The hate-monger Father Coughlin used radio through the 1930s to blame every trouble the world ever saw on Jews. Gangs of enlightened "Christian" hoodlums trashed Jewish stores, beat up Jews, and ran Jewish families out of neighborhoods. The Ku Klux Klan, wearing hoods as pointed as their pointed little heads, enjoyed a smashingly good time.

These were days of "restrictive covenants." When a gentile bought a house, the restrictive covenant in the sale agreement stated that he could never sell the house to a Jew or a Negro. Such covenants would be struck down by the Supreme Court after World War II.

Hatred of Jews did not exist only in Germany. There's a long tradition of oppression in all of Europe. In America, the tradition was not as consistent, but had been around since the eighteenth century. During the 1930s, and during World War II, anti-Semitism bloomed like a dark flower. I can recall, as a kid, going to the barbershop on Saturday, and, while waiting my turn, listening to men talk. If I heard it once, I heard it fifty times: "I don't like this sonovabitch Hitler, but you got to admit he's right about the Jews."

Schulberg's book is about Shmelka Glickstein, who changed his name to Sammy Glick, and who was raised on Rivington Street in New York's Jewish ghetto:

> He had fought to be born into the East Side, he had kicked, bit, scratched and gouged first to survive in it and then to subdue it, and now that he was thirteen and a man, having passed another kind of *bar-mitzvah*, he was ready to fight his way out again, pushing uptown, running in Israel's [his brother's] cast-off shoes [which never fit, so that he was often barefoot], traveling light, without any baggage, or a single principle to slow him down. . . .

Sammy grows up, gets a job on a newspaper, is always running, and passes himself off as a writer by selling another writer's story. He goes to Hollywood and plays the Hollywood game, jumping every fence, succeeding, getting higher and higher pay. He plays politics, is ruthless— Schulberg's ironic word is "blitzkrieg"—and the book ends with Sammy looking into the desolation of success. Having gained it all, he has gained nothing. But he owns forty pairs of shoes, and all of them fit.

The following is a key to the whole book. The narrator, a newspaperman named Al Manheim, sits in a bar. The bartender's name is Henry:

I was sitting in the corner at the end of the bar and, like all thinkers who are on the verge of a great discovery, feeling miserable.

Henry leaned over the bar and picked up my empty glass.

"Henry, do you know what I've been doing for the past two hours?" I asked.

"Yes," said Henry, "getting plastered."

"No," I said, "working out a theory that will end hate in the world."

"That's the same thing," said Henry.

"Now, Henry, I want you to listen carefully," I said. "Because Fate has chosen you as the first one to hear my message. Do you remember Sammy Glick?"

"Do you ever let me forget him?" Henry said.

"Okay," I said. "When Sammy Glick first walked into my office he turned my stomach. But just think if when he had walked in I knew as much about him as I do now." I punctuated my speech with thoughtful gulps. "We only hate the results of people. But people, Henry, aren't just results. They're a process. And to really give them a break we have to judge the process through which they became the result we see when we say So-and-so is a heel. Now the world is full of people hating other people's guts. Okay. Now, Henry, answer me this, what if each of them took the time to go down to Rivington Street—I mean each person's particular Rivington Street, Henry? We would begin to have compassion in the world, that's what. Not so much soda this time, Henry."

"I don't think you better have any more, Mr. Manheim," Henry said.

"Okay," I said, "you patronizing bastard. No great thinker is ever appreciated in his own time."


## ARTHUR MILLER

As we've seen, the idea that people are formed by pressures in the society had been around since the aftermath of the Civil War. From the 1940s onward, it became the same as religious creed among lots of Americans. In 1945, Arthur Miller published *Focus*, which did to prejudice against Jews what Sinclair Lewis' later *Kingsblood Royal* did to prejudice against Negroes.

*Focus* is about a man named Newman (Tully to his wife), who is not a Jew, and who lives in a neighborhood with only one Jew: Finkleman, who owns a newsstand and store. Newman badly needs eyeglasses. The minute he gets glasses, he looks like the stereotype of a Jew. Since he works in a company that hires no Jews, management wants to move him away from public view. He resigns, finds a lesser job, and marries a woman who may or may not be a Jew, but who looks Jewish. None of this goes down well in his "pure" neighborhood, where kindly neighbors begin tipping over his garbage can and spreading garbage across his lawn.

Then Finkleman becomes a target for an organized group of haters. Newman's wife wants to demonstrate that she and Newman are not Jews by joining the anti-Semitic crowd. Refusing to join, Newman gets a chance to understand his own prejudice, which he has worn without much thought. The ending is not very pretty, but it is a victory.

Schulberg and Miller stepped to the fore in portraying characters as products of society, as well as of religious culture. Other writers would not only explain the Jew, but handle the heavy remorse from World War II. After World War II, Americans Jews were not the only ones to ask why they were still alive when so many were dead; but the question became special to them. The question necessarily carried a certain amount of guilt.

Six to eight million people, the majority of them Jews, died in the extermination camps of Germany or lay in mass graves throughout Europe; graves to which they had been dispatched by bullets.

Many Jews in the United States were immigrants, or the children and grandchildren of immigrants. They had family members in Europe. The question after World War II was "Am I my brother's keeper?"

An answer came back in the form of a question: "Since you are your brother's keeper, why didn't you do a better job?" The answer did not come from living Jews, but from the mouths of the dead. Nothing that writers of horror stories can come up with will be worse than trying to answer that unanswerable question. It is unanswerable because it comes from conscience. It makes no difference that there was not one thing American Jews could do during World War II to mitigate what happened. The question was still there, as was the answer.

## JOANNE GREENBERG

Our writers handled the question. Joanne Greenberg's *High Crimes and Misdemeanors* is a collection of stories. Of these, one of the best is "Certain Distant Suns," about a favorite aunt who stops believing in God. Then she stops believing in money. Then she stops believing in electricity. Her television still works, although there's no electricity in the house. It broadcasts amazing stuff. Meanwhile, the aunt stops believing in gravity. She can no longer leave the house because she floats. Then she can no longer watch television because now it also carries commercials featuring two rabbis—one angry, the other gentle and sad. Between them we feel the awfulness of a loss of faith.

The other story that is so compelling is "On Tiptoe They Must Leave, The Pious of Israel." A Jewish couple moves into a neighborhood just loaded with liberal gentiles. The only other Jew, an old lady, tries to hold them up for a contribution to a Jewish hospital on Long Island. The hospital is filled with ancient, traditional Jews. The couple reveal that they have contributed to hospitals in Israel, but will not contribute to a conservative Jewish hospital in America. They are liberal.

The old lady then decides to use extortion. She tells them if they do not contribute, she will tell the neighbors they are Jews. They say, "So what!"

She says the neighbors will cultivate them, want to understand the "Jewish Point of View" about everything. She explains that the neighbors even take Boy Scouts to all the different churches in behalf of religious understanding. The neighbors will want understanding so badly the couple's life will not be their own. Sarah, the old lady, speaks:

"I wouldn't even have to say you were observant Jews. They know that Jews are all alike, that Jews believe deeply enough to have come from Mt. Sinai to Minsk to Miami without losing a single one of their own except to the gun and the gas oven."

"It's crazy, it's just plain arrogant and crazy."

Sarah smiled at them, conciliatory wrinkles wreathing a sad mouth. "What am I asking of you? That your sons be Bar Mitzvah? That you *bensh licht* Friday nights so that I can see from my old woman's house my history moving past me? That you have a Seder on Pesach and a menorah on Hanukkah and invite me? All I want is fifty dollars for some stubborn old Jews who are too stupid to die quaintly in Russia. Hey," and she grinned at them, "the black people hate us, and we give them money. The Israelis despise us and we give *them* money. These old Jews hate and despise us more than any of them could in his wildest moment. Who can hate like a brother? Now, if we Jews must pay everyone who hates us, why, we should make these old men princes, walking jewels!"

"Fifty dollars?" Mr. Waldman said.

"Fifty dollars. I wouldn't tell a soul."

## BERNARD MALAMUD

Short-story writers are often the poets of fiction. The short story is far closer to the poem than to the novel. Of writers who worked in this period, Bernard Malamud deals with problems of guilt. Malamud published a lot of wonderful stories, but I like "The Last Mohican" best. In that story, the failed painter Fidelman arrives in Rome to study the works of the Renaissance painter Giotto. He has already written the first chapter of his study. He meets Shimon Susskind, a man who knows a diaspora when he sees one:

"[I] knew you were Jewish," he [Susskind] said, "the minute I set eyes on you."

Fidelman, who did not look particularly Jewish, chose to ignore the remark. "Where did you pick up your knowledge of English?"

"In Israel."

Israel interested Fidelman. "You live there?"

"Once, not now," Susskind answered vaguely. He seemed suddenly bored.

"How so?"

Susskind twitched a shoulder. "Too much heavy labor for a man of my modest health. Also I couldn't stand the suspense."

Fidelman nodded.

"Furthermore, the desert air makes me constipated. In Rome I am lighthearted."

"A Jewish refugee from Israel, no less," Fidelman said good-humoredly.

"I'm always running," Susskind answered mirthlessly. If he was lighthearted, he had yet to show it.

"Where else from, if I may ask?"

"Where else but Germany, Hungary, Poland? Where not?"

"Ah, that's so long ago." Fidelman then noticed the gray in the man's hair. "Well, I'd better be going. . . ."

Susskind wants money. He wants a suit. Fidelman avoids him. Fidelman's first chapter disappears. Fidelman discovers where Susskind lives, is appalled at the poverty, is saddened, depressed. Fidelman's first chapter is being used, page by page, for the lighting of candles. The ending comes crashing, and the power of the story gives shape and form, if not forgiveness, to the great grief and death of World War II.

## ALLEN GINSBERG

In the 1950s books by and about Jews glowed like the finest roses with the longest thorns. Here is the voice of Allen Ginsberg in *Kaddish*, a poem for his mother, Naomi Ginsberg, dead in 1956:

Strange now to think of you, gone without corsets & eyes,
    while I walk on the sunny pavement of Greenwich Village.
downtown Manhattan, clear winter noon, and I've been up
    all night, talking, talking, reading the Kaddish aloud, listen-
ing to Ray Charles blues shout blind on the phonograph the
rhythm the rhythm—and your memory in my head three years
after—And read Adonais' last triumphant stanzas
    aloud—wept, realizing how we suffer—
And how Death is that remedy all singers dream of, sing,
    remember, prophesy as in the Hebrew Anthem, or the
    Buddhist Book of Answers—and my own imagination of
    a withered leaf—at dawn—

Other writers stepped out smartly. Sam Astrachan's first novel was *An End to Dying*. He then published *Rejoice*, and his big, generational novel, *Katz/Cohen*. Philip Roth published *Goodbye, Columbus*. Stanley Elkin published *Criers and Kibitzers, Kibitzers and Criers*, which contains the amazing story "I Look Out for Ed Wolfe." Many Jewish writers would also begin work with the fantastic, but the only one I've encountered who combined the fantastic with Judaism would arrive much later. Mark J. Mirsky wrote *The Secret Table* in 1975.

## SAUL BELLOW

Saul Bellow published *Herzog* and many other books for which he is rightly famous. When he published *Mr. Sammler's Planet,* I knew that an entire era had been summed up and set before us. The end of the book shows the power of the Witness; and all of us, gentile as well as Jew, may stand witness to a century that, finally, we need not accuse because it accuses itself. Budd Schulberg stands at the beginning of a period that took on the case of the Jew, and Bellow stands as its summation, a summation that includes all of us.

## JOHN P. MARQUAND

Questions about the power of society were not limited to Jews. From the 1950s through the 1970s, the social sciences reigned in much the same manner in which evangelical preachers reigned a hundred years before. And, like many of the preachers, a lot of social science amounted to less than the gabbling of geese. The strongest statements about the power of society came from our writers.

In the 1950s, social realism had its immediate roots in a brilliant novel published in 1937, *The Late George Apley,* by John P. Marquand. Like most writers, he wrote what he knew, and what he knew was lives of the Boston Brahmins. It will cause young writers no harm to read *Apley,* which won the Pulitzer Prize, but it is a book written so adroitly, so filled with artistry, that one really needs to have written a few novels in order to appreciate just how much goes on. One also needs know something of New England history and the history of the New England mills. The level of sardonic understatement in *Apley* is such that, without a knowledge of the violent history, much of the tale seems that of a dull and rather worthless people.

Dull they are, and ruthless, but even sharks and wolverines have uses. Marquand's portrayal of a man formed by old money, and by the Puritan heritage of New England, gives us a key to understanding the established rich wherever they live. If you have ever struggled for a living and wished yourself born with the legendary silver spoon in your mouth, Marquand gives reasons for joy because it didn't happen. I have never been charitable enough to pity the rich. I have, through Marquand, come to understand the trap enclosing them.

Marquand wrote other books. The next best known is *Sincerely, Willis Wayde* (1955). It is about a businessman, and the gradual destruction of morality and ethics in the face of "practical decisions." It's about betrayal of trust, manipulation, and the feeble self-justification of a man who knows he is wrong but refuses to accept the fact.

Of all our writers, Marquand is probably the best social historian. The literary crowd has always had a difficult time handling him because, among many elements of the literary crowd, sociology and psychology are items for laughter. It is true that both of those disciplines are often refuges for lazy or unfocused minds, but then, so are writing and literature. It is also true that when first-rate minds engage with those disciplines, history takes on greater meaning, and so does art. Marquand was a genius in portraying society.

## MORRIS PHILIPSON

Morris Philipson's best book is *The Wallpaper Fox*. It concerns the spiritual decay of a man named Henry Warner who resists temptation in a crooked business deal, yet gets thrown into an ethical situation where he fails. Side issues include Warner's heritage of old money and long history in New Haven, and the fact that his wife is a Jew.

His son accidentally kills a young friend in a hit-and-run accident. The son confesses to his father, and Warner (protecting himself, his son, but especially his wife) advises the boy to say nothing. The end can only be dreadful, and is.

Philipson wrote other books, including *A Man in Charge*. That book also deals with moral and ethical problems in the context of power, money, and society. In Philipson's view, life becomes compromised because integrity has been compromised. It's a view with which one can but agree.

## STEPHEN BECKER

Becker's best-known book is *A Covenant with Death*. It attests the legal rights of individuals as well, or better, than any other novel in American literature. It does so because it goes all the way back to the idea of the social contract as espoused by Thomas Hobbes.

A man is accused and convicted of murder. On the scaffold, he runs blindly into his executioner. The executioner falls from the scaffold and is killed. Evidence then arrives proving that the man could not have committed the original murder. The state then tries him for killing his executioner. The story is told by the trial judge.

Becker is one of our least appreciated but most brilliant writers; a genius with language, both English and French. He published eleven novels, twelve book translations, and a history, *Comic Art in America*.

## AGAIN, JOANNE GREENBERG

Another genius is a writer already mentioned. Joanne Greenberg published *I Never Promised You a Rose Garden* in 1964. It is a novel about a young girl in a mental ward, and equally about her psychiatrist. Greenberg takes her readers so deeply into the world of madness that they do not emerge from the book completely sane. It is also a book of social commentary, and it catches much of the fear of the 1950s, as well as the fear arising from worlds of the insane.

*The Monday Voices* (1965) is about Ralph Oakland, a social worker who deals with physically crippled, and consequently, mentally crippled people. His job is to help them live by getting them back into useful work. As with *Rose Garden,* the book goes far beyond normal expectations. Ralph Oakland, idealist and pragmatist, is so committed to his work that he has the social worker's main problem—i.e., how to keep from shutting down his emotions and his ideals. The reader feels, at the end of the book, that Oakland is not the kind of man who will begin cutting deals with himself, but Oakland feels that way. He finally settles for having worked at the top of his skill, and at the top of the profession, for five years. The attrition among social workers is probably higher than in most other occupations.

## REVISITING STEINBECK

Steinbeck, who reacted to tides of change, and to social conscience, which he resisted, reminded Americans of private conscience and individual morality in *The Winter of Our Discontent*; and the moral possibilities of our national and biblical histories in *East of Eden*. The books evoke strengths from our Puritan past. In the furious present, we can appreciate them now even more than they were appreciated when they were published.

That new force, social conscience, rose from a subterranean level of consciousness to the forefront for a number of reasons. The most important reason is that America finally, irrevocably, left the farm. People could literally not go home again because home was gone. On a nearly inarticulate level, society understood that it must undertake the role once held by the extended family. It seems a simple equation, but society, and our politicians, still haven't brought it to proof.

Preoccupation with society, and latterly with self-identity, arrived in part because people were scared to six inches under their toes. Reasons came partly from social change, partly because of the Cold War.

The Soviet Union remained busy inventing itself, and our government remained busy inventing Russia. Looking back on those days, it's hard to say which government engaged "in distributing the most taffy," as Mark Twain used to say. But a wad of taffy distribution went on. In a Grim Reaper sort of way, it was actually kind of wry. Almost everybody in the nation now lived in cities. According to the U.S. government, it was a slam-dunk that cities everywhere were prime targets for nuclear bombs.

In order to survive the aftermath of World War II while living a normal life, people had to go where there was work. Work lay in the cities, which were said to be automatic targets. This resulted in plenty of tension, plenty of social analysis, and subsequent contemplation of God, bombs, and belly buttons. It also gave rise to a variety of writing that would produce, among others, the greatest science-fiction novel of the century, a novel to which we may now turn.

# THE WRITER AND NUCLEAR HOLOCAUST

THE PEACE MOVEMENT arose as fear of nuclear war became a centerpiece of world history. In the 1950s, nuclear warheads were tied to missiles. As the Cold War raged, Americans heard from government and the press that nuclear war could only be avoided by preparation for nuclear war. This argument was justified in response to the acts of Joseph Stalin—never as colorful as Hitler, but even more ruthless and effective. The USSR, and the U.S.A., turned into deadly dangers for the entire world.

The resulting arms race turned ridiculous. Our military would finally claim the capacity to kill every living thing in the world from seven to ten times (overkill). Americans were told that the Soviets owned missiles so accurate they could hit a dinner plate perched on second base at Yankee Stadium. The U.S. Congress prepared bomb-proof hidey-holes for itself, while saying, "Rats on the American people," and lots of Americans responded by building their own bomb shelters.

From the 1950s into the 1980s, threat of nuclear war came and went in its immediacy on the American mind. As late as 1988, when I taught writing to sailors and their wives at a college in Bremerton, Washington, people reported in class papers that their children's main fear, when the blast came, was that dad would be at sea and mom would be at work. Children accepted early death and feared only dying alone. If this seems outrageous and cruel, it is. It is also true. Complaints may be addressed to what former president Eisenhower called "the military-industrial complex."

## WALTER M. MILLER, JR.

The finest book of the Cold War, and certainly the great science-fiction book of the century, is *A Canticle for Leibowitz,* by Walter M. Miller (1959).[1] Miller, a serious Catholic if a doubting one, gave voice to our fears. He kept the noise level high enough to let politicians and generals know themselves as fundamentally helpless and under surveillance. *A Canticle for Leibowitz* can easily be seen as the cornerstone of the peace movement.

The novel begins after a nuclear holocaust. An order of monks strives to preserve records of the now-dead American civilization. They make copies of written fragments, be those fragments notes to "stop off and buy bagels on your way home from work" or blueprints of parts for machines now long disappeared. Since most knowledge was destroyed when all civilizations were destroyed, no one knows what the fragments mean.

The novel is in three sections. In the first section a young novice at the abbey of Leibowitz, in Utah, discovers an old bomb shelter in the middle of the desert. There is some reason to believe it holds personal memorabilia of a man named Leibowitz, once an engineer, who is headed toward sainthood in the church. In addition, the novice meets an old pilgrim in the desert, a wandering Jew, still waiting for the messiah; a wanderer who also supplies comic relief. The Jew's appearance is somewhat magical, as is his disappearance. News of the wanderer upsets the entire abbey because canonization of Leibowitz is serious business, and the wanderer seems both mysterious and fanciful. No cheap miracles are wanted. Meanwhile, the novice faces deep religious questioning. In this passage, he recalls being quizzed by his abbot:

What is your opinion of your own execrable vanity?
*My execrable vanity is like that of the fabled cat who studied ornithology, m'Lord.*
His desire to profess his final and perpetual vows—was it not akin to the motive of the cat who became an ornithologist?—

[1]The best English book about the Cold War is *On the Beach,* by Nevil Shute.

so that he might glorify his own ornithophagy, esoterically devouring *Penthestes atricapillus* but never eating chickadees. For, as the cat was called by Nature to be an ornithophage, so was Francis called by his own nature hungrily to devour such knowledge as could be taught in those days . . .

Francis must study history:

It was said that God, in order to test mankind which had become swelled with pride as in the time of Noah, had commanded the wise men of that age, among them the Blessed Leibowitz, to devise great engines of war such as had never before been upon the Earth, weapons of such might that they contained the very fires of Hell, and that God had suffered these magi to place the weapons in the hands of princes, and to say to each prince: "Only because the enemies have such a thing have we devised this for thee, in order that they may know that thou hast it also, and fear to strike. See to it, m'Lord, that thou fearest them as much as they shall now fear thee, that none may unleash this dread thing which we have wrought."

But the princes, putting the words of their wise men to naught, thought each to himself: If I but strike quickly enough, and in secret, I shall destroy those others in their sleep, and there will be none to fight back; the earth shall be mine.

Such was the folly of princes, and there followed the Flame Deluge. . . .

Each section of the book traces a stage of development as the human race rebuilds. The second section begins in the Year of Our Lord 3174. In the abbey of Leibowitz, in Utah, one of the brothers has built a crude generator:

The vigil on the stairs descended to take their posts. Four monks manned the treadmill. The fifth monk hovered over the dynamo. The sixth monk climbed the shelf-ladder and took his seat on the top rung, his head bumping the top of the archway. He pulled a mask of smoke-blackened oily parchment over his face to protect his eyes, then felt for the lamp fixture and its thumbscrew, while Brother Kornhoer watched him nervously from below.

"*Et lux ergo facta est,*" he said when he had found the screw.

"*Lucem esse bonam Deus vidit,*" the inventor called to the fifth monk.

The fifth monk bent over the dynamo with a candle for one last look at the brush contacts. "*Et secrevit lucem a tenebris,*" he said at last, continuing the lesson.

"*Lucem appellavit 'diem,' *" chorused the treadmill team, "*et tenebras 'noctes.' *" Whereupon they set their shoulders to the turnstile beams.

Axles creaked and groaned. The wagon-wheel dynamo began to spin, its low whir becoming a moan and then a whine as the monks strained and grunted at the drive-mill. The guardian of the dynamo watched anxiously as the spokes blurred with speed and became a film. "*Vespere occaso,*" he began, then paused to lick two fingers and touch them to the contacts. A spark snapped.

"*Lucifer!*" he yelped, leaping back, then finished lamely: "*ortus est et primo die.*"

"CONTACT!" said Brother Kornhoer, as Dom Paulo, Thon Taddeo and his clerk descended the stairs.

The monk on the ladder struck the arc. A sharp *spffft!*—and blinding light flooded the vaults with a brilliance that had not been seen in twelve centuries. . . .

The third section begins in 3781. The abbey of Leibowitz seems about to be destroyed because the world has advanced to a stage of nuclear armament and nuclear war. The old Jew is still in the neighborhood. A mutant woman, a new mother of God, seeks christening of her second, vestigial head. Great powers have risen along with great weapons. The world is already at war, but does not quite realize the fact. Abbot Dom Zerchi switches off a radio with the sure knowledge war is certain:

. . . Listen, are we helpless? Are we doomed to do it again and again and again? Have we no choice but to play the Phoenix in an unending sequence of rise and fall? Assyria, Babylon, Egypt, Greece, Carthage, Rome, the Empires of Charlemagne and the Turk. Ground to dust and plowed with salt, Spain, France, Britain, America—burned into the oblivion of the centuries. And again and again and again.

*"Are we doomed to it, Lord, chained to the pendulum of our own mad clockwork, helpless to halt its swing?"*

This time, it will swing us clean to oblivion, he thought....

Many books are holy. *A Canticle for Leibowitz* is far more holy than many parts of the Bible.

## MARK RASCOVICH

A second powerful book, and one in the mainstream, is *The Bedford Incident,* by Mark Rascovich. It is a retake of *Moby Dick.* The commander of an American superdestroyer plays hide-and-seek with a Russian nuclear submarine. It took a lot of nerve to write because of the catastrophic end dictated by the white whale, and fairly summed up in this exchange between a navy doctor and the captain of a tanker that services the superdestroyers. They talk about Finlander, the captain of the *Bedford.* The tanker has just fueled the *Bedford.* The *Bedford* broke off the fueling operation because it picked up a live contact on sonar:

"Are you asking me to tell you about Finlander, Captain?" Hirschfeld asked him, cocking one of his sensitive black eyebrows.

Larsen shrugged. "Everybody's curious about Finlander, aren't they?"

"Yes, he's a remarkable officer," the young surgeon told him in his flat, unemotional voice. "Yes, he's a genius at antisubmarine warfare. And because the cold war is not a real war, he's like Captain Ahab sailing his *Pequod* through a closed season on whales." He contemplated the dregs in his empty cup, dropped his tone to a whisper and added: "But Ahab finally met up with his Moby Dick, didn't he?"

Captain Larsen looked perplexed for a moment, grunted and walked out of the navigation office, thoughtfully crossing the darkening wheelhouse to one of the windows. The *Bedford* was a blur dissolving into the distant murk, leaving only a ghostly white furrow to linger on the swells....

In stories of the Cold War, *The Bedford Incident* is the only mainstream book I've encountered that equals work done in science fiction.

## M. K. WREN

If *A Canticle for Leibowitz* marked the beginning of novels about nuclear holocaust (and there were hundreds), M. K. Wren's *A Gift upon the Shore* serves as culmination. It was written in those same late 1980s when schoolchildren feared dying alone, and was published in 1990, when the threat of massive nuclear war had receded in the public mind. The novel shares the greatness of *Leibowitz* because it, too, tells of the enduring spirit of humankind. A small group of women arrange to save books that will preserve the record of a dead civilization. They know they may be the last survivors in a blasted world. They live in support of each other. That support is a silent comment on the strength and ingenuity of women, although feminism is not really an issue.

Wren gives the reader a gift beyond the book by including a list of books the women chose to save. That list is contained in the inside dust jacket of the novel. It's a good reading list; a fine port from which any writer or reader might profitably embark.

## THE GOD THAT FAILED

In writing about the Cold War, the twentieth century's faith in science began to develop leaks. At the very same time that science seemed godlike, it also appeared that science, as defined by the popular mind, would soon be the death of us all.

In the early years of this century, science promised and delivered a lot. It rid our world of at least twenty killing diseases, and produced technology to handle sanitation in rapidly expanding urban populations. Science developed mighty weapons. It served as a base for development of communication equipment, allowing us to converse easily and instantly around the world. It produced refined combustion systems for automobiles, trains, ships, planes, and rockets by which we visit the moon or explore our solar system. It developed synthetics, from rubber to textiles, and it replaced metal with plastic in great numbers of applications.

We can understand the rate of advance by remembering that the twentieth century opened with the whinny of horses, the clopping of hooves along unpaved streets, and relative silence even within cities. It will close with more than 1 percent of the American landscape covered by roads, and with the clang and bang of urban areas. Science gave much. We became accustomed to receiving fruits of the miraculous. We learned to expect miracles, and are even resentful when they do not appear as promptly as we wish.

For example: In the next century, genetic engineering will doubtless make our present treatments for cancer look like butchery. The scalpel and chemotherapy will be little used or unused. If, today, we were unkind enough to say this to a cancer patient, we, and the patient, would demand, "What is taking them so long? It's needed yesterday."

"But," you may rightly protest, "because miracles do not arrive timely is no reason to depose the Creator." I agree, but perhaps others do not.

An additional problem rises because science is thought to have made a promise it has not kept. Whether the promise was actually made, or no, makes little difference in popular perception.

Through technology, science promised to provide us with a world of wonders, a high civilization in which all would be happy. Total nonsense, of course. Throughout history, some people have been happy, doubtless even people named Ab and Ug who lived in caves. Other people have been miserable, even astronauts and tennis pros. Science and technology have nothing to do with happiness, but the promise of happiness seemed real to many people, and the promise has been broken.

In addition, a scientific metaphor changes as the century progresses to its end. Science, as I've suggested, no longer seems omnipotent in the mind of America, and science has become remote. Personal contact with science mostly comes to the public via television that carries children's shows, or scientific investigations reported out of context: examples, the operation of space carts on Mars, or speculations on how Egyptians built the pyramids; information on the order of illustrated encyclopedias. Inventors of the stature of Thomas Edison may exist but they are not celebrated. A great multitude of people have no scientific or inventive heroes.

Faith in science will not die, but faith in science as a divinity carries its own dialectic. As the interests and abilities of science change, faith must also change or go elsewhere.

## THE REINVENTION OF SCIENCE

It appears that science in the twenty-first century will center around genetic and biological research, genetic "engineering." A second major interest deals with research on particulate matter. A third major field will be astronomy. Future ability to manipulate genetic structures, combined with further understanding of the structure of matter, and structure of the universe, shows that an entire scientific metaphor is changing. Philosophically, science points toward understanding and use of creation, rather than invention. As the scientific metaphor continues to change, faith in science as a divinity will either continue to fade, or change.

I'm sure disenchantment with science grew as the total destruction of nuclear war was a continual threat. I think the feet of clay began to crack with national fear occasioned by McCarthy's witch-hunt, and I also think it a scary matter when any deity passes from the scene.

## REACTION

When gods die, new ones are always created. It took a while for reaction to set in, but when it did our society went looking for alternatives. And, because this is America, a lot of those alternatives were religious.

During the 1960s and onward, we would see more than a routine number of cults and gurus. Many individuals would make excursions along the periphery of Eastern mysticism. We saw renewal of fundamentalist religions, and the rise of political movements using religion as a cover. Other causes were pursued with the fervency of religion: the environmental movement, feminism, civil rights, among those most admirable.

Changing definitions of sex were another alternative most religiously pursued, together with changing roles of gender. Science-fiction writers made a large contribution.

# SEX AND GENDER

THE 1950S, AS we've seen, were fueled by practicality. People raised their children as designers, builders, engineers, and as small-businessmen. That a few businesswomen existed, together with women in general, promised societal problems next in seriousness to atomic bombs.

Roles of the genders, and attitudes toward sex, were changing. Science fiction would be first in dealing with innovation in roles, although many mainstream writers were critical of American sexual mores. Michener published *Sayonara,* James Jones published *Some Came Running* and *Go to the Widow-Maker*. Philip Wylie published *The Disappearance*. Although they had little to say beyond complaint, these authors, and others, tied sex to society, with society as the controlling feature.

Traditional male and female roles came under attack because they could not hold up well in the postwar world. They were tailored for rural life, and Victorian life. Change also appeared because many women experienced financial independence during the war. Very, very few women—and almost no men—understood in which direction matters drifted. Into this temporary confusion stepped American business, which assured each and every one that it knew exactly what was wanted.

## THE NEW WOMAN

In the 1950s manufacturers of home appliances touted The New Woman, a revised version of the 1930s urban matron, now wearing a stylish housedress. She invariably displayed a smile, a cute little snub nose, and breasts encased in a brassiere so pointy that she could doubtless injure someone. She always stood beside a new refrigerator or washer or air conditioner. Her home was her kingdom, her modern kitchen a place in which, somewhere, surely lay stashed the Holy Grail. Her children, when trotted out for commercial purposes, stood smiling, washed, and slightly starched. Through all of this The New Woman managed to give the impression of being 100 percent government-inspected, grade-A virgin.

And, if manufacturers were not enough, Hollywood (in a frenzy of righteousness because Joe McCarthy scared all pinkness out of it) painted the world in baby blue. The boy-girl movies of the 1950s always show the man in titular command, even if he's a complete goof. The woman may be far more competent (one of the humorous themes), but the dear child gets her way only through the use of womanly wiles. Those movies managed to deny every practical human value, and do it during a period when people prided themselves on practicality.

## THE NEW MAN

The New Man was every bit as unreal as The New Woman. All of the BEMs (bug-eyed-monsters) of science fiction cannot come close to the surrealism of The New Man, as portrayed when advertisers began to see men as consumers, not producers. Advertisers could now sell men something beside tractors, farm equipment, and seed corn.

The New Man dressed in Brooks Brothers, or something equally fine. He drove something large and beautiful that sported fins. He had a quart of Jack Daniel's in the backseat, a deck of rubbers in the glove compartment, and was followed by bevies of beautiful maidens. Traditional male roles deriving from land, from the frontier, from war, and adventure, and as defender of the family, were discarded. We were left with The Stud.

You can meet him in old copies of *Esquire* magazine, and in the infantile visions of such moral incubi as Hugh Hefner, who, in his pursuit of some obscure sex-cathedra, managed, in the pages of *Playboy*, to reduce the image of the American male to that of a poor lad sitting in the backseat of a badly used Chevrolet, getting the girl's blouse off, and thinking himself as near heaven as, for him, would ever come to pass.

## SEX AND THE FANTASTIC

Writing of the fantastic, as we'll soon see, would soon become more real than the stuff being touted as reality.[1] The reality of the early 1950s amounted to a mixture of passion and fear. Women and men of today probably cannot imagine the fear of sex (read pregnancy) in a society prepared to think of women in terms of the 1950s. Women were either "pure" or "fallen," with no in-between. In addition, a residual fear of pregnancy remained from days of the Great Depression, when very few births were planned. During the Depression, few could afford the luxury of a planned pregnancy.

When the birth-control pill was announced in 1957, stirrings of uncertainty entered many minds. An interesting genie had just popped out of the lantern. Social analysts foresaw everything from doom to glory. Myriad jokes, starting or ending with "don't forget your pill, dear," did not do much to ease the situation.

Because of the pill, the seven-year-itch became easy to scratch as an expanding nation centered on urban life. In the city, one could walk around a corner and become a stranger. Social controls of small town and country no longer held much starch. Hormones fought with old-time morals. Another joke of those days claimed that it was high time to get sex out of the movies and back into motels where it belonged.

In addition, a generation born after World War II would shortly enter puberty, a generation raised to startling, perhaps unreal, expectations. Those kids were raised by parents who knew about economic depression and war. The parents' mantra went: "My kid is not going to have to put up with what I went through." They were generally good

---

[1]Not all movies were boy-girl, and not all magazines published casual fiction. Marilyn Monroe, a fine actress who was rarely allowed to act, found herself touted as a "sex goddess" (whatever in the world that is), but handled reality in *The Misfits*. Marlon Brando became the darling of young women because of a movie with motorcycles, and *Cosmopolitan* published serious fiction. I mourn the loss of Monroe and the old *Cosmo*, while continuing to applaud Brando.

parents and good people. With that attitude, they raised a generation that would produce much that is wonderful, but a generation raised to spectacular expectations. Prosperity was pretty much everywhere. Kids were raised with luxuries never known to earlier American generations. Being kids, they naturally took abundance for granted. Because of that abundance, combined with protective parents, a higher-than-average percentage of spoiled brats emerged. Such folk generally expect to be given the world without obligation of payback. The pill arrived most timely.

As the 1950s opened, though, and in the middle of a deluge of sweater girls and prissiness, America had little except Kinsey[2] as a reference point for sanity about sex. Then–to the horror of mothers everywhere–*Galaxy* magazine began dealing with sex and became a second point.

Writers created worlds in which three and four genders were necessary. The idea of metamorphosis between sexes became a standard theme. There's a good bit of birth and rebirth stuff in those old pages, although the covers, of course, go no further with sex than the display of chesty women in the grip of lascivious space critters.

Sex would appear in stories through the 1950s and early 1960s, but I know of no serious book examining roles.

## URSULA K. LE GUIN

The breakthrough book: Ursula Le Guin wrote *The Left Hand of Darkness* (1969).

The difference between Le Guin's book, and other books dealing with sex, came because Le Guin is a writer of the first rank. Most pulp writers dealt out cheap imaginings of a paradise in which existed no egg, or sperm, or consequences; only ejaculation. Le Guin dealt with character.

For that reason, *The Left Hand of Darkness* is not simply an investi-

---

[2]Alfred Charles Kinsey, a zoologist at Indiana University, scooped the world of social science by publishing *Sexual Behavior in the Human Male* (1947). This was the first work on sex done since the writing of Havelock Ellis's seven-volume *Studies in the Psychology of Sex* (1897–1928). And in 1944, a Swedish economist, Gunnar Myrdal, scooped American social science by publishing *The American Dilemma*, about American racial problems. The 1940s were hard on the social sciences, which suffered tiz after tiz.

gation into attitudes about sex. It investigates the fundamental human being beyond appurtenances of sex. In doing so, the novel gave form and sense to an emerging feminist movement that, at the time, consisted mostly of smoke and noise; as women burned brassieres and men fretted over fraying jockstraps.

On the planet Gethen, people are completely androgynous. Where need exists, anyone can become either male or female. Moral issues, as displayed in the book, consider the fundamental human, not the female human or male human. People may be mother to several children, and father to several others. ". . . Yet you cannot think of a Gethenian as 'it.' They are not neuters. They are potentials, or integrals. . . ."

On the planet Gethen, the idea of roles for sexes is impossible. Its absence forms a different way of viewing human endeavor:

> Consider: Anyone can turn his hand to anything. This sounds very simple, but its psychological effects are incalculable. The fact that everyone between seventeen and thirty-five or so is liable to be (as Nim put it) "tied down to childbearing," implies that no one is quite so thoroughly "tied down" here as women, elsewhere, are likely to be—psychologically or physically. Burden and privilege are shared out pretty equally; everybody has the same risk to run or choice to make. Therefore nobody here is quite so free as a free male anywhere else. . . .
>
> Consider: There is no unconsenting sex, no rape. As with most mammals other than man, coitus can be performed only by mutual invitation and consent; otherwise it is not possible. Seduction certainly is possible, but it must have to be awfully well timed.
>
> Consider: There is no division of humanity into strong and weak halves, protective/protected, dominant/submissive, owner/chattel, active/passive. . . .

For the nearly thirty years since, Le Guin has peopled the world with wonderful ideas rising from strange places. Her best novel is *The Dispossessed*. She has also written stories that captivate the old, and compel the young toward self-understanding. Her best such book is *A Wizard of Earthsea*.

The importance of *The Left Hand of Darkness* would become clear as American writing developed a wider perspective about sex, and as the feminist movement turned from complaint to analysis of female roles; as in Carol Orlock's *The Goddess Letters,* and Joan Didion's *Run River.*

## BOOKS FROM THE CLOSET

James Baldwin published *Giovanni's Room* and *Tell Me How Long the Train's Been Gone.* Truman Capote, who wore his homosexuality with the same intensity that produced some of the great stories of the language, published a little shocker (during those days it was a shocker) titled *Breakfast at Tiffany's.* It was about happy and profligate sex (though not homosexuality); at least, it was so received.

Capote made homosexuality an issue by his flamboyant manner, and flamboyant publicity. He lived a tough but flaming life. I mourned his passing in the same way I mourned the passing of William Saroyan; as I always mourn when bright spirits leave our world. Except for Ray Bradbury, no storyteller I know from those days could write poetry into prose so well as Capote.

Writing about sex continues, and should; as should analysis of male and female roles. This society is still a long way from understanding itself. Matters even slipped backward during the late 1980s and early 1990s, when many people thought it lovely to be seen as victims because of their gender. The problem with such indigent thought is that it retards lives. It also atomizes society.

Fortunately, our writers have a good deal of integrity, because integrity is a part of their business. Their art will be around long after society discards these latest separatist effusions.

# THE FANTASTIC IN
# FANTASTIC TIMES

IN AMERICA, MUCH writing of the fantastic has its roots in pulp, and pulp fiction has existed in one form or other since the invention of movable type, probably before. It deals with action-filled or sensational events. Characters have the depth of paper dolls. They are pictures of people, but without flesh, blood, intuitions, or mind. Pulp carries no concern with the meaning of events in the lives of characters.

Back in the nineteenth century, America was blanketed with pulp portraying sentimental romances between Victorian gentlefolk. Pulp also centered on adventurous tales of the West. In addition, there was a lot of "poor little rich girl" stuff, plus "destitute young man of integrity and grit rises to fame and fortune." Horatio Alger made his own fortune with these genre novels.

In the 1920s, pulp became a bit more daring. It suggested that people in love did not always remain completely clothed. Then, during the Great Depression of the 1930s, pulp imagined good times and sentimental romance; poor girls or poor boys hitting magnificent streaks of luck that brought love and riches. During World War II, there was a lot of battle stuff, most of it barely masked propaganda. By the 1950s pulp fiction dealt with space opera, or horse opera, or true confessions— the joke from the latter being: *I Was a Teenage Werewolf for the FBI with Good Posture and Found GOD.*

## The March from Pulp to Magic

Although writing of the fantastic had been part of mainstream fiction for well over a hundred years, most fantastic writing in the 1950s existed on the low level of pulp because serious writers of the fantastic found themselves in deep, deep trouble.[1] A tradition that had lasted in America since the days of Washington Irving was threatened by a combination of practicality and pulp. Practical people regarded anything fantastic as a threat. In addition, fantastic pulp was difficult to defend because on its surface it wasn't *about* anything. Pulp was treated as a danger by the larger society. It was seen in the same manner in which underground newspapers would be seen in the 1960s and 1970s, and for the same reasons; i.e., it represented low-down and revolutionary doctrine that hollered for change. In the case of pulp, the charge was a canard because pulp generally did not holler for change. It only hollered.[2]

Some of the best-known books of the early century vanished before puffs of practicality. It was a good day's work to find tales by H. P. Lovecraft and James Branch Cabell. My all-time favorite from those days, Robert Nathan, survived because he walked the edge of the fantastic, and because there is depth of affection in his work that almost everyone finds appealing. This affection not only preserved Nathan, but also spread wings on which the fantastic would soon soar. His small novel *The Weans,* tells of the excavation of America by African scientists in the seventh millennium. No one flew higher or better than Ray Bradbury.

## Ray Bradbury

Bradbury marks the clearest transition from 1950s pulp to serious fiction. He happily took on the 1950s through the 1990s and cuddled

---

[1]Pulp remains a staple of publishing. It's easy to write, and some young writers use it to get started. Even pulp, though, has seen a bit of change. Some comic books now comment on the meaning of events in the lives of characters and readers. *Amazing Spider Man* is a good example.

[2]In additon to dealing with sex and gender, stories in some pulp magazines anticipated the civil-rights movement. These stories were usually preachy. They resembled traditional pulp, but not fully.

them to his truly revolutionary bosom. While he is presently thought of as the grand old man of science fiction, he is more than that. Better than any other writer, he validated the Fantastic during a time when it might well have been discarded, or drizzled down to nothing.

Poetry marks the first difference between Bradbury and what normally appeared in the pulps. Bradbury is a master of evocation who echoes the best rhythms of Booth Tarkington and William Saroyan, among others. He sets spring breezes moving across new-mown fields, moving in tenuous moonlight, but strong enough to support the wings of owls and the imaginations of young girls and boys.

Here is a small example from Bradbury's story "The Fox and the Forest":

> There were fireworks the very first night, things that you should
> be afraid of perhaps, for they might remind you of other more
> horrible things, but these were beautiful, rockets that ascended
> into the ancient soft air of Mexico and shook the stars apart in
> blue and white fragments.

Bradbury writes romance during a time when romance has so suffered from effusions by sentimentalists as to be thought a useless form. In the classic definition of science fiction, Bradbury's work isn't science fiction at all, but fantasy. Whatever it's called, it amounts to wonderful romance.

The second, and even more important, characteristic of Bradbury is that he takes the human experience seriously. Emotions are real; ideals are real; ethics are compelling. There is no moralism in Bradbury, but there is the deepest respect for humans and human capacities. His work marks a turn for the Fantastic that would eventually produce some of America's best writing.

From the 1950s, when Bradbury started work, to the present, writing of the Fantastic gradually moved to the fore. One reason for its ascendancy would be reaction to a wide and powerful trend that began in the 1950s, one that has troubled many writers, including Bradbury. The trend is called relativism.

## RELATIVISM

After World War II, social realism worked to validate all Americans as equal. It introduced positive strains into the society. It also introduced relativism, which was the seed of its destruction. It worked this way:

Social realism leaned heavily on psychology. Psychology pushed the notion that people are but sum-total expressions of their backgrounds. Such a view (and from folk who purport to be scientists) amounts, as we've seen, to a warmed-over version of predestination. I find the position a trifle odd, but historically somewhat endearing.

Thus, in the 1950s, and at the very time when some of our best writers were using social realism to good effect, the society went overboard. This often happens when ideas get oversold. It seemed, in the late 1950s and through the 1960s, that no one was guilty of anything. In the late 1950s Americans began to encounter such arguments as:

"It is true this poor fellow murdered his father and mother, raped his brother, sold his sister into prostitution, and disemboweled the family dog; but his circumstance is mitigated because in first grade his teacher made fun of his box of crayons (which were too short)—while later, during puberty, people laughed at his squeaky voice. These awful happenings caused, in his mind, implied contempt on the part of society. His murderous actions, while regrettable, can be easily understood, and thus must be forgiven."

If the above paragraph sounds outrageous, it is. It is also not much of an exaggeration of messages pervading society during the late 1950s, and for many years thereafter. Such messages are also the reason why many writers gave up on social realism and turned to the Fantastic.

As the 1950s rolled into the 1960s, and it once more became okay for kids to believe in Santa Claus and the Easter Bunny, science fiction began making room for other fantasy: ghost stories, horror, magic kingdoms.

Those Fantastic elements arose because the Fantastic deals with good and evil, and is thus a direct contradiction to relativism. Most stories of the Fantastic operate on the level of morality plays—darkness combats light—light wins—but not always fully, and sometimes only sorta—

and thus a new struggle must begin. But win or lose, the fantastic almost always deals in absolutes.

If relativism suggests that no one is guilty of anything, then the concept of "evil" is equal only to the concept of "helplessness." The concept of "good" is reduced to something on the order of psychological mustard plasters. American society had become so immersed in relativism that it turned to the fantastic. It honestly needed to once more understand that good and evil exist.

Another reason for the rise of the fantastic came from cheapened entertainment. As times changed, and as our population doubled, television began peddling a brand of social realism that was really nothing but education in gratuitous violence. Common television stuff included people shooting each other, or men hitting women, or women selling sex to imitation tough guys.

This attempt at the seamy side of realism was presented as representative of American society. It was—and is—an exercise not in realism, but degradation. Because of time constraints television can only make overt statements about reality (or surreality), and even those statements are negated or watered down by commercial breaks. This causes a situation in which human emotion is downgraded to mere sensation. We see, for example, what purports to be a tragic event—for example, somebody's lover gets shot. The surviving lover weeps above the cooling corpse, and the scene breaks to commercial so that a couple of comic actors can sell soap. Television is thus no more or less than electronic pulp, whether it serves up attempts at realism, or attempts at fantasy.

Writing of the fantastic also became attractive to writers because, while it's a baby's task to outwrite television, it is a nice challenge to take a form television sometimes uses to degrade the human experience, and with it build something true; sometimes even beautiful.

## MAGICAL REALISM

Realism remains healthy, but magical realism has largely replaced social realism. Magical realism did not replace other elements of the Fantastic. Rather, it joined them. Magical realism arose because social realism was no longer a way of understanding reality. In very definite ways, social realism appears in each day's news broadcast, and each day's newspaper. Magical realism is a way of explaining the newspaper, of showing heart, mind, and soul of people trapped in violent events.

In the past two decades, important books using magical realism have come from Toni Morrison, Joyce Carol Oates, Alice Walker, Peter Straub, Rick Bass, Tim O'Brien, Peter Beagle, Thomas Tryon, Greg Bear, Lucius Shepard, and more than a hundred others. While the given reasons for the rise of magical realism seem obvious, another, cloaked reason seems likely.

Simply put, social realism no longer works because the national mind is in a period of change. Our society has turned to the Fantastic in much the same way that it turned to romance back in the Great Depression. Back in the Depression, when things were gray, romance served as an escape. Today, at the end of a century, magical realism suggests that the miraculous may actually exist, and may actually operate in the lives of a beleaguered people.

And beleaguered we are. Without quite understanding how or why, we still understand that something has either been given away or stolen. The move toward fantasies of all types, no matter if they originate from fiction, television, or films, may be seen as a search to reclaim something lost. If only we could figure what is lost, and how to go about getting it back.

# AT CENTURY'S END

THERE IS LITTLE more to tell. Writers write what they know and, if smart, don't fake what they don't. Other movements and stories crowd the period from the 1950s to present, but they are best portrayed by writers who lived them. I watched, but was too busy living among interests covered in this book. My sympathies did lie with writers whose characters sorted through the problems of cities. I admired those who wrote about conservation, and thought well of those who had stomach for the gnaw and chomp of politics.

Grief also entered the equation. When Martin Luther King, Jr., was murdered in 1968, a part of me died as well, and another part was born. The part that died, died gradually. It had hoped for greater affection between black and white than I then feared I would ever live to see, although these days optimism blooms in a new season.

The part newly born came from an understanding of my share of responsibility to the people of my country; people of all colors, and of all but destructive creeds. I felt no guilt over the legacies of history, but did feel (although in those days I did not understand) the power of history and the power of art.

Since leaders with the vision and ability of King do not appear in every century, it was clear our world would have to "make do" with what was left of King's presence, and with our own ideals of equality and unity. In the absence of a great leader, it was obvious that I, among others, must find ways to lead.

Nor was I alone in asking after responsibilities. Great numbers, black and white and Indian, did the same. It was not a question of skin color, because that could be overcome with ideals and frankness. It was a question of where to place individual strengths.

My passions run in private and quiet channels. I gradually understood that I could tell truthful stories, try to explain mythologies, and, latterly, stand before classes with complete dedication to writing, literature, and honesty; thus, complete dedication to humanity. I say "gradually" because the shapes of writers' lives are most often discovered, not planned.

Thus, joy, sorrow, and not a little chaos run through the years from the 1970s onward, both in private and public worlds. For the purposes of this book, and in a very general way, it's possible to sum much of what happened:

The nation's population continually grew and continually concentrated in cities. National leadership largely failed to unite the nation, although domestic policies received attention until the 1980s.

Media consolidated strength for some good, but mostly for ill. Advertising, which in the 1950s had been a steady annoyance, in later years became both saturating and demeaning as noise levels soared. The American world enjoyed general prosperity. Consumerism became not only a way of life, but actual identity for many.

As urban concentrations grew, so grew the numbers of drug deals, prostitutes, gang bangers, runaway kids, incidents of child abuse and domestic abuse; all of these coupled with shouts of accusation and guilt as special-interest groups vied for position on center stage.

On the joyful side, though, Americans began to construct new ways of viewing family and community. Alongside of great numbers of broken marriages were marriages in which couples redefined the family. These days, for example, we see fathers actively engaged in the care and raising of infants. Before the 1970s, that was rarely seen. In fact, before the 1970s, such interest by a father would have been taken by the mother as a reflection on her competence. The old-time roles are changing, and we are better for the change.

Severe pressures of urbanization brought out the brilliance of the American people. Church groups, community centers, women's centers, boys and girls clubs, athletic programs for kids, food banks, and other positive activity grew as leadership once more reverted to the American people. And, the American people proved themselves a very great people indeed.

"In other words," you might say, "the back end of the twentieth century somewhat resembles what you've told me was the situation at the back end of the nineteenth."

I do believe that much of the end of this century is a near-perfect copy of the century's beginning. There is, however, at least one difference.

The big difference arrives because the end of the twentieth century sees no coherent social movement, although a movement struggles to life.

In the late nineteenth century, the great social movement first appeared as a confrontation between labor and industry, with race and feminism intertwined. The meaning of the movement was not simply economic. The Western world had industrialized, but did not understand the awful power, and subsequent responsibility, of industrialization. America, England, and Europe would suffer at least two world wars and one major economic depression as our world came to terms with industrialization.

At the end of the twentieth century, our confrontations seem to be with ourselves. The self-absorption of many special interests, and the accusations flowing back and forth between the interests, seem both divisive and controlling.

Yet, basic interests are the same for all. From labor unions to racial interests to social interests like feminism and gay rights, even the most adolescent behavior still clamors after basic human values; dignity in the workplace, a strong context for families, and opportunity for education. The chatter and the insecure egos that cause divisiveness are really markers of a new movement that points toward understanding how we may live together comfortably in an urban world. The social movement heads in that direction because, for Americans, it's a matter of survival.

The movement is not yet coherent. We've missed coherence for at least two reasons:

1. We have to learn how to handle our massive system of communications. Incoherence comes, ironically, from a communications network so overwhelming that we can no longer communicate. That part of the communications system known as the media is contributory to in-

coherence. It is largely driven by commerce that either:

a. wants to sell us something, or
b. wants to interest us with sensationalism/controversy in order to gain our attention, and *then* sell us something.

The sum is an American world where the noise level rises as media work to gain and hold attention. We live in a world of such constant noise that silence, and privacy, have become nigh-unobtainable luxuries for many people.

The inability of society to communicate with itself arrives because there is precious little money to be made from tales of unity. Media much prefer controversy. Television will, for example, take a schoolyard fight over bubble gum—a fight between two seven-year-olds, one black, one white—and try to turn it into a major incident of racism. This is not an unreal example—at least, not where I live.

Sensationalism by the yellow press has gradually spread into mainstream media. It is not uncommon, at least in the Pacific Northwest, to see seamy incidents from the police blotter take the front page of once-serious newspapers; while international, national, and regional news gets shunted to the second or third page.

An additional problem arises because the volume of messages, combined with raised decibels, sends the subconscious message that nothing human is really important. Human actions are thought to hold only sensational interest. For example, we have all seen a situation in which a television reporter sticks a mike in the face of an hysterical woman while saying, "And tell me, Mrs. Jones, how does it feel to have three of your children burn up in the fire of your home?"

2. Our nineteenth-century mythology does not work in large cities. Metaphorically, we're beyond the point where we can afford to play cowboys and Indians, but we're still circling the wagons while doing more war-whooping than is, strictly speaking, useful or necessary. A nineteenth-

century mythology that dealt in "home on the range" and "the wide-open spaces" is not suitable to our present tightly packed urban condition.

A new mythology is wanted. In addition, a major symbol of the twentieth century is being replaced by a symbol of the twenty-first. Since that's a hefty assertion, I ask that your attention return to Henry Adams.

## HENRY ADAMS

At the end of the nineteenth-century, Henry Adams saw an old order, represented by the compassionate and loving Virgin Mary, being replaced with a new order represented by the dynamo. If we stop to reflect on changes wrought by industry and technology during the twentieth century, we'll doubtless conclude that Henry Adams had the situation nailed. We can also tentatively conclude that these days the dynamo represents the dying order.

In concrete, instead of symbolic, terms, we may say that the Middle Ages, dead in the books since the American Revolution, is finally, actually dead; and the Industrial Revolution, symbolized by the dynamo, kicks feebly as it departs the scene. A new symbol lies on the twenty-first century's horizon.

Were I as smart as Henry Adams, I could perhaps name it for you. As things stand, I can only guess. It is a symbol of both communication and, presently, of incoherence: the computer or, if one wishes to be grimly humorous, the motherboard.

The new symbol marks a change from human interaction on the local, regional, and national levels to international communication between private citizens. It also marks the end of most privacy, and it already displays a flood of information in biblical proportions.[1] Like the motherboard of a computer, the symbol promises a network of functions; including an electronic lap on which we all may sit for as long as we follow the rules of the domicile.

---

[1] Cruising the Internet these days is approximately like entering a massive library stocked mostly with encyclopedias for children; many of those encyclopedias written by people who present mere opinion as actual historical or statistical fact.

In addition, that library runs helter-skelter. There is no Dewey Decimal System. The Internet is magnificent and exciting because its very size dictates a worldwide social revolution. Revolutions, however, always end up invading someone's backyard.

The early twenty-first century will have to sort through the rules and, in sorting, will confront what historians and writers have confronted for centuries; use/misuse of power and information. In our own time there already exists a sort of "computer elite," people ranging from systems analysts to heads of software companies. They greatly resemble the middle- and upper-class members who caused the American Revolution, the French Revolution, and the Russian Revolution. How this elite uses and/or misuses power will surely be a concern of the early twenty-first century.

I do not envy the twenty-first century its problems. I do look forward to the ways American writers and artists will address those problems. Meanwhile, there is one situation we may address right now:

## WHAT HAS BEEN LOST OR STOLEN

Our loss is stated simply: As a nation, we have lost much of our sense of the importance of humanity. For the reasons already given, a nation with a mythology that celebrates individualism has lost a sense of the importance of the individual. Human dreams, aspirations, fears, loves, hungers have faded before the combination of forces that powered the twentieth century.

As we saw earlier, too many people, in too many ways, have been told that they are flawed: Darwinian theory, psychology, immense weapons that cause feelings of helplessness. In addition, these days, genetic engineering promises to demote individual differences to the level of solvable problems.

The message that everyone is flawed is as old as the Puritans. The message of unimportance is equally old and equally Puritan. It tells the national subconscious that no one is particularly worthy of any sort of salvation.

If my assertions are true, then, as writers and artists, we are given tremendous opportunities. As we've seen, there are other great ideas in America's past.

## THE AMERICAN WRITER

If we return to our first principles, we'll recall that art grants the ability for people to be humane in human affairs, but art is not an enforcer. No one says, "Experience this painting, or it's off to jail with you."

And no one says, "Understand this book with your heart as well as your head, or I'll kill you." The power of art is thus greater, and longer lasting, than any wielded by billy clubs, social movements, or scientific endeavors. Governments rise and fall, nations flower and fade; but human hope and dreams remain. The power of art is the power of displaying and endorsing human dreams.

And, first principles of the story hold that the story allows people to understand who they are and to pursue their understanding in a moral and ethical context. It makes no difference if the world goes mad in a flood of nigh-meaningless information. The story will still offer identity, ethics, and moral structure.

Further, first principles of the story join with first principles of American history. Those principles include the great ideas of Original Possibility and Original Good. From them a nation rose, a nation with ideas of liberty and justice; a nation of idealists who held Puritan notions of duty.

In addition to first principles of government and principles of stories (which are rational concepts), books and art change lives through emotional experience. Books changed *your* life. If books had not, you would not have read this far. You would not be a writer or other kind of artist. Since you are an artist, it follows that you have experienced reverence by way of emotions and ideas, even if you could not put the word "reverence" to them at the time.

"But," you may well ask, "what is a storyteller to do in a world saturated with film, video, and television—and books. Because when I walk into one of those massive chain bookstores, every message in the place says, 'Give it up, pal. Your voice amounts to a sneeze in a hurricane.' "

I answer in three ways. My first answer is based in a quote from a friend:

My friend says, when she is dead, she will miss reading most of all.

To which I reply, "You won't miss *me?*"

And she replies, "Of course, kid, but I *know* you."

Then she points out that when you read, you enter the world of another. A well-written story is not a report, or an imitation of reality. It is immersion in a world. We do not watch characters walking through those worlds. We walk through *with* them. We understand their minds and hearts because, since reading is creative, we create understanding with our own minds and hearts. The power of the book is the power of emotional understanding combined with thought. That combination requires more from readers than the ability to simply resonate.

Thus, writers have rarely changed the world through mass appeal; and when they have, the results were mixed. Writers speak to individual dreams. The story supplies original thought and validation of the reader's humanity. It does this one reader at a time; always has, always will. No other storytelling medium, with the exception of live theater, can even begin to operate in such powerful terms.

My second point is that books are not for everyone. They never have been, but the history of books in America is deceptive. Massive appeal of books in the nineteenth and early twentieth centuries made them seem like a universal medium. Books were literally everywhere. They served a number of functions.

In the late nineteenth century, for example, Edward Bellamy's *Looking Backward* served approximately the same function that television serves at the end of the twentieth. That book allowed uneasy people to feel somewhat reassured because they felt somewhat informed. Functions of simple instruction and amusement once supplied by such books are now fairly replaced by films and television, a fact that may actually relieve writers.

Our readership has been streamlined. People who do not like to think become bored with even the most powerfully written stories. They become bored because they have rejected all or part of the main tool required for dealing with stories—i.e., they have rejected much of their own creativity.

People who reject creativity do not change the world; or, if they do, their changes come through political or economic manipulation. Such changes, from such motives, are generally not beneficial to the greater good.

As writer-artist, and thus historian, you have more authority than you may believe. Your work appeals to those in society who are most likely to cause thoughtful change. When you appeal to the thoughtful audience of a great people, your voice becomes part of the mainstay of your civilization. You change the world by appealing to those people who change the world, who create substitutes for broken families, who defeat diseases, who study the cosmos; all of the important and affirming paths that people tread.

The majority of people are always greater than their governments, their religions, and their economic systems. The truth of the human spirit that you discover and display provides good cause for creative people to change crippled or outdated systems. It allows them (and you) to become humane in human affairs.[2]

My third point is that you are a part of the accumulating voice of America, and a part of the chorus; the voice of the Western world. Those massive bookstores, together with our massive population, intimidate most writers, including those who produce bestsellers. It is easy to feel lost. After all, if your first books only sell a few hundred or a few thousand copies, have you not failed the task?

Of course not. All honest books are marks of success because books are not videos. Books live a different life and have a different life span. On my shelves, and yours, stand books written one hundred, two hundred, or even two thousand years ago. A Greek tragedy is as powerful today as it was when first written. It holds that power because it displays truths of the human experience. In addition, the works of ancient Greeks hold power because they are among the founding voices in the chorus of Western civilization.

Your stories and books join that chorus. In the audience are many who will not read you now, and there are many as yet unborn who will someday read you. And, there are many who will not even read the ancient Greeks, although your voice and the Greeks' voice will sound through the other honest books they do read.

In the chorus, the Greeks will get more solos than you because they've been around a lot longer. As years pass, though, your readership enlarges. And it does that one reader at time, intimately, truthfully, effectively; always has, always will.

The chorus steps from one century to another, strides across centuries. When writers fail, the chorus falters or disappears, and so does civilization.

Few—perhaps none—ask you to work in writing or art, and only a few are likely to thank you when you work yourself to exhaustion; and there will always be plenty of people around to tell you everything you

---

[2] I do not mean to send an exclusive or precious message. Our nation clearly needs people who do not spend much time reading. While we need people who read widely, think through architectural visions, and produce cathedrals, we also need people who own little information, but who can scrounge up materials, borrow a hammer and saw, and, with only utilitarian intent, build an awkward but serviceable house. It is well to remember that even when people reject their creativity they do not necessarily reject their dreams. Writers validate Americans' lives, thus their dreams.

did wrong after your work is completed. I can say to you, though, what others will not. You may not be thanked, and you may be criticized, but your civilization cannot live without you.

## TOWARD A NEW MYTHOLOGY

The American writer is needed every bit as much as writers were needed after the Civil War. In support of this, I ask you to consider a proposition I believe true:

The glory of America and the American people is not that we continually succeed in meeting our democratic principles, but that we never stop trying. We are a nation of immigrants with a myth of the melting pot, although we've never really melted. Our strength comes from our heritage of many cultures and races. Our frailty comes because that heritage too easily brings confrontations and secularism in areas where such things need not exist.

Secular elements, behaving in the manner of subcultures, have more in common than in difference. A black child, a white child, an Indian or Japanese or Mexican child is, first of all, an American child, one of our, as Americans, children. As writer-artists, children may or may not be our immediate business, but secularism certainly is not. The defeat of secularism is one of our opportunities.

It is easy to say that we need build a new mythology. It is far more difficult to say what that mythology should be, because it must be discovered. We can, however, define the problem in order to make an approach; and to me it seems the mythology needs speak of unity, not division. Carl Sandburg set the stage for such writing in *The People, Yes*, and Langston Hughes did the same in "Freedom Train." Those poets, together with storytellers like John Steinbeck and Meridel Le Sueur, can surely serve as our teachers in spirit.

Young writers and artists are the explorers, the creators, and the newest makers of myths. Old writers, having already taken most of their shots, get to watch from the sidelines. While I would not dream of telling you in which direction to travel, I would ask you to mull what follows:

In addition to saying that we need a new mythology, it is also easy to say that America needs to preserve the best of its founding principles. Those are not difficult to find. The principle of equal rights, and the principle of unity, are two great legacies in American thought. At the end of this century both legacies seem healthy, but one is obscured.

## EQUAL RIGHTS

The principle of equal rights continues to grow and flower. No matter the many objections we hear, laws are on the books, and the laws are more often enforced than not. People who wail that the deck is stacked either deny evidence, or use their wails to gain political advantage. The great legacy of this century is the realization of principles contained in the U.S. Constitution. While we can never completely cure prejudice (because there is no magic pill that cures stupidity), we can cure discrimination. That is what America has been about since the 1950s. It's been a long haul, but it is succeeding.

## UNITY

At the beginning of this book I asserted that America could not reach its dreams because it is a democracy. In a democracy, everyone talks—generally, all at once. Controversy is built into the system. It is a price we pay for the greatest gift of the nation's founders, the First Amendment to the Constitution.

The principle of unity, however, is equally American and equally a gift from the founders. We see two ideals that stand, more or less, at cross-purposes. For that reason, American dreams stand too high to ever be completely captured. That's our American greatness, our strength, and often a very American problem.

At present, that problem seems large and dreadful, but it seems that way only because the real situation is obscured by noise. Thus, the principle of unity is one that American artists of all types may wish to consider. We may do so while holding two understandings:

First, we may understand that social problems are rarely cured, but are often treated effectively. Thus, there will always be some racial, economic, and religious demagogues; black racists, white racists, and religious bigots. There will always be men who bash women, and women who bash men; and in doing so, reduce their lives, their happiness, and their contributions to the nation. We do not have the power to make them stop. We have the power to show them what they

do, and to let them make up their minds. We also need understand
that such people often fight for their own survival because demagogues,
at base, are hollow. They may become subjects of our charity, but not
our attention. Perhaps they deserve pity.

The second understanding is more complex, but wonderful to view.
It's complex because half of it is obvious, and the other half is confused.

The obvious half is that people wish to live together comfortably.
On the West Coast, for example, heavy immigration from the Orient,
and from South and Central America, would seemingly dictate that
neighborhoods would be at each other's throats. On a grand scale, it
isn't happening. Massive numbers of people from different backgrounds live comfortably side by side, intermarry, worry about each
other's kids, and manage to handle their prejudices.

Trouble often rises on a local scale, not a grand scale. It comes from
gangs and drugs. While the gangs are often racial or ethnic, they are
not the majority. They are not even expressions of race and ethnicity,
but of commercialism, social unrest, and provocation by media. The
gangs are currently named "the underclass," and they are not new.
There has been an underclass in America since the first white settlement
and, in fact, among some tribes before white settlement.

Not obvious is the inarticulate movement of Americans toward
unity. Our universities might have given coherence to this movement,
and so might our media. At present, both are failing badly, and the
main responsibility for the failure lies with the university. The American university has failed to seize a main chance in aiding contemporary
culture. I do not report this with joy.

This is what happened: Social movements grew and made demands
that come under the general heading of "political correctness." The
university, which is supposed to concern itself with language, embarked
on a course that renders language not only silly, but meaningless. Euphemisms became the order of the day. For example: It was no longer
possible to be blind. The unfortunate person had to be visually chal-
lenged.

This type of thinking became endemic. It spread through our society
because it was well purchased by media.[3] When our universities ignored

---

[3]Members of media traditionally align with movements that suppose themselves
intellectual.

a main need in the culture, and settled instead for playing word games, the games gave rise to rules. Rules gave rise to minuscule feelings of power. The rules are puritanical, Victorian, and represent the old and too-human frailty that puts form before content. People who hold rules as of first importance express the mind of the seventeenth century, not the twentieth. Our universities, which are supposed to be concerned with the humanities, instead played ancient themes.

And yet, obscured behind those forces that seek to reduce language, and thus reduce thought, is a vast yearning among Americans; a yearning for unity. Simply put, our society understands—even if our institutions do not—that we can no longer afford divisiveness. Many people use rules in the felt, if not expressed, hope of causing a blessed state in which no one offends anyone. Their expression may be clumsy, but it is not ill intended. Once more, although largely inarticulate, the American people are smarter and greater than American leaders, or American institutions.

For the American writer and artist, that is good news. The need for unity is one we can honor. We can embark on one of the great tasks of art: to define situations, and to give voice to the voiceless. Thus, it's possible that at least some messages from contemporary art and literature may be like this:

Allow us to extend our understanding by showing you our hearts. If you have a problem with Jews, we will immerse you in the worlds of the children of Father Abraham, and if Negroes bother you, our blood pulses with the beat of Mother Africa. If Caucasians seem threatening, observe our blond hair and blue eyes, and if you fear homosexuals, we can be as queer as a seven-dollar bill. Do you detest females? We will show you woman. Do you shun males? We will display the hearts of man. Tell us who scares the liver-and-lights out of you and we will be that person, extending our understanding to you, our commitment to a humanity you may not even know you own. We will tell you a story of how the first people on this continent placed the sun in the sky, and then put the moon up there to follow her; or we'll give advice on how to behave should you meet a leprechaun hiding beneath leaves. We will yarn for you, and in our speech will be expressions from Spanish, Chinese, Lithuanian, Turkish, French, German, Filipino, Tlingit, Samoan.

Because, my friend, a fine way to succeed as an American is to understand the great forces of which you, too, can be a part. It is through our stories that you can understand those forces, understanding that cannot come from prejudice or cupidity, but only from your mind, as your mind is informed by your heart.

# Index